THEORY AND PRACTICE IN CHILD PSYCHOANALYSIS

THEORY AND PRACTICE IN CHILD PSYCHOANALYSIS

An Introduction to the Work of Françoise Dolto

edited by

Guy Hall, Françoise Hivernel, and Sian Morgan

Routledge
Taylor & Francis Group
LONDON AND NEW YORK

First published 2009 by
Karnac Books Ltd.

Published 2018 by Routledge
2 Park Square, Milton Park, Abingdon, Oxon OX14 4RN
711 Third Avenue, New York, NY 10017, USA

Routledge is an imprint of the Taylor & Francis Group, an informa business

British Library Cataloguing in Publication Data

A C.I.P. for this book is available from the British Library

ISBN 9781855755741 (pbk)

Edited, designed, and produced by The Studio Publishing Services Ltd
www.publishingservicesuk.co.uk
e-mail: studio@publishingservicesuk.co.uk

CONTENTS

Françoise Dolto, Paris, 1986. © Alécio de Andrade, ADAGP, Paris.

ACKNOWLEDGEMENTS

The Editors wish to thank the many people who have helped and encouraged us. In particular, FH and SM wish to thank Catherine Dolto for her support during the genesis of the book and fondly remember the afternoon spent in Granchester discussing the possibility of its production. FH wishes to acknowledge the sensitive editorial support of Christopher Wright. FH and SM wish to thank Roger Bacon for the conversations they had with him about Françoise Dolto over the years. SM wishes to thank the late Daphne Henrion for her help with translation. We would also like to thank the staff at the Archives Dolto as well as Annie Trassaert from Gallimard, who organized a mass sending of Françoise Dolto's books to England to start us on our project, and the staff of the Maison Verte. We would like to thank Fiona Sinclair for her work in editing parts of the manuscript. We have been encouraged and inspired by two conferences, one held in Rome and the other held in Paris at UNESCO, both in 2008. We would like to thank Walter Morgan for his artwork on the cover of this book, and Patricia Newcomer for providing us with a photograph by Alécio de Andrade. Our thanks go also to our families and friends for their patience and understanding.

The representation of Françoise Dolto in each of the chapters is specific to each author.

Copyright permissions

ABOUT THE EDITORS AND CONTRIBUTORS

Bice Benvenuto is a psychoanalyst working with both adults and children. She practised for fifteen years in London, where she also attended the Tavistock Institute's course in child psychotherapy and worked with children and parents at the psychology department of Great Ormond Street Hospital. She was a founder member and co-director of the Centre for Freudian Analysis and Research, as well as co-ordinator of the Child Analysis Working Group. A member of the Champ Freudien and Cereda in Paris, she has lectured widely in UK universities and was an honorary fellow at Kent University. She has been a visiting professor at the New School of New York, and at the Florida Atlantic University for many years. She is now practising in Rome, where she directs the Dolto Association and a Casa Verde, a centre inspired by Dolto's Maison Verte for the prevention of mental disturbance for both children and adults. She has published several articles in international psychoanalytic and humanities journals. She is the author, among other published works, of *Concerning the Rites of Psychoanalysis*, and co-author of *The Works of Jacques Lacan. An Introduction*, and *The Klein–Lacan Dialogues.*

Claude Boukobza is a psychologist and psychoanalyst, co-founder and consultant at the day-care centre Mother-and-Baby Unit at the Hôpital St Denis, Paris. She was trained by Françoise Dolto and Maud Mannoni. She is a training member and President of Espace analytique (founded by Maud Mannoni). She has directed the publication of five books, the last one being *Les Ecueils de la Relation Précoce Mère–Enfant*, coll. Mille et Un Bébés, (éditions Eres), and has written about thirty papers in various professional reviews. In English: "Maud Mannoni and the retarded child", in J. De Groef and E. Heinemann (Eds.), *Psychoanalysis and Mental Handicap* (London: Free Association, 1999).

Anne-Marie Canu is a psychoanalyst, psychologist, psychiatrist and pedopsychiâtre (child psychiatrist). Born in America to a French father and an English mother, she studied at the Sorbonne in Paris and at Georgetown University in the USA. She has been an *Accueillante* at la Maison Verte since 1985. She is the author of "La Maison Verte: Le Jeu des relations" In: *Françoise Dolto, aujourd'hui présente: Actes du Colloque de l'Unesco 14–17 Janvier 1999* (Paris: Gallimard, 2000).

Guy Hall is a psychoanalyst and rabbi.

Francoise Hivernel, MA, PhD, left France in 1971 to pursue her career in Archaeology at London University, where she completed her PhD in 1978. She has published over twenty papers and contributed chapters to several books on archaeology. She graduated from the Contemporary Freudian training of the West Midlands Institute in 2003 as a psychoanalytic psychotherapist and is a member of the Forum for Independent Psychotherapists. She works in private practice in Cambridge with adults.

Catherine Mathelin-Vanier, PhD, is a researcher at the Centre de Recherches Psychanalyse et Médecine de l'Université Paris 7—Denis Diderot. She is a psychoanalyst at the Hôpital Saint-Denis, Paris. She founded the Consultation des Buttes Chaumont in Paris, a psychoanalytic treatment and training centre. She is the President of Enfance en Jeu, an association for research and study in paediatrics, psychoanalysis, and pedagogy, and is a training member of

Espace Analytique, Paris. Dr Mathelin-Vanier has written several articles which have been published in journals and edited books. Her own books are: *Raisins Verts et Dents Agacées. Clinique Psychanalytique avec les Enfants* (Paris: Denoël, Collection Espace Analytique, 1994), translated into English as *The Broken Piano* (New York: Other Press, 1999); *Le Sourire de la Joconde. Clinique Psychanalytique avec les Bébés Prématurés* (Paris, Denoël, Collection Espace Analytique, 1998); *Qu'est ce qu'on a fait à Freud pour avoir des enfants pareils?* (Paris: Denoël, Collection Mediation, 2000); *Survivre en famille* (Paris: Albin Michel Jeunesse, 2000). She also wrote a Preface to *Comprendre votre enfant* (London: Albin Michel and the Tavistock Clinic, 2001).

Sian Morgan is a psychoanalytic therapist, practising as a therapist and supervisor in Cambridge for twenty-five years. She trained at the Guild of Psychotherapists and is a member of the Cambridge Society for Psychotherapy. She was Director of Studies for the Post-Graduate Diploma in Psychodynamic Counselling at the University of Cambridge for fifteen years. She has published many papers on psychoanalytic subjects and has contributed chapters to several books on psychotherapy. Her publications include *Phobia* (editor and contributor) (London: Karnac, 2003).

PREFACE

This book has a task that should strike us as odd: to introduce the work of an extremely famous French psychoanalyst whose name is a continental household word; a clinical and theoretical practitioner whose influence on the understanding and care of babies, infants, and children is unsurpassed, but who is virtually unknown in Britain. Why is Dolto unknown? The reasons are surely multiple, but the puzzle remains. Is there something alien here to British sensibilities? As her absence from our culture and practices is a serious problem, the question is worth asking.

An irritating aspect of the rational atheism of UK anti-God propagandists such as Richard Dawkins is the lack of any intellectual curiosity about the fact that most of the world's human population is religious or, at least, spiritual. If roughly 95% of the species is irrational and deluded, we are entitled (or, as psychoanalysts, obliged) to wonder why. I shall start with Francoise Dolto's Christianity, because it is with this that I am personally most out of tune and therefore with which I have had to grapple hardest; is this a personal dimension of a wider resistance?

Dolto's concern with religion was both her own active communicant faith and the observation that everyone has some belief.

France is a secular Republic filled with atheists; yet I think her Christianity may have some bearing on why Dolto is not known in the Anglo-Saxon world. The French, Italians, Spanish, and even many Germans (atheist or religious) are once-Catholics in a way that the British are *not* lapsed Protestants. Protestantism might be fundamentalist, but, whether or not we are believers, today it does not run through our blood-stream as does Catholicism, like wine through water, changing the colour of our thoughts. Specifically, although Dolto seems to have highlighted sin, desire, and the first communion, the place of the Virgin Mother-and-Child seems to me to have a salience that is not part of our British conceptual or visual imaginary. It is this icon, with Joseph and a Christian God in the powerful paternal background, that is Dolto's centrepiece. The actual mother-and-child of her socio-psychoanalytical practice joins a dominant cultural–religious image and this makes for a very different baby.

Dolto shares her infantocentrism with the British, but her child is not a walking–talking Dombey, but, rather, a being-spoken-to and *therefore* speaking and thinking small person. Donald Winnicott, her rival in this field, famously dismissed her as "too intuitive"; this is incorrect, because, like the object of her research, she is intensely engaged in the process whereby language turns feelings into thoughts. Dolto might be a populist rather than an intellectual in her presentations of her theories, but the child of her observation and of her theory is a thinker whose task of humanization is to have new thoughts. For instance, she addresses an infant desperately envious of another child whose mother has given it cake: "You want the cake that other child is eating? That is OK; you can have it, but then you must change mothers too". As with the surprise interpretations of adult analysis, this is enough to provoke anyone to think! This is different from the verbalizations Melanie Klein offered: Klein put infantile phantasies into words; Dolto is stimulating the intelligence even of the foetus.

Dolto's social–clinical observations became her theory and her theory is the explanation of the process of humanization. Religion, psychoanalysis, and human strivings are tied together in the concept of desire. Desire is shaped by the social prohibitions on it (manifold and repeated "castrations"). Words replace objects, and thus are the medium within which desire circulates. Although speaking is developmentally acquired, a condition of one's humanity is that one is spoken to and speaks. In language one knows what one wants and what one cannot have. Klein's "memories in feelings" must, therefore, be articulated. However, where Klein gives words to the baby's *sui generis* emotions, Dolto uses language as relational, definitial, and irreducibly a process of exchange. Thus, language is social, both immediately in the present and historically: what your great-grandparents did and what they said about what they did is transmitted down generations, and laterally across different experiences.

Shelley is reputed to have stopped a nursemaid on one of the bridges over the Thames to ask if he might question the baby. Shelley wanted to know what it felt like to be born. Dolto's baby, even if not yet able to answer, would have understood that the general uncertainty of its experience would have depended on what its Mum or Dad said of what they felt at the times when it was conceived, carried, and born. The general is always specifically experienced. This treatment of humanization taking place through and in language endorses the status of desire—the word is never the object, so it contributes to the constitution of desire that never attains an object. Because language is always a process of exchange, Dolto's empirical practice and theoretical stance are inextricably social: from conception, the human being is part of its society; it is within society that it must be humanized or therapeutically socialized. But, for Dolto, desire is not only constituted by what it lacks; it is also a kind of collective unconscious energy, a life-drive, which makes us a generic human subject beyond the specifics of our individual selfhoods.

Dolto's theory is simultaneously more concerned with the historical individual than Anglo-Saxon psychoanalysis is used to, and more general, arguing that there is a "beyond" (Freudian and Christian) each particular life to an all human constitution of desire; a naming of the "id" we each bring with us and each share. It is a social theory in its emphasis on family and peer interrelationships, and also in the almost diametrically opposite sense of the social in which we could say, we *many* are as *one* in God. The Imaginary preconscious individual self joins the Symbolic generic unconscious subject. The child who is asked to contemplate that being given cake goes with having this, but not with that particular mother, illustrates how to become human is to think; so, similarly, does Dolto's concept of the image raise again the question of the intellectuality of the psychoanalyst. "Image", as in Dolto's best known thesis of the "unconscious image of the body" is her personal pun: I–ma–ge is a play with "I" (identity/je/ego/I) . . . "ma" (maman/mother) "ge"/"je" (earth/je/Gaia), a triad of self, mother, and subject, which is the baby. Although this is not her ideological or political intention, from the acute sensitivity of her observation, Dolto, I suggest, is engaged in thinking through the complexities of the baby–mother–humanity nexus that is other than the maternal idealizations/denigrations of phallo- or patro-centrism.

The observations of Winnicott, Klein, and Tustin, on the one hand, and Dolto on the other, overlap or are compatible. The intellectual framework within which they are understood is different; the concept of the child is not the same. The cross-channel contributors to this volume have set themselves a crucial and difficult task: to introduce a writer who thinks differently. The result is fascinating and important.

Juliet Mitchell
Cambridge, December 2008

Introduction

The idea of writing a book about Françoise Dolto's work for the English-speaking public emerged slowly during 2006. A few enthusiastic psychotherapists (Guy Hall, Françoise Hivernel, Sian Morgan, Françoise Mouchet-Davis, Valerie Mortin, Fiona Sinclair, and Michaela Pisan) decided to convene in Cambridgeshire once a month for a morning of reading and discussions, in French, of French psychoanalytic texts. We read, among others, P. Aulagnier and M. Mannoni and eventually discovered the work of Françoise Dolto. It became apparent that her practice and thought had been seminal to a number of French child analysts, known to the English-speaking world. However, Françoise Dolto's own work had remained largely untranslated into English and was unknown to the English psychoanalytic community. This spurred us on to try to find out why this was the case. As we began to read Dolto, we discovered that she was extremely well known in French society; for example, a street is named after her, and a coin was issued in her honour. She published more than thirty books, and participated in many television and radio programmes. A play, *Allo Maman Dolto,* was written about her and performed in London in 2006. Although Françoise Dolto's work has been translated into many languages, only two of her numerous books have been translated into English, and both have been out of print for a long time. *Le Cas Dominique* was translated as *Dominique: Analysis of an Adolescent*, and first published in the USA in 1973; it was later published in the UK in 1974, by Souvenir Press. The other work, also published in the USA, in 1995, is entitled: *When Parents Separate*. A third book, "Flower dolls: Essays in Child Psychotherapy", should have been published in 1989 by Marion Boyars, but was withdrawn at a very late stage because of "problems with the translation". Dolto is the only member of a group of analysts close to Lacan not to have received attention in the English-speaking world over the last thirty years (Turkle, 1992, 1995).

Françoise Dolto lived through the major crises of the twentieth century. She was analysed by one of the first analysts in France. She qualified as an analyst in 1937, in Paris, and then as a paediatrician at the outbreak of the Second World War. She helped to bridge an important chronological gap when many Jewish analysts fled, committed suicide, or were killed (although not being Jewish herself). She worked as one of the first child analysts, using her highly developed intuition to work with children who might otherwise have been dismissed as untreatable. She was a colleague of Jacques Lacan and was a member of l'Ecole Freudienne de Paris. She lived and worked through another critical time in Paris, that of May 1968, and contributed to educational reform in France. Her broadcasts in France in the 1970s made her a household name, bringing the insights of psychoanalysis to ordinary families.

This book is a compilation of papers about Françoise Dolto's life and work. It has been written in the year of the centenary of her birth and the celebration of her dedication to the healing of children. In this book, the various contributors explore her ideas and practice. In writing this book, we hope to introduce Françoise Dolto's key concepts, which are as follows.

- The human subject is a function of language and, from conception, is a subject of desire. Dolto believed that infants understand much more than is commonly understood, and that infants are in receipt of their family history, which is transmitted unconsciously from generation to generation. As a consequence, infant experience needs to be made sense of in language and communicated to babies so that they are not left alone with what might traumatize them in the womb during the process of birth or after birth.

- A series of benign "castrations" is necessary to enable the infant to symbolize the inevitable separations and losses involved in coming into being, "castrations" that foster psychic growth and creative life.
- Françoise Dolto developed the idea of the "unconscious image of the body". She elaborated the use made of the "unconscious image of the body" as the support and agent of the emergence of the subject through language.

One of the problems that the editors faced in compiling the papers in this book was how to convey, in all its rich diversity, the theoretical and clinical ideas of Françoise Dolto. The matter is complicated by the fact that she is practically unknown in the English-speaking world and that the editors themselves, while being clinicians, only know of Françoise Dolto through her published books available in French. This is one of the reasons for inviting other contributors, who could add an extra dimension of experience, or who had known Françoise Dolto directly, to supply their particular insights. What makes Françoise Dolto so interesting is that she combines a variety of different psychodynamic therapeutic perspectives to enable the understanding of children and parents, rather than remaining in a conventional, analytically boundaried framework. She calls upon psychosomatic understanding, and couple, family, and group therapeutic resources within her work as a child psychoanalyst. She considers the consequences of trans-generational processes, suggesting, for example, that it took three generations to create a psychotic individual. She stresses the importance of prenatal influences on the child. Much of her later publications are in the form of conversations, and, along with some of the earlier works, these are not always systematic in the form of their presentation. Not everything can be adequately transmitted within the space of one book and the application of Dolto's work is more than the blind repetition of what she said. All the quotes taken from Françoise Dolto's work and reproduced in the various chapters of this book have been translated by the respective authors of the chapters.

It is not always easy to define and precisely distinguish some of the concepts that Dolto uses, let alone translate them from French to English. Yet, the very things for which she was criticized are those which make her so interesting to read. No one would pretend that one has to agree with everything that Françoise Dolto said, but her ideas and approach are so stimulating that one could scarcely be considered to be well educated in psychoanalytic literature without having read and understood some of her most important works.

The book includes chapters on some of Françoise Dolto's most original ideas, including reflections on the Maison Verte, a revolutionary institution of her inspiration, the intention of which was to provide a place within the community which was sensitive to the unconscious process of small children and their carers.

At the time of writing (December 2008), popular attention in the UK is fixed on the consequences of the death of Baby Peter, one of many atrocities involving the abuse of children which have recently occurred in the UK. Baby Peter, a seventeen-month-old child, had been consistently tortured and was eventually murdered by the three adults responsible for his care and well-being. The child had been seen twice a week in the eight months prior to his death, variously by social services, the police, and the medical profession. He was known to be at risk, but the child protection system failed to save his life: he was not taken away from those who most threatened him. Unfortunately, it was not the first time that such a situation has occurred. The government has promised action and to improve the existing system, but no undertakings have been given to reconsider any alternative ways of looking after children and parents. Baby Peter is a reminder of the dangers of investing resources only as cases become critical. Inadequate consideration is given to the unconscious transmission of trauma and of the sense in which abuse might escape representation and is thus subject to the repetition compulsion. Françoise Dolto's notion of preventative action could have an important role. The establishment in the UK of centres akin to the Maison Verte could establish a location for the containment and transformation of unconscious process and might make a preventative contribution to a whole range of potentially dangerous situations and anxiety-provoking relationships.

Many Maisons Verte have been established throughout France and have been introduced into other European countries. In a recent conference to celebrate the influence of Françoise Dolto in Rome, Adalinda Gasparini (2008), in a paper entitled "Dreaming the future", spoke of her experience in attempting to establish a Maison Verte in Florence, which entailed eliciting the support of the city administration. Françoise Dolto was interested in applying psychoanalysis to the social sphere, a desire that Gasparini shares in offering psychoanalytic skills to the city, which could challenge the "ownership" and hegemony of parents and schools over children. The intention is to establish a Maison Verte, a Casa Smeralda, in the Istituto degli Innocenti, Brunelleschi's Foundling Hospital, a sublime building, created in the fifteenth century, to house and care for the illegitimate children of Florence. The creation of the Istituto degli Innocenti was a visionary humanistic project, from which we have still much to learn. It may soon be augmented by Dolto's vision, which is a contemporary expression of similar humanistic ideals. The Foundling Hospital is also headquarters of the Unicef Research Centre. Just as the city of Florence once legitimized its illegitimate children during the Renaissance, so now it may legitimize a convivial, "ordinary space", for people of all social classes, including the city's many migrants, a space to facilitate the expression of the unconscious and the growth of the human subject.

We also attended a three-day UNESCO Colloquium (2008) in Paris, to celebrate the centenary of Françoise Dolto's birth, organized by the Dolto Archives, her publishers, Gallimard, and Catherine Dolto and her family; this also coincided with the 60th anniversary of the Universal Declaration of Human Rights "World Philosophy Day", which recognizes the child as a linguistic being, capable of thought and interrogation. The colloquium considered that the analytic work of Françoise Dolto is more significant than ever today, because of its radical subversion of social norms, and because of her insistence on the importance of truthful speech in the service of the recognition and respect for otherness, underpinned by therapeutic conversation pursued outside the agency of any social control. Dolto's ethic is increasingly relevant in a society that has become highly technical and "object-related", as a counter to the erosion of the liberal and humanistic values that society claims to espouse. The colloquium sought to support and defend what Dolto described as "the pathways toward humanisation" that she tried to create in her work with children, equally applicable in therapeutic work with adults.

The conference began with a consideration of the question of the transmission of her work, and how the major currents within her work might support the subject of desire for life, particularly within institutions, which are increasingly focused on the early diagnosis of the child, on the controlling of symptoms, and on the reduction of the subject to his behavioural traits. The conference also considered the effect of the increasing fragmentation of society on childhood, of divorce, described as *la transmission blessée*, of single parenthood, and of the new reproductive technologies. Consideration was given to the ways in which the creative thought, practice, and ethic of Françoise Dolto have affected workers within the field of psychoanalysis, how her ethic has affected their being, their work and how they may be influenced in the future. Her ethical stance was vital to her practice and to the understanding and compassion she transmitted to her patients and colleagues. Central to her ethic was her non-compliance with meaningless regression, in the face of which she showed considerable ferocity. She had an extraordinary capacity to speak to the most regressed, psychotic part of the child, but would only engage with such "malignant" regression in order to get the child back into relationship.

The conference was an astonishing, inspiring, and collaborative convention, which reflected the warmth and generous spirit of Françoise Dolto. We hope that you will find some of these qualities in this book. Our intention is to find sponsors to fund the translation of Françoise Dolto's work into English, so that we might be able to make available her challenging and innovative ideas and practice to all those who live and work with children.

Guy Hall
Françoise Hivernel
Sian Morgan

References

Baret, G. (1994). *Allo Maman Dolto*. Adapted for the theatre by S. Dupres, Paris and Avignon. Produced in the UK by C. Ha. Thuc and played by La Compagnie du Carreau, 2006.

Dolto, F. (1971). *Le Cas Dominique*. Paris: Le Seuil.
Dolto, F. (1973). *Dominique: Analysis of an Adolescent Boy*, I. Kats (Trans.). New York: Outerbridge and Lazard, 1974.
Dolto, F. (1988). *Quand les parents se séparent*. Paris: Le Seuil.
Dolto, F. (1995). *When Parents Separate*, D. Callimanopulous (Trans.). Boston: D. R. Godine.
Gasparini, A. (2008). Dreaming the future. Presented to the Dolto Conference: "Childhood and its Discontents: Words, Listening and Welcoming". LUMSA University, Rome, 22 November, 2008 (in press).
Turkle, S. (1992). *Psychonalytic Politics: Jacques Lacan and Freud's French Revolution*. New York: Guildford Press.
Turkle, S. (1995). Tough love: An introduction to Françoise Dolto's *When Parents Separate*. Lincoln, MA: David R. Godine.
UNESCO Colloquium (2008). Françoise Dolto—Actualité d'une pensée 1908–2008. Journée mondiale de la philosophie, 12–14 Décembre 2008 (in press).

CHAPTER ONE

Françoise Dolto: a biography

Sian Morgan

This chapter is presented in two sections; the first concerns the history and formative influences in the life of Françoise Marette Dolto, the second traces her career.

Background

Françoise Marette Dolto was born in Paris in November 1908 into an affluent bourgeois family. She was the fourth of the seven children of Henri Marette and Suzanne Demmler. She appears to have been, from her early years, an exceptionally independent spirit with an acute intelligence. Her family was religious, strict, and protective. Her mother, though loving, was controlling and demanding, while her father was more liberal, encouraging her inventiveness and desire for knowledge. She was educated in a *cours* within the kind of seclusion typical for girls of the time, pursuing her studies on her own, only having contact with other children at playtime. She was well known for being funny, jolly, noisy, and full of vitality. Reminiscing late in her life, in *Autoportrait d'une psychanalyste* (1989, pp. 209–210), Françoise Dolto remembered being told by an old family friend that when she was born she had remarked on her difference from the rest of her family: "How is this little frog going to fare amongst the ducks on this pond?" It is apparent from letters written to her parents from Deauville when she was five that she had considerable difficulty being good; her charming communications are a frank confession of a series of transgressions from a naughty little girl (Dolto, 2003, pp. 18–28).

She was already, as a small child, a considerable force, causing discomfort with her penetrating gaze and intuitive capacity. She was close to her siblings, particularly to her older brother Jean, with whom she felt 'twinned'. However, lively and communicative as she was, there was always an other-worldly quality to the young Françoise. Already fiercely religious, she soon developed an enquiring and rebellious theological mind, arguing with her priest before her first communion. Displaying a creative capacity to overturn conventional understanding and an unusually developed compassion for the scapegoat, she defended the integrity of Judas. She soon developed an awareness of mysticism, always sensing the protection of a guardian angel. After the death of her grandfather when she was four, she remembered daily asking the question, "What happens after death?" (Dolto, 1989, p. 69). Her memory included the regular walk taken over a railway bridge, during which she would become engulfed with the steam from the engines and would find herself transported to another world, where she imagined we exist before and after birth. It was after this that she experienced what she described as a schizoid crisis, not being able to tolerate the fantasies and dissociation in the adults around her towards the existential dilemma posed by death. Subsequent to this, her guardian angel came to her aid.

She had the sensibility of an artist and became a skilled painter, potter, and sculptor. However, her imagination also encompassed the sciences, and from an early age she became interested in the development of communication systems, encouraged by her father. As a child, she was an avid reader of technical journals, from which she taught herself Morse code and how to build a radio receiver. This served as a metaphor for her of how it is that humans can communicate unconsciously, without obvious material means. By means of her radio receiver, she could receive the exact time from the Eiffel Tower, which represented for her the phallic power of France and, along with her radio, represented her father's phallic strength with which she was identified.

Her relationship with her mother was often troubled. Her mother seems to have found her intelligent, irrepressible daughter, with her strange ideas and defiance of what was conventional for girls, incomprehensible. Françoise Marette loved her mother, but despaired at the monstrosity of her expectations. She had compassion for her, for her misogyny bred of a sense of inferiority, for her self-loathing, for her intolerance of her passionate nature that her mother misperceived as sinful. Her mother's guilt appears to have generated aggression towards herself and towards her children.

Her mother was preoccupied by Françoise's older siblings. Françoise, in the first months of her life, was cared for by an Irish nurse, thereby, perhaps, avoiding a primitive identification with her mother. However, this relationship was to be severed prematurely and brutally because the young nurse, though deeply affectionate towards her charge, would 'borrow' her employer's dresses and jewellery so that she could go to parties, accompanied by the baby. When her activities were discovered, she was peremptorily dismissed. Françoise was abandoned, deprived of the life she had known, and immediately succumbed to pneumonia. Her mother responded instinctively to the plight of her infant, holding her to her naked body and loving her back to life. Françoise was marked by the ambivalence of her mother's love; of the woman who had failed to live her own desires and who seemed to fear that her daughter might live out her desires in her place (Dolto, 2003, p. 217)

Françoise Marette resolved as a young girl that she would try to become a *médecin d'éducation*, a term of her invention that described a doctor who would understand the emotions and the relationships between human beings which underpinned what is expressed in illness. She already sensed that she had been born too early for her ideas to be easily accepted. However, she was to spend her life repeating with considerable success what she had failed to do in relation to her sister. She had acquiesced to her mother's demand that she should pray to bring her sick sister, Jacqueline, back to life. Jacqueline died. As a paediatrician and psychoanalyst, Françoise Marette Dolto was able to respond to the appeal of thousands of desperate parents with the healing words of a psychoanalyst.

Françoise Dolto is an *Athene* of French psychoanalysis: Athene, who, according to Bonnefoy (1991, pp. 86–88) sprang armed from her father's head, with her intelligence derived from her mother,

Metis, who was swallowed up by her father, Zeus. Athene is represented in the form of a large owl on top of a potter's kiln, facing a phallic dwarf, the bearer of the evil eye. When Françoise Dolto was asked in *Autoportait d'une psychanalyste* (Dolto, 1989, p. 217) what she might have been had she not become a psychoanalyst, she answered, "Certainly a potter." She was a skilled amateur, an artist with a powerful technical intelligence. The owl was a favourite motif on her pots and her collection of ceramic owls are now displayed in the Dolto Archives. Athene was the protectress of potters and was the mistress of fire, intervening to rid the kiln of a troupe of demons, the Breaker, the Cracker, the Indistinguishable, the Burster (Bonnefoy, 1991, p. 87). The domain of the potter and its protector offers a powerful metaphor for the art and craft of psychoanalysis. Athene also procured the bit that tamed Pegasus, the instrument that tames the wild horse, a metaphor for the unbridled desires and demonic forces of the id (Bonnefoy, 1991, p. 87).

Françoise became interested in madness early in her life. As a small child she challenged the limits of what could be thought, and was often the object of her mother's neurosis. Following the family's move to a new apartment overlooking the clinic for the insane founded by Dr Blanche, she became an observer of its wealthy inmates. She was an acutely perceptive child who enjoyed the foibles, contradictions, and eccentricities of the adults who surrounded her.

The First World War engendered a social madness. Her mother, Suzanne's, brother Pierre had been killed in action in 1916, a death that affected the whole family, particularly Françoise, who was his god-daughter. Françoise adored him. In a letter dated September 1915, aged seven, she writes:

> I would like very much to marry you, next year, but I can't yet because I am too small, but yesterday when I was out walking, I blew on Monsieur le Cure's candle and everything was all at once blown out so perhaps all the same I might even so be able to marry you but I don't know if this candle lied. [Dolto, 2003, p. 48]

And again, in a letter to him dated June 1916,

> The other day I did see the building of some houses occupied by the Bosch and I visited them and they were very pretty and I chose one for you and me and our four children. I will have two girls and

> two boys or if you really want, we could each have a boy and a girl. Hurry up and ask for permission that we may get married because I am about to set off for Deauville. I had to use my umbrella this morning because it was raining. [*ibid.*, p. 66]

Within a month, Pierre had been killed in action at the Sphinx de la Tête des Faux. Françoise's mother and grandmother were bereft, as was Françoise. No further mention is made of his death in her *Correspondances* until her supplication for intercession for her prayers to save her sister Jacqueline's life. In 1928, there is a post-card to her youngest brother, Jacques, sent from the Vosges, where Pierre had been killed, of a little girl carrying a toy soldier in her basket, containing a powerful allusion to her relationship with her uncle and its fate. Françoise had considered herself a war widow. The whole of France had fallen into mourning following the First World War. The Marette family's grief was intensified by the death of Jacqueline in 1920, a crisis which had precipitated their mother Suzanne into a period of madness that inevitably burdened her younger daughter with a sense of guilt. It was the time of Françoise's first communion, when she was twelve and her sister was eighteen. When Jacqueline became seriously ill her mother began to use her daughter, Françoise, as a kind of psychoanalyst. Jacqueline had been her mother's favourite, being blonde with blue eyes, like her mother's father, leading Françoise to speculate that, in her mother's fantasy, Jacqueline was the child of that incestuous union: on the other hand, Françoise was dark like her mother, which led Francoise to believe that, in her mother's fantasy, *she* should have been the one to have died. While Jacqueline was dying, her mother demanded that Françoise should pray for her, because it was the eve of her first communion and only a miracle that might occur on the day of a child's first communion might save Jacqueline's life. So, Françoise was charged with praying to save her sister. Her mother was half Catholic and half Protestant, but also held superstitious beliefs and now she was desperate. She asked Françoise to rescue her sister through words communicated to God: of course, Françoise failed.

In the *Correspondances 1913–1938*, this extract from a notebook describes her plight, but also I think betrays a sense of humour, even in this situation.

> May 1920
>
> I have asked Oncle Pierre to intercede so that my prayers may be heard. In the first place, I have asked that Jacqueline may recover and I am sure that she will have her operation because I heard a voice that said that my prayer would be granted. Secondly, I ask for Papa to be converted and I noticed that yesterday he got up early to come to mass with us. I ask that God might make his will known to me and that he give me the courage to respond. I promise that I will do whatever I am able, not to commit a mortal sin. I then want to pray for Dan-pe and Oncle Pierre, if they are still in purgatory and if they are in heaven, to ask them to intercede on my behalf with God and to strengthen me against the devil, so that I can be reunited with them in heaven.
>
> Resolutions
>
> I will get up in the morning resolved not to be lazy. I will always pray. I will always make my bed. I will tidy my room. I will say a little prayer before working. I will do up my boots. I will say a prayer before and after my meals. In the mornings, I will take a little time to meditate. I will do everything I can to be obedient, to not contradict, to not lie and to stay calm. Every evening, I will say a prayer and I will say a dozen Hail Mary's in my bed. Every time I fail to do one of these, I will impose upon myself a penance. [2003, pp. 104–105]

A letter from her maternal grandmother describes how Françoise was regarded within the family and condescends to her efforts for self-improvement: "I understand that you are making efforts to control yourself and to bridle your wild horse nature" (2003, p.107).

In the years that followed her sister's death, it is as if Françoise was stricken by a form of survivor guilt, which was in intense conflict with her passionate desire for life. Her letters to her parents at the time are long and affectionate. Many betray a sense of abjection. Her letters to her mother demonstrate that she had, as an adolescent, taken up the role of healer. The letters display a reparative need for not having been able to rescue Jacqueline, even for not being Jacqueline, for not being the daughter her mother yearned for. After the birth of Jacques Marette in 1922, the baby who, by his name, indicates the desire for a substitute for Jacqueline, Françoise, aged thirteen, writes to her mother:

> Mademoiselle has told me that you cannot be doing with this fifth boy. I understand your dismay but perhaps it is for the best. If it had been a girl, you would not have been able to leave her for one minute for thirteen years and maybe you would want the freedom to travel and then you would not be able to launch her in to the world until she was 20. Whereas although this may be hard for you for 5 or 6 years, after that I will get married and will stay with you and I will provide you with many grandchildren particularly lots of granddaughters. Since you have mainly boys, I will have girls. And you will come and stay with me and I will look after you and you will be loved by your grand-children. You won't need to be vexed by me because I will never leave you. I will choose a husband who will want lots of children and will never move far away from you . . . Now I am nearly 14, I have a little more than two years of study, then I will stay with you. [*ibid.*, p. 130]

She spent many years looking after Jacques. Her letters are poignant, and full of repeated reassurances to her mother:

> It grieves me that you feel that you won't later on gain as much support and consolation from having had boys. I understand that it isn't the same only having one big girl, compared with what it might have been to have two grown daughters, but I assure you that I will be a true daughter to you. I will try as hard as I can to replace Jacqueline. I will help raise my little brother so that he will be affectionate and will substitute in part for the little girl you might have had. And I will get married and stay close to you . . . I see now how much you cruelly suffered two years ago. I am sorry that I did not understand well enough at the time. I must have seemed thoughtless and ungrateful to you, when you saw me being full of life when you were so sad . . . I hope that wherever Jacqueline is that she will forgive me, that she will aid and protect me, because I didn't understand the bad things I was doing. [*ibid.*, p. 131]

Françoise had been a brilliant student and had been ready to sit her *Baccalauréat* at the age of fifteen. She had found herself under pressure because her mother's intention was that she should complete her studies by the age of sixteen; in order to forestall her daughter's bid for independence, her mother had intervened and, without consultation, instructed her teachers not to enter her for the exam. Françoise, on discovering this, had become enraged with her parents, one of the few times in her life she suffered what she described as a white rage, a rage which was incomprehensible to her mother but which her father understood only too well. He subsequently made it possible for her to sit the exam. Neither her mother nor her two older brothers, nor various friends of the family, could understand her, for, as far as they were concerned, a girl with qualifications was branded for life as a black sheep. Françoise passed her *Baccalauréat* with a commendation, but her mother continued to oppose her progress. She was willing for her to train as a nurse, but did not want her to enter a *lycée*, where she might meet people of a lower class. Françoise was tolerant of her mother's possessiveness. She understood that her mother's demands and control were a consequence of her grief; her grief about Jacqueline but also about her own frustrated ambitions and fixated development. Her mother had wanted to be a suffragette and to have studied medicine, but had been overcome by neurosis and inhibited by the limitations of the age in which she grew up. Françoise had to fight her prejudices ferociously but with compassion, in the knowledge that her mother was terrified of loss and abandonment and was blind to her giftedness: "I have only one daughter, I do not want to have to sacrifice her to her ridiculous studies" (Chérer, 2008, p. 130).

In spite of her mother's protestations and manipulations, Françoise registered for her second *Baccalauréat*, at the *Lycée Molière*, in philosophy. When it came to her examination, the examiner asked her, somewhat sarcastically, to tell him what she knew about psychoanalysis. He was not expecting the elaborate and sophisticated response that ensued from a sixteen-year-old, but she impressed him to such an extent that she was once more passed with a commendation. Succumbing to her mother's desire for her, from the age of sixteen to twenty-one, she did not pursue her studies. She was held and protected within the family, typically for a young woman of her age; she played the piano, painted, and read. The society within which she found herself did not esteem clever women; their role was to be dutiful daughters, then dutiful wives if they were fortunate and obedient. She was biding her time until the moment was right to enter medical school, for which she prepared herself by training as a nurse, acceptable to her mother as sufficiently feminine. She entered the nursing school of the Croix-Rouge in

November 1929. Interestingly, this was the year that followed her visit to the battlefield where her uncle had been killed, as if she had now been able to let go of her grief, and her self-imposed status as war widow. In June 1930, she obtained her nursing diploma.

Her letter to her future sister-in-law, Yvonne Hurel, who was to marry her brother Pierre, describing her nursing training, again betrays with characteristic humour her considerable anxiety about not being sufficiently feminine:

> I greatly admire you for being slim and slender. You must know by now from my parents and from Pierre that unfortunately for me I am of considerable proportions! I regret profoundly not being more decorative. I am very lively but a boisterous fat person is comical and ultimately ridiculous . . . I hope that you will not pay too much attention to my physique, but that you will nevertheless love me . . . I understand from what has been said that you are very much a woman. I admire you very much and wonder if you could give me some advice. I have always been surrounded by boys, and in character and attitude I am not very feminine. Mother must have told you how it is that I often think and feel. I try with all my might to change and feminise my nature. You can help me. Since you are close to me in age you can tell me what I need to do. Always be honest with me. Don't hesitate to tell me the truth however unpleasant it might be. [*ibid.*, pp. 234–235]

In *Autoportrait d'une psychanalyste*, Françoise Dolto describes the summer of 1931, when Suzanne Marette took Françoise to visit the family of old friends of Jacqueline, in Provence. She was asked to stay while her mother returned to Paris. Following her return, her mother wrote to her every day betraying an obsessive jealousy: "Why did you accept their invitation? It is because you do not love me. You prefer anyone to your mother" (Dolto, 1989, p. 94). She enjoyed her stay, in the company of two young women and their brother, sharing a delight in poetry, music, and nature. She interpreted the Greek myths to the young man from a psychoanalytic perspective, speculating on the nature of Medea in the human psyche. Françoise felt a platonic love for him. However, he fell in love with Françoise, but she could not reciprocate in kind. It soon became known to both mothers. Suzanne Marette insisted that the relationship could continue only if they became engaged. Françoise agreed in order to continue seeing him, but refused her mother's demand that they kiss in front of her and stated that she would only get married when she finished her medical training. Her mother was completely uncomprehending, ending by calling her daughter a monster. In this way, Françoise's mother placed her daughter in a bind. If you leave me, you do not love me; if you do not leave me and love him, you do not love me. In addition, it soon became apparent that the young man, D, did not want his future wife to pursue her studies. Françoise soon told him, in no uncertain terms, that for her the pursuit of a medical career was far more important than marrying him. Her mother persisted in forbidding her to study medicine. As a consequence, Françoise, with characteristic *bravura*, insisted that she would register at the Sorbonne, but to study Italian. In an uncharacteristic *volte-face*, her mother suddenly gave her permission, in part because Françoise's younger brother Philippe intended to register at the faculty of medicine. In November 1931, Françoise began her medical studies, accompanied by her brother Philippe, who was to act as her chaperone. Yvonne and Françoise's other brother, Pierre, had given birth to a daughter, Nicole, on the 6th of July 1931, a niece for Françoise and the first grandchild for Suzanne and Henry Marette, a much wanted granddaughter. It might be that the birth of a granddaughter for her mother helped to free Françoise from her guilt towards her mother and her sister. Françoise was also becoming increasingly aware of how destructive had been the effect of her mother's grief and her ferocious jealousy, an awareness that was soon to be magnified by her encounter with psychoanalysis.

It was Marc Schlumbereger, a fellow student who had been in analysis with Nunberg in Vienna and later Laforgue in Paris, and who had spent some time at Summerhill, who introduced her to the experience of the practice of psychoanalysis. Hitherto, it had been only a philosophical system of ideas for Françoise. In the first place, it was for her brother, Philippe, that she looked to psychoanalysis for help. Françoise was the more brilliant student, but she sensed that her brother was in some way inhibited. Schlumberger suggested that Philippe consult with Laforgue. Within a fortnight of analysis with Laforgue, Philippe was working well, and both Françoise and Philippe passed their end of year exams. Meanwhile, Suzanne Marette was once more disgruntled that her daughter was happy and flourishing in her pursuit of a medical career. Françoise had not ceased to defend herself against her fiancé's disapproval of her desire, and, at the beginning of the second year of her studies, she became weary and overwhelmed with guilt and shame, no longer able to sleep or work effectively. So it was arranged that Françoise should become a patient of Laforgue's and that her father would pay. Her father's support had been invaluable to Françoise, and his paying for her analysis would enable her to become free of the yoke of her family and to develop her extraordinary ideas and psychoanalytic practice.

However, it is clear that a letter dated 15th May 1933 betrays her father's disquiet as to how she is changing:

> Since you began your medical studies, you appear to have changed and your attitude can cut me to the quick. Your attitude towards your mother and I reveals a Vava [pet name] who is very different from the person we knew as being straight forward, modest, affectionate and so tender. You seem to regard us as old spoilsports, and you are hardly able to be polite, in fact you seem to regard us with impatience. Alas, you are the only daughter left to us and you should be, in spite of your studies, a fond companion for your mother. It was a beautiful dream amongst many others that your mother has had stolen from her. . . . My poor child I see terribly clearly but you are elusive, being gratified by these new ideas, and the blandishments offered you by sadistic dilettantes who are squandering your attention . . . You are succumbing to the most terrible pride and I hope that you will see that it is only in your parents that you can trust . . . Intelligence is not everything. It comes to nothing either serious or lasting without a considered moral framework. [Dolto, 2003, p. 354]

Françoise took several months before directly answering her father's complaints. When she did, in a letter written in July 1933, she is clearly weary and contrite: "My greatest desire is to get to the end of this tiresome treatment as this would be the best way to thank you, by becoming a proper woman" (*ibid.*, p. 382).

She later writes letter to her mother with similar sentiments:

> I realise only too well what humiliation I have caused you, of the profound wound I have inflicted this year . . . After all that you have done for me, I want you to be one day proud of me and that

> without hoping for as much, that you will understand my affection and desire to become a woman worthy of you, even if I cannot be entirely like you. I realise every thing that is lacking in me in comparison to you, but that having received so much from you, when I get better, I will be able to establish a family in which every one will be able to be happy. [*ibid.*, p. 385]

Her mother's reply is deeply affectionate, appearing to accept their differences, telling her not to identify with her but to find in the depths of her being her "true self" (*ibid.*, p. 386). Françoise's thrice weekly analysis with Laforgue lasted three years, unusually long for the time. He forbade her any involvement with psychoanalytic theory so that she might understand the experience of analysis 'from the heart'. She was impatient to finish her analysis and, at times, does not have appeared to have relished the experience. "The atmosphere is heavy, when every word and gesture is interpreted" (*ibid.*, p. 535). She came to believe that her analysis would not be finished until she had ceased to narcissistically identify with her patients, when she no longer found herself saying, "It is just like me". Her guilt towards a sibling was repeated as a consequence of her analysis with Laforgue, and in this respect she is critical of him, for having taken her as a patient when Philippe, her brother, was also his patient. She felt that Philippe had once more been displaced by his elder sister, even attributing the severity of his tubercular illness to her 'invasion' of his analytic space (Dolto, 1989, p. 120).

Her analysis lasted from 1934 until 1937, the focus of it being her sense of entrapment by her mother and her consequent moral dilemma as to how she should be in relation to her family. In *Autoportrait d'une psychoanalyste*, she expresses her debt to Laforgue and explains the helpful way he interpreted her relationship with her mother (*ibid.*, p. 243). She describes herself as having begun her analysis in despair, grief, and overburdened with guilt towards her fiancé and towards her mother. Laforgue never blamed her mother, but always spoke to Françoise of her own sense of guilt. This was in spite of her mother's punitive behaviour, including her attempts to sabotage Françoise's medical studies. Laforgue challenged Françoise's defensive avoidance and submissiveness, saying that nothing was worse for an obsessional neurotic, like her mother, than for others to collude with their obsessional ideas. He suggested that Françoise forbid her to speak to her in the way in which she had become accustomed. Françoise was at first too anxious to challenge her mother because she was too self-critical, but after some time in analysis, with the support of Laforgue, she took the risk of speaking to her mother:

> I forbid you to speak to me in this way. You haven't the right. I have never dishonoured you. I am an honest, hard working young woman. I know what I want and it is not forbidden by the law. I have the right not to be treated by you as a slut or to have you spread malicious rumours. [*ibid.*, p. 244]

In reaction to her daughter's newfound sense of authority, her mother backed down. Reflecting on her mother's capitulation, Françoise realized that her mother needed someone stronger than herself to curtail her passionate excesses because, although she was very intelligent, she sometimes behaved like a child and, like a child, she needed firm boundaries. This way of thinking and communicating was to help Françoise in her development as an analyst. In a letter written to her father in 1938, she expresses her full fury towards her mother and her grief at what she had suffered: "I have lost ten years of my life, without having had a true youth. I have had to wait to be thirty to become a real woman" (Dolto, 2003, pp. 528–529).

She now visits home less often. A rift has opened up between her and her brother, Pierre, whom she claims speaks on behalf of her mother's insinuations; he had made what seemed to be an anti-Semitic attack on psychoanalysis. Françoise attempts to explain her mother's neurosis to her father. She describes the force of her mother, of her demand that Françoise be dutiful, of how she feels charged with so much blame. She tells him that she believes Jacques was born to be a substitute for Jacqueline, and how such a strategy was destined for failure; that it was her attitude and containment that prevented her mother from collapsing into self-destruction after Jacqueline's death. She speaks of how she has been prepared to sacrifice her desire for medicine because she had perceived that it had been her mother's desire, but also of her own wish to be equal to her brothers and to have a man's profession. What is remarkable about the letter is its honesty and the hope which is contained within such an angry communication that there is sufficient love between the members of the family to survive her attack. She evokes a deep sense of sadness at her own loss. Françoise Marette emerges from her analysis as a forthright and courageous young woman, who could be seen as a young Athene preparing to fight on behalf of the abandoned and disturbed children of France.

Life as a doctor and psychoanalyst

Responding to Laforgue's encouragement, Françoise began her training as a psychoanalyst in the Société Psychanalytique de Paris, attending seminars given by Spitz, Loewenstein, Nacht, and Hartmann: at the time there was no child analytic training. Meanwhile, during her medical training, she had decided to specialize in paediatrics. After completing a psychiatric placement, she remarked, "It is too late to make a difference with adults who are so impaired; the work has to be done with children to prevent later disturbance" (Dolto, 1986, p. 60).

During her studies, she became an extern for Professor Heuyer, a child neuro-psychiatrist at the Hôpital Vaugirard, the only such department in France. She was horrified by what she witnessed: children in a state of semi-incarceration who were treated with a complete lack of empathy. No one seemed interested in understanding these children, no one, that is, apart from a psychoanalyst, Sophie Morgenstern, whom Heuyer had employed, in spite of his ambivalence towards psychoanalysis. Sophie Morgenstern listened to her young patients, making links between their symptoms and family history, confirming Françoise Marette's intuition that certain physical symptoms were psychosomatic, caused by unconscious tensions within the family. In 1937, she became an extern at l'Hôpital des Enfants Malades, where disturbed children were sent for assessment. Here, Françoise began to conduct psychotherapeutic sessions using drawing and modelling to help the children put into words what was troubling them. At this stage in her career she had no intention of becoming a child analyst: her desire was to be a paediatrician.

She qualified as an analyst in 1938. She completed her medical training in 1939, with the submission of her thesis, *Psychanalyse et pédiatrie* (Dolto, 1939). Her intention in researching her thesis was not to promote psychoanalysis as such, but was to develop a new approach in child medicine. Her desire was to find an application for psychoanalysis within paediatrics. She submitted her thesis at 1.00 p.m. on 11th July 1939 and, unconventionally, an hour later she went immediately to register as a doctor. She was aware that war was imminent; the Second World War was declared on the 3rd September 1939. Had she registered any later, she would not have been able to practice until after the war was over. She stayed in Paris during the war, at first substituting for doctors who had been called up at l' Hôpital des Enfants Malades. Simultaneously, she began consultations as a psychoanalyst. Many Jewish analysts had been obliged to flee, leaving their patients. In *Autoportrait d'une psychanalyste* (1989, p. 134) she describes the terror in Paris when war was declared: ". . . the siren wailed, scenes of madness broke out and women screamed". The hospital she was visiting flooded with hundreds of raving people who had to be sedated. It was in this atmosphere that her career as a psychoanalyst and paediatrician began. She was passionate about her consultations with children, many of whom had been sent to her because others had failed to help them. Her practice was regarded as eccentric, but her method worked with little bed-wetters, anorexics, children with nightmares, obsessions, tics, stammers, vomiting, tummy aches, and other unexplained sickness. In addition, now that war had been declared, she received the orphans of war, those who had lost their parents to camps, their fathers to the army, and those who were frightened by occupation. When Paris was invaded, her supervisor, Sophie Morgenstern, killed herself. Françoise Marette was forced to become independent, developing a way of working that was revolutionary, but there were many already who thought she was mad, calling her *la folle*.

In 1940, she began working in the department of neuro-psychiatry at l'Hôpital Trousseau, in Paris, establishing the first psychoanalytic consultancy in a neuro-psychiatric department of a children's hospital in France. She worked there until 1979. She was never officially employed by the hospital, but held the position without ever having been an official member of staff and was never paid. It was here that she carried out her research and did her most creative work. In 1942, she married Boris Dolto; the marriage produced three children, Jean Chrisostome (1942–2008), Gregoire

(1944), and Catherine (1946). Boris Dolto was a Ukrainian doctor, whom she had met during a discussion group on the subject of the "waking dream". He was an immigrant from Russia, after the revolution. He worked to pay for his medical studies, qualifying in orthopaedics, and eventually founded the first French school of physiotherapy. During the war he was interviewed by the Nazis and made to strip naked to see if he had been circumcised. He was not, so was declared not to be Jewish, but the humiliation of this act lived with him all his life. He participated in the Paris Resistance, caring for injured members, while two of Françoise Dolto's brothers, Pierre and Jacques, were also in the Resistance. Both Françoise and Boris supported the Resistance, providing refuge and donations of money.

Francoise Dolto found solace within the Russian Orthodox faith of her husband. In contrast to Catholicism, which designates the authority of man over woman, the orthodox liturgy establishes the equality of man and woman as subjects before God and the law, because the law of the Orthodox faith is not a law that demands justice, but is a law based in charity. The law, its rituals and institutions, were made for man rather than that man should serve the law. She did not support a church that institutionalized sadomasochism; rather, what she upheld in Christianity was its radical subversion of power, a God who does not judge, who does not blame, but who encourages the overcoming of obstacles which bar the realization of desire. Her spiritual nature led to explorations of different faiths, including Hinduism, and she and her husband were part of a group that met with Swami Siddheswarananda during the war. They had been introduced to the group by Louis Renou, professor of Sanskrit at the Sorbonne, who was an admirer of Françoise Dolto's work.

The Société Parisienne de Psychanalyse (SPP) was in disarray during the war years and did not reconvene until September 1946. Françoise Dolto was the object of prejudice and criticism within her own society; she was particularly undermined by Lebovici. In *Autoportrait d'une psychanalyste* (1989, p. 138) she attributes Lebovici's attitude to fear based on his rivalry with her for power within the medical establishment. She asserts that she was not ambitious for titles; indeed, she considered such desire for advancement as being incompatible with being a psychoanalyst.

After the war she was involved in many projects, in addition to her hospital work. In 1946, she worked in collaboration with Georges Mauco and Juliette Boutonnier at the Lycée Claude Bernard, where they set up a psycho-pedagogical institution to research and provide help for students with learning difficulties. The research later informed the reform of the education system in France, introducing psychoanalytic ideas into education.

Dolto's father died in 1947. She left the Lycée Claude Bernard in 1949 to join Jenny Roudinesco at a clinic in the Boulevard Ney. Dolto was beginning to establish herself as an influential communicator, participating in radio broadcasts and publishing articles in the journal *Psyche*. In 1949, she was a contributor to the *Dictionnaire de Psychanalyse et de Psychotechnique*. In the same year, she gave a paper at the first International Psychoanalytic Association (IPA) congress since the war, the XVIth International Psychoanalytic Congress at Zurich, giving a seminal paper entitled, "The *Poupée Fleur*, used in psychoanalytic treatment". The *Poupée Fleur* was an invention of Françoise Dolto's, for use in the treatment of a little schizophrenic girl. She had noticed how frequently flowers were depicted in the drawings of children with narcissistic disturbances and among anorexics. She made a doll that had a flower face but no features, and no hands or feet. The *Poupée Fleur* served as a mirror to stimulate a primitive, aggressive oral transference and to unblock communication. Her creativity with children began to excite the interest of an international audience.

Lacan, who was now on the training committee of the SPP, responded to Françoise Dolto's paper:

> Doctor Lacan feels strongly that the Poupée Fleur of Madame Dolto has a bearing on his researches into the Mirror Stage, the narcissistic body image and the disintegrated body. He thinks it is important that the doll has no mouth, would like to stress that it is a sexual symbol and that it masks the human face. He would like to finish by saying that one day he would like to make a theoretical contribution in response to Madame Dolto's offering. [Dolto & Nasio, 1987, 2002, p. 57]

Françoise Dolto responded by saying that the *Poupée Fleur* did indeed connect to the mirror stage, but only on condition that the mirror stage could be understood not only as reflecting what is visible, but also included what is heard, felt, and intended. The mirror stage, for Lacan, brought with it a sense of narcissistic jubilation, whereas for Françoise Dolto, the mirror stage brought with it the experience of castration and a sense of sadness, of not being the image reflected by the mirror. The mirror, for Françoise Dolto, was a mirror of all the senses, which formed a basis for what was to become her major theoretical contribution, *L'Image inconsciente du corps*, "a mirror of the being of the subject in the other" (*ibid.*, p. 59).

Meanwhile, in Paris, a schism was opening up in the SPP. The main source of dissension within the organization hinged on Lacan's unorthodox psychoanalytic practice: specifically, his shortened sessions. Françoise Dolto was also the object of criticism, partly because she allied herself with Lacan, but also because, in her own right, she was a creative non-conformist who had little respect for the rigidity of the rules of the psychoanalytic institution. Françoise Dolto was not a Lacanian, but she recognized the revolutionary nature of Lacan's ideas. She was impressed by how the analysands of Lacan were able to work effectively with children because Lacan had an acute ear for primitive states within the adult. Lacan, for his part, held Françoise Dolto in esteem and frequently referred to her patients he found too difficult.

In December 1952, Jacques Lacan was elected provisional director of the new Institute of Psychoanalysis that had grown out of the SPP. This overturned an election earlier in the year, deemed unconstitutional, which had appointed Sacha Nacht as director. Sacha Nacht and his followers wanted to reserve the diploma in psychoanalysis for those who were medically qualified. This was opposed by the analysands of Laforgue, who included Daniel Lagache and Françoise Dolto. In 1953, Lacan became president of the SPP and Nacht was re-elected president of the Institute. There followed a period of dissension amongst the students, led by Jenny Roudinesco, resulting in a petition delivered to Nacht and Lacan, complaining about the undemocratic nature of the institute, the paternalistic control exerted over the training, and demanding codification of the Institute's rules. Françoise Dolto supported the students, who wanted to ensure that students who were in receipt of bursaries would have the right to choose their own analyst. Lacan found himself in a minority on the training committee in his support of the students, so was forced to resign as president and was followed by Françoise Dolto, Daniel Lagache, and Juliette Favez-Boutonnier. In June 1953, Daniel Lagache formed the Société Française de Psychanalyse. None of the analysts who resigned from the SPP realized that in so doing they would lose their membership of the IPA.

It was during the XIIth IPA congress in London, at which Françoise Dolto was to speak, that the president, Heinz Hartmann, refused membership of the IPA to those who had resigned from the SPP. Françoise Dolto was not allowed to speak. A commission was set up to investigate the practice of each member who had resigned, including Lacan and Dolto. This commission included Winnicott, who was to interview Françoise Dolto to judge whether she was worthy to remain a member of the IPA. During this investigation, Lebovici made a public declaration that Françoise Dolto was a member of the communist party. This was a lie. In fact, it was Lebovici himself who had previously been a member of the French communist party, before resigning in order to pursue his career as a consultant psychoanalyst. Lebovici's assertion was very damaging at the time when McCarthyism was rife in the USA and Europe was also terrified by the spectre of Soviet communism. He also defamed Françoise Dolto's character by claiming that she spent her weekends in the company of her patients, which was also a lie. In addition, as if it were a sign of moral turpitude, he accused her of being a Jungian. Again, this was untrue. She had been let down by her fellow analysts, including Hartmann and Lagache, who knew her practice to be honourable; they had been present when Lebovici slandered her and said nothing. She was disgusted by the narcissism of psychoanalytic institutions, and astonished by the falseness of people who by rights should be true to themselves, who seemed to be afraid, in her words, "of being alive" (Dolto, 1989, pp. 141–142).

The committee of inquiry set up by the IPA, chaired by Winnicott, interviewed Françoise Dolto. Winnicott is said to have commented that he was interested in her work and found her innovative, but he reproached her for her *wild creativity* and said that "She has too much intuition and not enough method to be a teacher" (Roudinesco, 1986, p. 329). Thus, Françoise Dolto was excluded from the IPA, as was Lacan. It is puzzling as to why Winnicott was so damning of Dolto, especially given that they were both paediatricians working in the same field of primitive psychosomatic disturbance. Perhaps there was an element of rivalry in the decision. It is likely that the commission was suspicious of her association with Lacan; also, that they would not have known what to make of a child analyst without the affiliations that they recognized, to Anna Freud or to Melanie Klein. Perhaps there was an element of machismo and fear in reaction against this clever, outspoken woman who was not afraid to speak from her intuition.

Dolto never practised short sessions. In fact, she was very much against what she thought of as a potentially sadistic practice. In *Autoportrait d'une psychanalyste*, she speaks of how important the idea of "method" (p. 183) is to her in the practice of psychoanalysis. She always took notes of her patients' dreams, annotating them like a musical score, always noting the detail, the repetitions and the transference. The "method" entails finding out what a particular remark recalls of the past and how it relates to history of the drives and the libidinal stages, to evince what period in the relational history of the patient is being relived in the analysis. Also, she observed closely the psychosomatic communications within the analysis, the emergence of bodily dysfunctions, often relating them to the earliest experiences of life, before or after birth. She describes a compassionate and classical approach within psychoanalytic sessions, paying close attention to what her countertransference informs her of the patient's unconscious process, being very sensitive to the effect she has on the patient, as a person and as an analyst.

Undeterred by exclusion from the IPA, the SFP began to find its own voice. In 1953, Lacan gave a seminal paper in Rome, "La function et le champ de la parole en psychanalyse", which Françoise Dolto responded to by saying:

> With or without words, there is language . . . an infant, a few days old . . . expresses his contentment with responsive and meaningful noises . . . And if the mother mimics the same sound, echoing him, the infant receives and considers it. This exchange, this language . . . is a creative language which enables the infant to structure its sensations . . . which enables him to develop not into a mere digestive system but into a human being. [1989, p. 919]

Thus, she began to declare her profound belief in the vital nature of language, a belief which had already led her into talking to babies, and so dramatically relieving their anguish. For the next seventeen years she and Jacques Lacan had a fruitful, if uneasy, professional relationship. She remained within the organization that Lacan founded in order not to be alone, because she believed that to be an analyst one has to communicate with others, as otherwise the lure of narcissism may be too powerful. The positive aspect of no longer being a member of the IPA was that it freed her to think for herself. In the years that followed, she developed her central and original contribution to psychoanalysis, *L'Image inconsciente du corps* (Dolto, 1984). It followed on from her work with very regressed children, in the course of which she noticed that their drawing displayed images of archaic foetal life and of the body as sensed within the first days of life. If the child is not born into language the *image du corps* is abandoned, resulting in severe disturbance. Throughout the1950s, she held seminars for trainee analysts, extracts of which are to be found in the *Séminaire de psychanalyse d'enfants I* (1982a). In this time she also developed ideas about feminine sexuality, which she spoke about in a Congress in Holland in 1960, later published in *Libido féminine* (1982b).

Yet again, in 1961, the IPA refused the SPF membership. A new schism began to open up within the SPF, with certain members wanting to submit to the demands of the IPA. In 1962, Françoise Dolto's mother died. In 1963, Lacan and Dolto were excluded from the list of teachers at the SPF. Rather than accept the conditions imposed by the IPA, in December 1963, Lacan, followed by Leclaire, Dolto, Aulagnier, Aubry, Octave and Maud Mannoni, and many others, left the SFP, establishing, in 1964, l'Ecole française de Psychanalyse later to be called l'Ecole Freudienne de Paris. Françoise Dolto led a seminar at the Ecole Freudienne for clinicians, supervising their work with difficult cases, many of which are recorded in her *Séminaire de psychanalyse d'enfants II* (1985).

There followed a long and creative period of working as a clinician, teaching, broadcasting, writing, and involvement in social projects. In 1967, she gave a paper on a psychotic boy, Dominique, in a conference on infantile psychosis organized by Maud Mannoni in Paris. This conference was attended by Ronnie Laing and other members of the anti-psychiatry movement in Britain. Later, the paper was published as *Le cas de Dominique*, and has been one of only two books written by her hitherto published in English. Dolto was able to understand, by listening to Dominique's words, the meaning of his illness and its place within his family history. She describes how his psychosis is a function of not having experienced the humanizing effects of benign castration, which had resulted in a malignant regression to an archaic body image.

From 1969 Dolto began to broadcast on French radio, first as Doctor X on Europe1, to parents about the conflicts of childhood. In 1970, she participated in a programme, on France Culture, on the role of the father. In 1971, she participated in a televised debate supporting a new proposed French law to improve the legal status of children born out of wedlock. She is most well known in France for her broadcasts on France-Inter, *Lorsque l'enfant parait*; she broadcasted for twelve minutes every day of the week for two years, answering parents' questions. She received about a hundred letters a week, which, if she could not deal with on air, she would reply to personally (Dolto, 2005, p. 925). It is interesting to note how her childhood love of the radio found its way into communicating her passion for the welfare of children.

Meanwhile, the EFP was in the throes of internal conflict; both Dolto and Lacan were growing old. In 1979, Françoise Dolto had retired as a practising psychoanalyst and was unwell. Certain members wanted to dissolve the organization because of Lacan's authoritarian rule. Jacques-Alain Miller and Eric Laurent defined what was truly Lacanian, dismissing Dolto for turning psychoanalysis into "Good News", presumably an allusion to a certain evangelism in her attitude. Françoise Dolto opposed the dissolution of the school, but spoke out against what she perceived as a violent dogmatism that had developed amongst the followers of Lacan. She was in conflict with him, but remained his friend. In 1980, Lacan dissolved the EFP. Françoise Dolto never again belonged to a psychoanalytic organization. In 1981, Jacques Lacan died, a few months after the death of her husband, Boris Dolto.

Françoise Dolto was now approaching the end of her own life. She spent much of her time writing, publishing many books on her life's work. She had also been able to create a work group which met regularly to discuss the problems particular to deaf children, which eventually, in 1983, became an association, *Communication Précoce Entendants et Non-Entendants*. Her flat was next to a school for deaf children, and she had long felt a deep concern for the plight of the deaf. After the dissolution of EFP, she held her seminars in this school, l'Institut des Jeunes Sourds.

Dolto realized one of her major life achievements in 1979 with the opening of the first Maison Verte, in the 15th arrondissement in Paris. The Maison Verte was an original idea of Françoise Dolto's: it was to be a place where children younger than the age of three might socialize and play, without having to separate from one or other parent or carer, where their identity was respected, and where parents might speak of their anxieties with psychoanalytically informed staff. It was to be a place that was neither educational nor medical, without bureaucracy, with payment according to means, providing a space for the unconscious within the community. Since the opening of this first Maison Verte, more than a hundred have been opened throughout France and all over the world.

Conclusion

Françoise Dolto is an important figure in the development of infant and child psychoanalysis in the twentieth century. She was a brilliant clinician, particularly in her work with children who were severely disturbed. That she is not an influence in Anglo-Saxon countries is an enigma that this book seeks to redress. That she became unacceptable to the IPA may be explained by her departure from strictly orthodox practice, by her loyalty to Lacan, and possibly because of the conflict between the nature of her religious beliefs and classical psychoanalytic theory. Given the deeply perceptive nature of her thinking and her success as a clinician, this does not reflect well on the effect of the institutionalization and bureaucratization of psychoanalysis. It could be argued that she did not defend herself sufficiently well against malicious rumour and the unfairness of her treatment, both by senior members of her own training organization and by members of the IPA who were charged with investigating her practice. Indeed, there does appear to be a repetition in the behaviour of her colleagues towards her, notably Winnicott, and the dismissive and sometimes contemptuous attitude her mother held towards her. It may indeed be that she was afflicted by a form of survivor guilt, which meant that she never felt that she was fully entitled to belong to her family of origin. Whatever the reason, she was able to use her position as outsider creatively and productively, challenging the institutions of France, the family, the church, hospitals, schools, and universities to think psychoanalytically about the minds of children and young people and the suffering that they endure from the earliest days of their existence, in a way that is unparalleled in Anglo-Saxon countries.

Françoise Dolto was deeply spiritual, a practising Catholic, and had always been a committed Christian. Her ideas about the subject of desire are radically different from those of Jacques Lacan. She believed that psychoanalysis could only have been created by someone from a Jewish spiritual tradition, within which Christianity finds its roots. Within these traditions there is no subject without God. She explains:

> There is no subject without God. If I exist, it is because God exists. I cannot exist without God. It is very curious that psychoanalysts do not realise this. Clearly for Lacan the subject is a hole; he was frightened of this void that was his version of the subject. But it is not true! What is true is that we will never know what the subject is if we do not recognise that it is a part of God incarnate. But the desire for life is God in each one of us. It is the subject before the word that appears with the word, not only the spoken word but that which comes into being with every significant act. So, to be incarnated is a meaningful act of a subject God. I don't see how it is possible to think otherwise. From within Christian folklore, not the thinking of the church, the meaning of the subject of the word or of the subject speaking to God, or of God responding, within the Bible, is equivalent to our understanding of the unconscious. [Dolto, 1989, p. 158]

She claimed that it was the experience of psychoanalysis that gave her faith, the capacity to live according to an unknowable truth, while accepting that which is unique and unforeseen: to have the ability to be aware of the awesome quality of life which destabilizes and disturbs.

Françoise Dolto had an inspired and fruitful life. She had a long and happy marriage and enjoyed her children and family. She died, according to her daughter Catherine, "lucid, joyful and serene", on the 25th August 1988.

References

Bonnefoy, Y. (1991). *Greek and Egyptian Mythologies*. Chicago, IL: University of Chicago Press.

Chérer, S. (2008). *Ma Dolto.* Paris: Editions Stock.
Dolto, F. (1939). *Psychanalyse et pédiatrie.* Private publication, 1940 [reprinted Paris: editions de la parole, 1961].
Dolto, F. (1982a). *Seminaire de psychanalyse d'enfants, tome I. (en collaboration avec Louis Cadagues).* Paris. Le Seuil. Coll. "Points Essais", 1991.
Dolto, F. (1982b). *Libido féminine.* Paris: Editions Carrère, 1987.
Dolto, F. (1984). *L'Image inconsciente du corps.* Paris: Le Seuil; coll. "Points Essais", 1992.
Dolto, F. (1985). *Seminaire de psychanalyse d'enfants, tome II. (en collaboration avec Jean François de Sauverzac).* Paris. Le Seuil. Coll. Points Essais, 1991.
Dolto, F. (1986). *Interview par J. P. Winter.* Direction editorial et réalisation E. Noblecourt, 2008 MK2 S/A.
Dolto, F. (1989). *L'Autoportrait d'une psychanalyste, 1934–1988.* Paris: Coll. "Points", Le Seuil, 1992.
Dolto, F. (1990). *Lorsque l'enfant paraît, I, II, III.* Paris: Le Seuil.1977, 1978, 1979.
Dolto, F. (2003). *Françoise Dolto. Lettres de jeunesse. Correspondance 1913–1938,* C. Percheminier (Ed.). Paris: Gallimard.
Dolto, F. (2005). *Une vie de correspondances, 1938–1988.* M. Djeribi-Valentin (Ed.). Paris: Gallimard.
Dolto, F., & Nasio, J. D. (1987). *L'Enfant du miroir.* Paris : Rivages Coll. "Petite Bibliothèque Payot", Paris: Payot, 1992.
Lacan, J. (1977). The mirror stage as formative of the function of the I. In: *Ecrits. A Selection,* A. Sheridan (Trans.). London: Tavistock.
Roudinesco, E. (1986). *Histoire de la psychanalyse en France (1925–1985), 2.* Paris: Fayard, 1994.

CHAPTER TWO

Françoise Dolto's contribution to neonatology

Catherine Vanier

When I began my work in neonatal care, I worked with Françoise Dolto. I encountered much prejudice. Françoise Dolto supported and encouraged me when I said to her: "They treat me like a witch. They want me to work in a broom cupboard." This was a fact, because the first office in which I received a mother was indeed a broom cupboard, with a broom for a witch. I went to complain to Françoise Dolto, whose advice to me was: "Just hang on in there. When I started work, doctors, even psychoanalysts, treated me as if I was crazy." Eventually, they realized I was right. From the moment of birth something has to be taken care of, alongside bringing the body to life. From the moment of the baby's arrival, as a team we care for the baby, not only as a body, which has to be helped to maintain a continuity of being, but we also have to care for the baby's humanity, for him as a bearer of a history that precedes his coming into hospital. This history, of which his stay at the neonatal care unit will be only an episode, will continue into the future as long as there is no trauma to interrupt it. So often the tear of a premature birth testifies to a breaking of the chain of signifiers that prevents symbolization, making it impossible to carry the child. The neo-natal team has to bear in mind the context of gestation that is greater than the link between the mother and baby alone.

We are far from being merely skilled practitioners and observers and our emphasis is on making a place for the child in the world and delivering him into true speech. It is this speech that has power over the body. The medical care provided by doctors as bearers of a desire to live is not always enough. To live, one must also inscribe oneself in speech: otherwise the human being dies. If a human being is inscribed, or inscribes himself, into mad speech he might collapse into madness. Two children born at the same time, of the same weight, and demonstrating similar symptoms will not necessarily evolve identically, even if they benefit from the exact same quality of care. It is the impossibility of generalization that challenges us, but we should not necessarily believe that medical practitioners ask themselves the same question. Every single body inscribed with different speech is as a consequence completely different. Medical knowledge (*savoir*) that speaks of the body in generalities thus clashes with the truth of every human being's unique body. It is the link of truth between speech and the body that the analyst within a medical service comes to question. This variety of truth is different from medical knowledge, in that it raises the question of desire and of fantasy.

Hospitalization means different things to different families and for doctors it has yet another meaning. Medicine can, at times, "undo" something of that which has the quality of a curse.

I am going to tell you briefly a story of a little girl, whom I will call Zora, whose mother was of Arabic origin. The mother gave birth by Caesarean section, very prematurely, at twenty-seven weeks. It was her first child. Zora had already been in the unit for three days and her mother, in the maternity ward of the same hospital, did not want to come see her. She was crying. She was crying in her bed and, as mothers separated from their babies often do, she said that after the operation she was only able to get herself together slowly and that the wound was not healing well. "It's a girl," she repeated ceaselessly. "It's a girl. She's too small. I don't want to see her." When I saw her three days later, she had not come to see the baby but she did come to the appointment that I systematically offer to all mothers. She explained to me that she was the sixth and last daughter of a mother who herself had been in despair at not having a boy.

"At home, you know, it's very important. You have to have a boy. It's our culture, our tradition. Otherwise you're not a good wife. By the way, my husband is still in our home country and I haven't dared to talk to him about it. I haven't called him. I pretended as if nothing was happening. I would rather think she was not yet born, that it hasn't happened yet."

And she was desperately shedding her own tears, and the tears of her mother who cried at her birth; she refused to see Zora, turning away her eyes when we took her to the cot. But the nurses were not discouraged. Day after day they would try to talk to her about her little daughter: at the entrance, in the hallway, not rushing her, letting her come slowly.

This little girl was just ravishing. She was cheerful, endearing, and she quickly made a place for herself in the service. Everybody really liked her, all the more so given the fact that she demanded a lot from the staff because she was refusing the bottle! Even after resuscitation and in spite of having caught up with the full-term children, she still would not drink.

During this period, every time I met up with Zora's mother, who was beginning to suffer a bit less from the wound in her stomach, she would talk to me about her other wound; the wound of her childhood, of her own mother's violence, of her phobias of impulsive acts which paralysed her, because she truly believed that she was capable of killing her child. Then, slowly, she started to talk about the little girl, to ask questions. "I wonder how she's getting on?"

I replied, "When you want to you can go to the unit and see her. She also must be wondering how you are."

At the same time, the mother became aggressive towards the hospital staff. The more aggressive she became towards them, the more she would talk about her despair, of the impossibility she felt of being a mother, and so the more she would begin to speak, with tenderness, about her wish to see the baby.

Since the mother had kept refusing to come to the cot, the staff first decided to talk to the baby themselves about her and her mother's history. But every day, the mother would come closer and closer to the cot; she was becoming a bit tamer.

The staff were providing a link between the two, talking to one, then talking to the other: "Maybe your mother wants to say this"; "I think your little girl wants to tell you this". Slowly, but gently, the mother would allow herself, too, to speak to the baby, to touch her, to take her in her arms.

Then something amazing happened: one day we were standing around the incubator when Zora began to cry. Suddenly the mother said, "Ah, but I know what she wants. She's hungry." She was a baby that would never take a bottle. We quickly found one and gave it to the mother. This was the first time that Zora drank a whole bottle. The mother told me, "She now looks like a baby to me. That's why I thought that she was hungry. Before, I preferred to think of her as if she had not yet been born, as if the nightmare of childbirth hadn't happened. Now I know that she is here, that she calls me."

From this moment on she was able to be a mother. It was a month and a half after the baby's birth. One day, a nurse said to Zora's mother, "You know, she really is beautiful, your little girl. One day she'll have beautiful children, just like you." To hear this promise was very important for the woman, because what she heard in it was the possibility of repairing the wound her own mother had dealt her. She then slowly became more able to welcome her daughter, who in turn could begin to inscribe herself, without shame, in the family's history.

There is no doubt that, during the period of hospitalization, with appropriate intervention, some things can be prevented. What might have happened to this mother and to Zora had they stayed from the beginning alone and together? Leaving the hospital, with Zora in her arms, the mother called in at my office, without an appointment. She said to me, "I just wanted to tell you something: tell the nurses not to be angry with me. It is true that sometimes, for days, I was bad to them. But you see, this bad thing was in my stomach. I managed to get it out. Now, Zora and I, we are going to try to live." It was very important that the staff accepted this mother the way she was, rejecting her daughter and being aggressive towards them, without trying to enforce at any cost a mother–child attachment, in order to make a link before the mother was able to speak about what in her own history was making it impossible for her to be a mother. Only then could she hear the cry of her daughter as a call, and so to enable her baby to be a subject.

Here is another story, of a little boy whom I will call Steve. In the hospital unit, there are mothers who are labelled as unsympathetic, obnoxious, and aggressive. This is very difficult, because there is an idea at large of a "typical good mother"; a mummy who is "all love". It is unthinkable that there should not be love between a mother and a baby. (I think that the idealization of the mother–child relationship remains one of the last bastions of repression in our society.)

At birth, Steve weighed 900 grams. He was systematically refusing to make contact with us. With some babies, you are alerted of the risk of a movement towards autism, of the baby sliding away, of not being really present any more. Since his birth, Steve was, however, very present, very attentive. As soon as he could, he would smile a little, which was very soon, despite his 900 grams. But, on the other hand, once we began to try to give him a bottle, he would interrupt all contact with us. From this moment, he did not want to hear anything from us. He refused to be bottle-fed and would throw up his meals. The staffs were getting worried. By chance, they noticed that there was one particular nurse from whom he would take a bottle.

She was a nurse who was unlike the others. She was more distant; she would give him the bottle, but with the child at the very edge of her lap, with the bottle as far away from her as possible. She never gave him a cuddle. She would talk to him, saying, "You don't want to . . . but now you're going to drink." In fact, she was very pleasant, but she was not inclined to show love. She did not glue the child to herself. The staff were surprised to see that it was this nurse that Steve wanted. Each time he would not take the bottle from us, we would say, "We will ask her." And she would come, saying to him, "You're such a pain. Come here!" And then, he would start drinking. The staff were surprised by this. Only a long time afterwards, when we had understood Steve's history, in listening to his parents as they were telling it to us, did we say to ourselves, "In order to survive, this little boy needs to put this distance between us and himself." He knew that love is not so simple.

The parents told us that within two generations there had been two crimes of passion. And here was this little boy—do not ask me how or why—who knew that love is not just to do with pleasure but that love can kill. Some babies and children have an uncanny sense of the dangers involved in loving.

At which point in time will a mother be able to think of her baby as a subject? That is what happened as a result of Zora's cry, her call to her mother.

At birth, the baby only exists in and through his mother—his mother, or any other person who touches him, who speaks to him, who names him, who tells him whom he is: whoever defines him as a boy or a girl, who intimates what he is feeling or what he is thinking, whoever it is who is able to understand him. In the beginning, a little human being is not a subject, in spite of what is sometimes said. The subject is in the other. The little one is not a subject. The subject of the unconscious is constituted first in the other: the one who speaks and who speaks to him, who speaks to him as a function of his own desire. The baby exists and he is a human being, but he is not yet a subject. We might say that he is an object, or, according to Lacan, "an object of *jouissance*" (1977a). If all goes well, the child is an object of *jouissance*, valued, rendered "phallic" by his mother: in the mother's eyes the infant is transformed from an object of desire into a subject of desire. This first joyful encounter, the mother's response to the call of her baby, is essential.

If the baby in question is born prematurely, what happens to the mother's libidinal investment? It is difficult to feel really happy, really proud and fulfilled. A prematurely born baby of 500 grams is traumatic to see, when glimpsed in the incubator. Is it possible for a mother to be narcissistically gratified by a premature baby? Most mothers experience a sense of disappointment that leaves them feeling invalidated.

The initial stage is essential, when the infant is "phallicized", made into a subject of desire by the mother. However, when a mother beholds a baby who is too small, she feels ashamed and guilt-stricken and suffers a breakdown in her imaginative capacity. The separation that is indispensable to the formation of the baby as a subject becomes problematic because the symbolic will fail him. Without lack, without separation, no demand is possible.

During the process of resuscitation the baby does not experience the need to make a demand. The small, premature newborn is connected to a machine, a machine that is always there. There is no rhythm in the lives of these babies, there is no discontinuity, there is no night and no day. The child is never hungry. By what means is this baby going to satisfy himself?

Obviously, there is something of a presence and absence provided by the staff. Does this coming and going function as a basic rhythm, when the doctor arrives, when he departs? A nurse may come to perform an aspiration, to give an injection, or to take blood, all of which are unpleasant procedures. How then does rhythm establish itself for such a baby? The presence of mothers within a resuscitation unit is not without problems. Often these mothers are in a traumatized state of mind. An enormous amount of time is spent in trying to help them recover, in order for them to be able to be really present with their babies. They are like ghosts; mostly they visit infrequently because they are unable to hold themselves together for very long. They stand there, not daring to touch the baby, or even to move, not daring to speak to the baby. The staff have an important function, which is not merely medical, to bring the baby to life. It is often these first care-takers who give him "a taste of desire".

But let us get back to the more specific problem of feeding. Zora's cry was identified by her mother as a call, a demand to be fed, and seems to have triggered within Zora a desire to drink.

The question arises as to what role the oral drive might play in the process of resuscitation. In *The Four Fundamental Concepts, Seminar XI,* Lacan makes an incredible statement:

> Even when you stuff the mouth, the mouth that opens in response to the drive is not satisfied by the food, the food is in the service of the pleasure of the mouth. The oral drive does no more than order from the menu. For the oral drive it is not a question of food but of the breast, the object that stimulates desire. [1977b, p. 167]

The issue of feeding in the resuscitation unit strikes at the heart of this problem. To orientate ourselves at this point in this we must first get out of a psychologizing tendency that confuses the drive and the instinct. For Freud, the drive (pulsion) is a key concept, because it gives human beings their life force. It is the drives that give us the force to live and which give neurotic symptoms the energy to constitute themselves.

In the beginning, Freud distinguishes between two groups of drives: the sexual drives and the drives of self-preservation. The latter include thirst and hunger, which support the subject's survival, not only at his reproduction. However, herein lies the problem: Freud indicates that the preservation of the ego does not completely fit into the register of need, but that the question of desire arises. This is really troubling because, as far as need is concerned, we know what that is, but desire is another question! It is not enough to say "it is good to desire, or the desire of the mother, or the desire of the baby". By definition, we never know what desire is because it is always unconscious. We feel that there are things that we want, we have the idea of perhaps wanting this or that, that we like this or that. In fact, we do not really know: desire is unconscious.

As far as the question of desire is concerned, Freud complicates everything. In 1920 he imposed the duality of the drives, of the life drive and the death drive, on all drive theory.

We are thus confronted with the question of desire. What desire induces a 500-gram baby to either live or die? What, beyond the body itself, are we trying to resuscitate? We are now very far from it being merely a question of nourishment. Rather, it indicates that we should allow for the loop that leads the child to make a demand to be fed, to be established. It is not a question of encouraging the child to desire. It is more a question of making the child desire to desire, because that is what keeps us all alive, that we desire to desire. And we never stop, that is why we are here every morning, why we love, why we hate, why we make bonds with others.

We do not stop desiring for a simple reason: because we never have what we want. You have all noticed it: it is never what we thought we wanted. We know only too well that the object of the drive can never be reached. What one wants, one cannot have. One is impelled towards the object but the object eludes us. We fail to reach it not because of particular conditions but for structural reasons. The drive misses its object, creating a loop, which then leads it back, rekindling its source, and once more setting off on its trajectory. In this way, one always desires and one always is—to use Dolto's expression—in one's 'going–becoming' *allant–devenant*, in the spirit of one's gender. One moves forward.

This story of a loop of desire which provokes desire and yet more desire and which ensures that we are alive rather than dead, is, however, not something mechanical: it requires the involvement of another human being. And for premature infants, it is indeed more complicated. When I first arrived at the unit, the infants were referred to as "mechanical children", to indicate that they were connected to the machines. A mechanical baby! What can be done to ensure that a machine does not replace the presence of another?

There is no registration of the drive without the demand of another: there is no nourishment, no satisfaction possible unless the question of the other's *jouissance* is taken into account. There must be another and even more than that, there must be another able to witness his own *jouissance* in the baby's presence, in response to the fact that the baby eats, that we feed him. The world surrounding the baby is received by the infant as real, as a kind of a thing, that in the beginning he is merged with. That which surrounds him is the real, and it is himself. We know, for example, that babies who are no longer ventilated breathe more easily if the noise of the machine is preserved in their environment. For weeks the baby had been hearing this noise, and if it is left on there is more chance of not having to reventilate them. This is really incredible. It probably means that the baby has confused himself with this machine.

He has become the world, and like all other babies who become the world that is imposed upon them, he became this machine. He became this machine, and is spoken to by its noise. He is the object of this absolute other, who is already there. This other who makes of the infant a mere toy of its mechanical language, since the noise in question is a sort of speech. But when the noise in question is just noise, well, then, it is much more complicated for the loop of desire to establish itself.

All the work done in the resuscitation unit is undertaken with the aim of giving relationship to a human being priority over relationship to a machine, in order to avoid the serious psychological repercussions, which are always a risk, even if the baby survives resuscitation physically.

For the newborn, the other is, in the beginning, not separate and, most importantly, does not make sense to him. It is only at the time of separation that the child will become a subject. The separation from things, from the surrounding world occurs when one begins to say to oneself, "Oh, look, I am different." His separation from the machine will have to be worked with, and it will be necessary to put intermediaries between the machine and the infant, the doctors, the staff, the parents, to replace the noise with words. The separation will only occur following this first alienation, but the subject who is separating himself will suffer yet another alienation because he will try to deny the separation at any cost. We spend our lives trying to deny separation—to use an object to plug the hole of this loss: the object of the oral drive, for example, or of the anal drive, and of all the other drives. This object, which is now cut off from him, because he does not have it any more, is now the cause of his desire, so that he has a desire to find it again, to find something. And it is here that the fantasy is formed and that is what feeds the mouth.

The time spent in the resuscitation unit undermines the process of alienation–separation. To be the object of the maternal other's *jouissance* is not a simple thing, if one's mother regards one as a catastrophe. What is the mother's desire concerning the baby? Separating oneself from her and finding one's meaning as a subject through the effect of another signifier, that of the paternal function, is really not so simple. Fathers also find themselves invalidated by premature birth, if only because they cannot hold their place alongside their wives, whom they fail to contain and reassure. It seems that in the separation from the mother, in these premature births, the cut of birth is doubled and cancels itself out. Remember Zora's mother's words: "She has not yet been born."

It had occurred to us that the service itself was, in fact, made to position itself as this third function, as the paternal function, thereby allowing separation. It seems to us important to emphasize not the preservation of a mother–child link at any cost, but that time should be taken so that work can be done to effect a real separation; that there should be recognition of lack, of loss, so that a desire for desire may be established.

In order for the baby to be hungry, that he may then drink, he must be first given this taste of desire. During resuscitation, the baby's desire is brought to life. It is a question of resuscitating this desire.

One day, Françoise Dolto, to whom I was again talking about my work, said to me, "Well, you really are doing a peculiar job. You have managed to create for yourself an insane function: you are a psychoanalyst who resuscitates."

Medical staff are now beginning to recognize that the most sophisticated protocols will not suffice to resuscitate an infant. Even if the effects of language on the bodies and the being of infants appear to them to be mysterious or even like witchcraft, the medical staff know that paediatrics must take psychoanalysis into account in order to receive and welcome the child, a welcome that the infant needs in order for the desire for life to establish itself. In addition to acknowledging the scientific progress made by modern medicine, doctors may now acknowledge their debt to the thinking and practice of Françoise Dolto.

References

Lacan, J. (1977a). The signification of the phallus. In: *Ecrits*, A. Sheridan (Trans.). London: Tavistock.

Lacan, J. (1977b). *The Four Fundamental Concepts of Psycho-analysis*, A. Sheridan (Trans.). London: Hogarth.

CHAPTER THREE

Childhood psychosis

Sian Morgan

Several French psychoanalysts influenced by Lacan have written on childhood psychosis and autism, including Françoise Dolto, Maud Mannoni, and, more recently, Catherine Mathelin Vanier. Very little of their work has been translated. *Le cas Dominique* (1971), the case of a pre-psychotic adolescent boy, is the only one of Françoise Dolto's thirty-four works available in translation into English. Much of Françoise Dolto's writing focuses on childhood psychosis and autism; in her writing, the term autism is used to describe a form of severe childhood psychosis. Dolto's interest in child psychoanalysis grew out of her work as a paediatrician in a children's hospital in the 1930s, which influenced her research and contributed to her medical thesis, entitled *Psychanalyse et pédiatrie* (1939). She held an unpaid position as a child psychoanalyst at the Hôpital Trousseau in Paris from 1940 until 1978. Here, she supervised the cases of trainee psychoanalysts that later informed her seminars on child psychoanalysis, published in the 1980s. Donald Winnicott and Françoise Dolto were contemporaries; both were paediatricians and psychoanalysts, both were extremely sensitive to the developing mind of the infant, and both shared the same interests in primitive emotional disorders. Thus, it is surprising that Winnicott is known to have dismissed her as being too intuitive. English psychoanalysis has persisted in being deeply suspicious of Lacanian psychoanalysis, and this accounts in part for the lack of interest in Françoise Dolto's work, which, within France, has had revolutionary effects on childcare.

Françoise Dolto's ideas on the nature of childhood psychosis developed throughout her life. At first, she focused on the role of regression within a disturbed relationship between mother and child. Subsequently, she took into account the family dynamic and the child's place within the family unconscious. The focus of her analysis was on that which is misunderstood and/or unspoken within the family. Her theoretical originality lay in her emphasis on the regression to an archaic body image that she perceived as occurring in childhood psychosis. Françoise Dolto believed that children vulnerable to psychosis are among the most sensitive and precocious members of society; infants who in some significant way are not responded to appropriately, who then become shut off and turned in on themselves. She recognized that the origins of psychosis are complex.

Although she did not consider herself a Lacanian, and indeed many of her ideas were radically different from his, Françoise Dolto worked alongside Jacques Lacan and was influenced by his theories. There follows a brief outline of some of Jacques Lacan's ideas that have influenced Dolto and are relevant to childhood psychosis. (I owe a debt to my colleague Roger Bacon for clarifying some of Lacan's ideas.)

For Lacan, there is no such thing as a preverbal period or a prelinguistic world because, before an infant speaks, it is spoken to and spoken about. When an infant is born, he is born into language, a language that has been prepared for him by both his culture and his inheritance. The infant is born into and through language, the language of the other, and the psychic survival of the infant is dependent on language. From the earliest days, the infant demands a response; without a response there is no language acquisition and no infant.

There is no identity outside of language not created or conferred through language, and the truth and falsehood of identity lies in language, not in the person. The infant absorbs and is absorbed by a language that, in Lacanian terms, constitutes the subject, the subject of desires, demands, expectations, images, identity, and of the various responses it evokes. Long before it can actually speak, its speech is filled with the speech of others.

In 'The Child, his "illness" and the Others', Maud Mannoni emphasises that a child is born into a pre-existing discourse to which he has to submit. It depends on the nature of the unconscious parental discourse as to whether or not a child may have access to his own speech.

Analysis is, thus:

> Not a dual relationship in which the analyst offers himself as the object of transference. The most important factor is not the interpersonal relationship but what is going on in the process of communicating; that is the locus from which the subject is speaking; whom is he addressing and for whom. [1970, p. 53]

The function of analysis is, therefore, to free the patient from a predetermined language, from the alienating words of others, which is inevitably a painful procedure. Before a child is born, its family will hold preconceptions about the child, many of these unconscious, which leads to misrecognition of identity. That which is expressed in the language of the other, who gives birth to the subject, is the possibility of recognizing or of denying the truth of the subject. The subject may be given respect and recognized as separate and different, or be merely an image or reflection of the other's desires and demand.

A patient of mine, who came to see me as an adolescent, felt burdened by parental expectation. She performed brilliantly at school but did not value herself or her achievements. Both her parents had been loving and supportive, but she had experienced her father as demanding her understanding of his emotional pain when she had been a small child and, at the same time, she had experienced her mother as depressed and anxious. My patient was the second child, and had been born a few weeks early, as the result of an elective Caesarean because a previous child, two years older, had been damaged in the course of labour. My patient displayed a prematurity in many aspects of her development and found the process of transition from one stage of life to the next unbearably painful. She did not feel entitled to her own life, as if she was living in the shadow of another's. It transpired that her mother, the eldest child, had suffered terribly when her baby brother, the second child, had died when she was two. She had suffered the most terrible grief, jealousy, guilt, and lack of entitlement to her own life, which had been transmitted to my patient. My patient unconsciously bore the consequences of the baby's death alongside her mother. As a child, she had felt charged with bringing the dead part of her mother and father to life. In the course of the analysis, it was possible for my patient to separate from the mistaken identity conferred on her inadvertently, by both her parents, so that she became free to pursue her own creative life, rather than feeling that she had to compulsively bring others to life.

Françoise Dolto describes the process of recognition of the separateness of the child by the parents as entailing an acceptance by the parents of their own *castration* in the face of the birth of their child. At different stages in the child's life, the child also has to accept various benign castrations. The child can only do this if the parents accept the castration of his birth, after which they must respect their child as a separate and equal human being, who has his own intelligence about living and his own desire. The history and the nature of the parents' subjectivity might, however, fix the child as an "object" of desire, who then receives the parents' history as his own.

Françoise Dolto was a consummate clinician. She worked with children using drawing, painting, modelling, and toys. She believed that it was not the production of art in itself that healed, but visual representation as something that could be talked about, first by the child, and only after this by the analyst. She did not infantilize children, or even babies. She spoke to them with respect, even the tiniest infants, explaining to them the nature of their plight. Her most astonishing discovery was of the precociousness of the child's sensitivity to speech. She would converse with foetuses and newborn babies, convinced that infants can listen, register, understand, and remember the essentials of what is spoken. She believed that although the ego might be slow to understand, the id, the unconscious subject, can know and understand. In her sessions, she revealed the most distressing and embarrassing truths to her little analysands, because she recognized them as suffering critical problems, whether to love or to hate, to grow or not to grow, to live or to die. She believed that the suffering of children is nearly always linked to that which is unsaid, to implicit lies, even if these have been proliferated for the good of the child.

She had remarkable success in calming troubled infants by speaking to them. The school of psychoanalysis to which she belonged believed that the child is, from the beginning, capable of being in a human relationship. The child is not in a chrysalis, which, with the aid of good enough mothering, will become a full human subject. As a consequence, psychopathology is not seen by these French analysts as a breakdown in the process of evolution into adulthood, but rather as the subject's deceit or deception of his own humanity, as the annihilation of his own desire in favour of the Other's will. The analyst, therefore, is not a substitute parent, but is a speaker of truth. The *I* of the baby is immature but his unconscious is equal to that of an adult. To become a subject and to represent himself symbolically, the child has to be helped to separate himself from the desire of the Other.

L'image inconsciente du corps (the unconscious image of the body) is a central idea of Françoise Dolto's. In a dialogue with Dolto in *L'Enfant du miroir* (1987) Nasio asks what she exactly means by *l'image inconsciente du corps*. She replies, explaining that the phrase contains play on words, embedded in the word "image":

> The first letter "I" is also the first letter of the word "Identity".
>
> The second syllable "ma" is the first syllable of "maman" or mother.
>
> The last syllable of "image" "ge" signifies the earth, our base or our body. [1987, p. 12]

The *image inconsciente du corps* is an unconscious representation of the primitive experience and emotional history of the infant, which is structured by language. It is not just a specular image, like the mirror image. Dolto's conception of the mirror stage is different from that of Lacan (1977). For Dolto, the mirror stage is traumatic, wounding the infant's sense of self. The mirror stage establishes a separation between the baby and the mother, with the consequence that the scopic image substitutes for the *image inconsciente du corps* that becomes unconscious. After the mirror stage, the *image inconsciente du corps* is repressed in favour of the mirror image The mirror stage entails a castration of sensory experience, of the world of touch, smell and taste, privileging the visual image, which might deceive. After the mirror stage, the unconscious image of the body only manifests itself in dreams; otherwise it underpins and integrates the psyche–soma and guarantees authentic being. Françoise Dolto believed that the unconscious image of the body breaks through traumatically in psychosis.

While looking at the drawings of children, Dolto realized that everything they depicted was an aspect of themselves and, more specifically, of their *image inconsciente du corps*. The unconscious image of the body is not just a representation of sensations, but is affected by language and desire, by satisfaction and frustration, by losses and ghosts; it is a function of relationships with other bodies, particularly that of the feeding relationship with the mother. *L'image inconsciente du corps* is the first rough outline of our eventual psychosomatic constitution, an outline of the unity of the body discovered by the subject in the mirror stage. It is a representation of the effects of the drives through the various libidinal stages, associated with a specific personal history. She describes the unconscious image of the body as: "the symbolic incarnation in the unconscious of the desiring subject" (Dolto, 1984, p. 22).

It is a form of psychic container, in which emotions are inscribed in a living form. The psychotic child does not move out of primary narcissism into a relationship with a more evolved body image. The psychotic child is inhabited by archaic and primitive body images, which result in a basic narcissism that is poorly anchored to the body. As a consequence, there is a risk of developing a phobic state of mind. Dolto understands phobia as being the result of the threat of dissociation from the *image de base du corps*. The following is an account sourced from *Introduction à l'oeuvre de Françoise Dolto* by Michel Ledoux (1990).

> *L'image de base* is associated with conception and foetal life and the desire for survival. It is foundational, constituting primary narcissism and links the subject to life; it is realised within the first relationships that accompany the first breath. It is what allows the experience of a self-sameness and a continuity of being. The basic body image ensures narcissistic cohesion and is located primarily in the perception of respiration and cardio-vascular function. [p. 95]

Françoise Dolto believed that what we term psychosis is often manifested as phobia. Dolto, in contrast to Klein and Lacan, perceived phobia as lying at the heart of psychosis. Psychosis is an elaborate defence against having to suffer the grave threat of a loss of connection between *l'image*, elaborated as *ici-moi-je'* (Dolto, 1987, p. 20), or 'here I am', and the body. At the beginning of life, at the source of life and the drives, within the body, there is a danger of dissociation. Psychotics are those who are in the grip of a phobia that invades all contact with others (*ibid.*).

She observed that, hitherto, to designate someone psychotic was also to diagnose them as outside of the possibility of being treated psychoanalytically. She believed that such a diagnosis might constitute a resistance in the therapist to his own psychotic core. It betrays a misunderstanding of the nature of the psychotic defence, which she believed was a defence of the basic body image (*ibid.*, p. 21).

She illustrates a case of a young, phobic schizophrenic in *Séminaire de psychanalyse d'enfants II* (1985, pp. 167–173) and in *L'Enfant du miroir* (Dolto & Nasio, 1987, pp. 83–91) The case concerns a thirteen-year-old adolescent boy who was adopted, having been born to a mother who was sixteen years old, a girl who had never known her own father. She had had an affair with a married man who was a teacher, who said he could never see the child although he was prepared to take financial responsibility for him. Her mother had wanted to abort the child. However, since this was not possible, an adoption was arranged with the adoptive mother being named as the birth mother. Neither the boy nor Dolto knew of the intention to abort him, nor had they been informed of the adoption when she first saw him. Dolto described him as a *grand* phobic; he was frightened of everything that was pointed, including pencils, that he believed could be murderous weapons. Dolto concluded that the phobia was a function of his grandmother's desire to abort him of which he consciously knew nothing. Dolto soon disabused him of his phobia, simply by persuading him to prick her with the point of a pencil; to his surprise, she did not die. When he came to his next session, he began to speak with two distinct voices, one that was shrill and fretful and one that was sombre and aggressive. The one voice cried *but I want to keep him*, while the other screamed, "No, you slut, if you keep him I will strangle him with my own hands. This will be your eternal punishment". Dolto had been amazed to hear his uncanny reproduction of the voices of what she had eventually found out to be his grandmother and his mother, since he could not have known what they felt about him other than by hearing them when he was only forty-eight hours old. A few days later, his adoptive mother phoned to share her astonishment that, after the session, the boy had come home and had slept for thirty-six hours, having never slept for any length of time, and that he had become calm and co-operative. Dolto told her what the boy had spoken. His mother then broke down and divulged that she had been at the clinic when the boy had been born, and had heard the argument between the boy's mother and her mother. The words had marked the boy's body with a prohibition of life and forbade the unconscious foetal body image from assuming a life outside the womb, denying it the breath of life.

The deadly words had been inscribed in the body and could only be dislodged in the transference, through the boy's words, and by the emotions the words induced in the analyst. Subsequently, the boy forgot the words he had spoken, suggesting that the trauma could only emerge safely within the containment of the transference. His phobia was a phobia of the death drive; it was relieved by the analyst's capacity to enter into a bodily transference, a fusional transference that revived a primitive, traumatized, unconscious body image. In the transference, the analyst suffered the impact of his words, which enabled the boy to accept his death drive and to sleep peacefully and securely (Dolto & Nasio, 1987, pp. 83–91).

In the case of this boy, the kernel of his psychosis lay in the foreclosure of the screen memory and the phobia of sharp objects; it is interesting to note that the boy later became a tailor. Dolto proceeds to explain that what had been foreclosed was the Name of the Father (Dolto, 1985, p. 171) The child was born to a mother who had not resolved her Oedipus complex, having conceived him in fantasy with her own father.

Dolto is ill at ease and confusing in her use of the term foreclosure, which, for Lacan, is central to his understanding of psychosis. In a discussion on the subject of foreclosure (*ibid.*, p. 177) she asserts that everything leaves a trace in the unconscious, unlike Lacan, who believed that what was foreclosed had never entered the unconscious. Her description of foreclosure is looser than Lacan's definition, which asserts that what is foreclosed is that which symbolizes castration. Sometimes, she states that there is always foreclosure at the root of psychosis; sometimes, it seems that she is saying that foreclosure is a name given to the resistance of the analyst. Dolto believed that, in the transference, one can successfully lift the prohibition which blocks a memory if it brings to life an archaic unconscious body image hitherto petrified. It is this primitive unconscious body image which is involved in that which has been foreclosed. In the unconscious, an element of experience has been registered but not symbolized; it has no resonance within the history of the subject because it has no links to language. An experience of rupture may be represented in the unconscious, but it is not symbolized as a castration. She believed that what has been foreclosed can be overcome in analysis, within a regressed transference (*ibid.*, p. 179).

Dolto emphasizes the importance, in the transference, of the sensitivity of the body of the analyst to the words of the patient; that it is in the body, or the unconscious body image of the analyst, that the transference is consolidated (Dolto, 1987, p. 99). In working with children, the analyst can lose a sense of a part of the body. In response to resistance, the analyst may defend himself by infantilizing the patient, denying that his communication has meaning we should respect. Or, if the other refuses to speak, we may deny that the patient has anything to communicate or that there is nothing to be heard. Infants are not outside language; they do not speak, but that does not mean that they do not understand language (*ibid.*, p.100).

Dolto understood psychogenic autism, as did Frances Tustin (1981), as a response to a perceived or actual traumatic premature separation. Psychogenic autism can be conceived of as an extreme form of childhood schizophrenia, in which there is a withdrawal into an autistic state. Dolto emphasizes how damaging experiences of separation and loss can be at any age, but particularly early in life, if these traumas are not spoken about at the time they are happening. In *Séminaire de psychanalyse d'enfants II* (1985, p. 69), Dolto talks about autism as entailing a very early rupture in the mother–infant relationship, before or after birth, a rupture that has never been spoken about and which has left the infant with no alternative but to relate to a part of his own body, in a masturbatory relationship. Autism entails a rupture in the narcissism of the subject; the Other is reduced to a part of the unconscious image of the body, which is traumatized at the foetal or early oral stage. The only law is a cosmic law, associated with intra-uterine life: the infant resides in a state of fusional desire, unseparated from a *ghost* mother and is menaced by death, which is warded off by mimicry (Dolto, 1984, p. 225).

She believed that if ruptures and separations were not spoken about, the infant or child was left in a state of non-being, as if the parent no longer existed. If and when the child renewed a relationship with the parent, it is as if the parent comes to incarnate death; her face, her smell, her voice are mere apparitions. She becomes dead inside the child. The infant regresses massively, maybe retaining an obsessive interest in an animal or in inanimate objects. Psychogenic autism is associated with a terrifying sense of dislocation and loss of direction, with the disruption of sensory experience and the loss of anchoring of desire. The self or subject is out of reach. There is a lack of cohesion between the subject and his body, and dissociation between the subject and the unconscious image of his body.

She illustrates her theory with the case of a baby, called Sebastien, who fell into an autistic state when he was five months old. He had recently been weaned and had suffered three changes of nurse in a week. She describes how, alongside the loss of his mother, there was a loss of her smell, of the rhythm of her body, and an ensuing disturbance of his image of the alimentary track, of digestion, and of his lungs and respiration. She then describes how these losses mobilize the death drives on to the body image and how the death drives are a significant feature of psychosis. They are a product of a body that is no longer affected by desire because desire is exhausted. The death drives lead to a state of passivity, inertia, and sleep. In despair, the infant folds in on himself and loses a feeling of existing within space and time. Such autistic children appear to live by a code that obeys cosmic rather than human rules. The drive is to quiescence and fusion, a drive towards incestuous cohabitation within the mother. In the autistic child, Dolto perceives the specifically human desire for communication to have been perverted: "In these children, the oral and anal drives are satisfied alone, in a masturbatory mode, in an imaginary world" (1984, p. 219).

Autism entails the "unhooking" of language between the parents and the child. The child becomes

> . . . the locus of a cancer of symbolisation, an imaginary tumour, formed of a symbolic function that has entered a void, without a relationship to a human being who might recognise the child's drive. The child is an isolate because the parent is perceived as absent or psychically out of reach. [*ibid.*]

In *Tout est langage* (1987), Dolto suggests that if a child is left alone for too long and is not spoken to, he will, in his symbolic function, be running on empty. She gives a rather beautiful example of what she means:

> A child is left in his cradle. He appears to be calm, left in the garden, but he wants to have fun with someone, someone who will to talk to him . . . if not this well-behaved baby becomes undemanding. He no longer desires a feed, he just accepts it indiscriminately. He ceases to have to do with human beings; his language becomes cut off from human words. A bird flies by, at the same time as the curtain of his crib billows, at the same time as the baby experiences a colic and a rumble in his tummy. The meeting of these perceptions in his mind, his loneliness is spoken by his tummy: a little colic becomes associated with the crying of the bird, the signifier for the squawk of the bird and the movement of the curtain. These synchronised meetings of external and internal events and states take on the meaning of language, composed of signs, coincidentally strung together. [1987, p. 29]

The baby's sensations are not symbolized. The work of psychoanalysis is to decode the language that has disturbed the regulation of the developing body.

Speaking more generally of childhood psychosis, Dolto understands its dynamics as being very complex. She describes psychoses that grow out of traumas suffered over generations in families, of feelings of despair and hatred, of misunderstandings and secrets, of pain and anguish that has never been talked about. She writes about psychoses that arise out of physical defects and out of severe trauma at critical stages of libidinal development, when hope of growth and development is refused for and by the child. She describes psychoses that arise out of severe maternal depression after birth. In *Séminaire de psychoanalyse d'enfants I* (1982), she describes the origins of psychotic states that may result from symbiotic confusion.

> . . . for the new born, maternal depression exerts a massive appeal [to the child] which provokes him to want to restore her life, so that later he may not feel the right to let go of her and to leave her . . . these infants perceive that their mothers reproach them for having given them life, so they feel themselves guilty for having taken the life of their mothers. [p. 170]

Thus, the infant becomes fusionally attached to the mother; he puts his entire libido therapeutically at her service. "He exhausts himself in giving back to his mother that which he believes he has taken from her, that is, himself" (*ibid.*). In this way, the child becomes trapped in regression, in a passive womb-like state of being that results in the death of his individuality.

In *Séminaire de psychanalyse d'enfants II* (1985, p. 160), she talks about the effects of the death of a parent on a child. The danger for such a child is that he might want to die too, in order to find his lost parent, and that in the child's identification with the ideal ego of the dead parent, his drive towards death might be stimulated. She emphasizes that the child feels extremely angry with the parent who has been insufficiently strong to resist death and that the expression of his anger must be facilitated. Other members of the family might find it very difficult to accept the child's fury, but it is only in the expression of aggression that the child will find the desire for life. She suggests a form of expression that might help an orphaned child choose life.

> They haven't thought about you enough but the fact that you have survived demonstrates that you have enough of the strength given to you by your mother and father to go on living. And now it is up to you to represent the family. [*ibid.*, p. 60]

She manifests a respect and toughness in the face of tragedy, based on a genuine faith in the capacity of children to find emotional and spiritual resources within themselves. She states that all our losses revive our early experiences of separation and loss, beginning with the cutting of the umbilical cord and the loss of the placenta and the womb, and that we have to express our aggression to restore our damaged narcissism and to save us from falling into depression. She emphasizes that it is vital, when working with abandoned children, to have faith in their capacity to sustain their sense of loss; if they are supported and told the truth, their loss can then be symbolized.

Dolto describes the ways in which each of us can be caught between drives towards a non-life, in the repetitive, addictive meeting of need, and, on the other hand, the drives towards life and the drives of desire. For Dolto, the concept of desire has overtones of faith in God: as a devout Christian she believed our longing for completion should be directed towards God. Need is distinguished by its repetitive nature, whereas desire brings something new. It is through words that it becomes possible to transform the desire of the body-to-body relationship with the mother into cultural expression.

Desire arises out of the acceptance of castration, in both the parents and the child. If, for any reason, the parents are unable to accept the necessity of their castration, it may become an invitation to the child to turn back and to become psychotic. The relation of castration to desire can be understood as the cutting of unlimited boundless desire; in the acceptance of boundaries, desire becomes contained, focused, and capable of realization.

In *L'Image inconsciente du corps* (1984), she describes castration as:

> A prohibition of desire in relation to certain means of gaining pleasure; the castration has a harmonising and progressive effect in so far as the desiring subject is enabled to integrate the law which humanises him. [p. 301]

The various castrations, umbilical, oral, anal, and phallic bring changes because they have symbolic effects, and they then generate new ways of being. If they have pathological effects, it is because they are not delivered with respect, confidence, and in truth. From the beginning, the child should be recognized as separate and different and not as an image of the parents' desires and demands.

Dolto's view is that a psychotic child is only loved if he exists within the death drives, deprived of a right to live autonomously. He is only loved as the product of his mother's body, unmarked by the father's lineage. The formation of the "ideal ego" is disturbed: the "ideal ego" is, according to Laplanche and Pontalis (1988),

> the, as yet, unorganised ego, which feels at one with the id, and corresponds to an ideal condition. In the course of his development, the subject leaves this narcissistic ideal behind, but aspires to return to it—a return which occurs mainly, but not exclusively in the psychoses. [pp. 201–202]

It frequently appears that there is a disturbance in the erotic relationship between the parents, who form a neurotic couple who close in on the child. As a consequence, the psychotic child is not able to symbolize, as part of his ideal ego, a parent who is part of a sexually desiring couple (Dolto, 1984, p. 242). According to this description, the child becomes an eroticized part-object in relation to his parents.

Le cas Dominique (1971, translated into English as *Dominique: Analysis of an Adolescent Boy*, 1973) is an account of an analysis by Françoise Dolto of a young adolescent boy who had been diagnosed as mentally defective and schizophrenic. He was seen for twelve sessions, during which he emerged from a psychotic regression, in reaction to which his father withdrew him from analysis.

The history of Dominique was enacted in the analysis through fantasies, recounted in stories and in clay models. Dominique was the second of three children. His behaviour was described as normal until the birth of his sister, Sylvie, who was nearly three years younger. He became insanely jealous, suffering uncontrollable rages. He soiled himself and was still wetting his bed at fourteen. He was passive and a dreamer, refusing contact with people. He forgot to eat, to dress, or to wash. He had no memory. He was phobic and obsessional, and shied away from all physical contact.

His mother's relationship to her children was full of incestuous longing, confusion, and regression. Françoise Dolto thought that Dominique functioned as his mother's phallus. Dominique's father was largely absent. His parents had sad histories. His mother was rejected by her parents and his father had suffered traumatic losses; unbelievably, his brother had died as the result of swallowing a toy train, and Dominique's first drawing was of a train. His father's older brother had disappeared on a mountainside. It transpired that both parents had wanted Dominique to be a girl. Dolto thought that, in his father's mind, Dominique was identified with his dead baby brother, so that it was impossible for Dominique to identify with his father or to be in a straightforward Oedipal relationship with him. The role of the father was foreclosed by the mother, who claimed the children as her products and possessions. After the birth of his sister, Dominique was usurped as the object of his mother's desire, so, in order to placate him, he was allowed to persist with breast-feeding alongside his baby sister, resulting in what Dolto describes as an erotic and devouring contact. His mother was still tied to her own mother by her many phobias. Dolto suggests that because she felt unloved by her own mother, she had herself been unable to overcome her own primary umbilical castration, so that, for her, her children were like warming fetishes, given to her by her husband, who was more like a motherly, older brother.

Dominique was sent away to stay with his grandmother when his sister was born. In Dolto's words, he became like "a disaffected fetish", losing all his points of reference. Birth and new life came to signify for him something that damaged his narcissism. He came to live in a passive, paranoid world in which he was unable to separate from his mother's body. He began to experience anxiety about his cannibalistic and incestuous desires, but his anxiety was not recognized. Dolto suggests that:

> When parents through their words and deeds allow a child to view incest, murder or cannibalism as possible desires, kept from him only because he is a child . . . they are submitting him to a traumatic experience. [1973, p. 30]

Dominique was unable to develop an ethical sense because he did not have to renounce the pleasure of breast-feeding after his sister's birth. Because of this, Dolto says that he lost access to the phallus. The account of the analysis is impressive in its illuminating and detailed accounts of his mad stories, illustrated by his drawing and modelling.

At the end of the story of "The sacred cow and the nomad", Dominique bids farewell to his "kiddie", his *biquette* (a slang word for penis in French) (*ibid.*, pp. 54–67). Dolto interprets the story as being to do with the mutilation and loss of his penis. She believes that Dominique had always been his mother's part-object, her imaginary penis: her parents had rejected her because she was female. Thus, Dominique's desire was alienated to satisfy his mother's perverse and narcissistic desire. The "kiddie" is his penis, which during his protracted experience of being breast-fed, was closed off to his desire. As an extension of his mother, Dominique found himself with no one who was like him, no one to identify with, and all he could do was regress into bodily dependence.

He had only become himself in so far as he accepted his own body as a penis, the part object of another: a typical metaphor for the foetal relationship (*ibid*., p. 67).

The nomad

In the first stage, the nomad has become the Maharajah (Figure 1).

In the second stage, the Nomad is leading his cow. She is called Miss. He has a blob for the head, a blob for the body, a hat, two eyes, two pigtails, and a beard that grows and trails the ground (Figure 2).

Figure 1. First stage: the nomad as Maharajah.

Figure 2. Stage 2: the nomad leading his cow.

By the third stage there is an evil man, or perhaps the tired-out nomad. Only one eye, one opening, a slit in the hat, a flattened-out blob for the head. Two other cube-like masses below, something sticking out of the chest, or abdomen (Figures 3 and 4).

The camel

However, his was not a growing foetal relationship, but one that threatens psychic death. The underlying symbolization seen in the bottom drawing suggests the foetus attached to a placenta. Elsewhere (1982) Dolto suggests that the psychotic child is searching for a "double", at the level of the placenta searching for a foetus. The story is not just about the loss of his penis but also about the fantasy of the annihilation of his birth. With Françoise Dolto and through his story, Dominique is able to put in to words what he experienced as a catastrophic loss of part of himself. Although Dominique was taken out of his analysis prematurely by his father, Dolto later discovered that Dominique had become a potter, suggesting that he

Figure 3. Stage 3 in 'The sacred cow and the nomad".

Figure 4. Stage 3.

had found his "double" in his analyst, because making pots was Françoise Dolto's other preferred activity.

In Dominique's story, he is bidding farewell to his "double", which could be seen to be represented by the placenta, which once completed him. A successful transition after birth entails a weaning from the womb, in order that the baby should be left with a sufficient sense of primary containment, enabling a body memory of a safe womb place and a memory of connection to the "double", the placenta. The placenta is a genetic double, the prototype of a soulmate, that eventually in unconscious fantasy merges with the breast and becomes part of the unconscious body image. In *Au jeu du desir* (1981) Françoise Dolto describes the infant being merged with the lost object. In the beginning the lost object is the self. It is only after the Mirror Stage that the subject becomes 'a me for you', a 'me with you'. The 'double' constitutes the other within oneself, thanks to which we can feel contained and complete, or, on the contrary, wounded if it is not symbolized. The securing of this symbolic connection is necessary for the establishment of healthy narcissism and of an ideal ego that promotes growth. The parents of the psychotic child put their own need for a "double" on to their child, and thereby make it impossible for the child to establish a sense of his own "double".

Françoise Dolto recounts in *L'Enfant du miroir* that in her work with severely anorexic children (Dolto & Nasio, 1987, p. 29) she was led to believe that it was essential to engage with the unconscious body image of the child. So, for example, instead of saying, "You do not want to swallow", you might say, "You are refusing to swallow because it is blocked at your pharynx". Such a child wants to return to foetal life to re-establish his body image so that his mother comes to occupy for him the role of a placenta. Dolto describes how, in analysis, a patient may want to graft himself on to the analyst, creating a placental transference (*ibid.*, 1987, p. 34).

In *Séminaire de psychanalyse d'enfants II* (Dolto, 1985, pp. 153–165), she discusses the significance of sleepiness in analysis. It is not always a sign of defence when drowsiness intervenes within a psychoanalytic session. It may be a sign that the death drive is attempting to induce a profound therapeutic sleep, peaceful and untroubled by desire, within which the patient may be able to accept death without fear. She describes how, in the treatment of psychotic children, the analyst might be seized with a desire for sleep. This should not necessarily be interpreted as a defence, a rejection, or a collapse, but it might indicate that a deep trust has developed in the unconscious of both the child and that of the analyst. It can lead to healing. In allowing sleepiness, the analyst submits to the libido of the child, and it may be a means of permitting the child to benignly castrate the analyst, enabling the child to create its own structure. The child becomes master and, for a while, the analyst submits to his death drive. It can give the child confidence that his sadistic drives can be contained within this unconscious communication in security. He can receive in the analyst's drowsiness an alleviation of his anguish and can feel entirely accepted. The here and now of the psychic relationship between two subjects when the analyst is sleepy allows the child to fully experience his drives while the analyst submits to his own death drive. The relative absence of the analyst enables the psychotic child who is habitually absent to become present and to have an effect.

Sleepiness of this kind is never due to weariness, but is bred of a desire to better understand the child. It is necessary to enter into relation with one's own death drive because it is within the death drive, a drive which habitually disturbs the psychic structure of the psychotic child, that we can help him find authentic communication with another being. A psychotic child who has not undergone appropriate castration has a barely formed ego; such a child will endure intolerable frustration, in the presence of someone whom they feel to be strong and desirable, because he is terrorized by his own projected sadistic impulses. He is abandoned to the desires of the death drive, in a life that is unconscious of the body and its erogenous zones. If the analyst can give up his position of being the subject of the desire for life, the child may be able to find in the drowsy analyst a subject who can become for him a support, an extension of himself. The child finds calm, order, and security, and is able to play peacefully, overcoming his previous state of agitation, because, at a deep unconscious level, he feels recognized. The analyst accepts that, by yielding to drowsiness, he becomes an object, so that the child may become a subject. Drowsiness in a session is part of countertransference and, as such, also belongs to the patient. It needs to be spoken about to give it meaning.

Sometimes, the experience of lethargy denotes aggression; sometimes, it does not. Sometimes, it represents a refusal of being; sometimes, it is a desire for peace. The death drive expresses itself as the serenity that is found in deep sleep. When desire is exhausted, it may be found again within the death drive. When the subject is eclipsed in sleep, having let go, the play of desire takes over. There is no aggression in the death drive, whereas, by contrast, the aggressive drive is part of the life force of an individual who wants to kill, which is frequently turned inwards on the other within the self, on the enemy within the body.

Dolto counsels caution in relation to the desire for sleep, and suggests that each therapist should be aware of its meaning for themselves and their patients. She suggests that drowsiness may signal the absence of a language. It is necessary to clarify the nature of the transference and the countertransference; to ask how old the child is in his regression, and what he is trying to find once more, in the here and now, in his relationship with the analyst. What position is he putting me in, in whose place? We have to be open to the psychotic elements within ourselves in order to be able to make contact with the psychosis in our patients. When we speak of psychosis, we also mean that a necessary code is unknown, is unavailable. The lethargy of the analyst may derive from being inarticulate in the face of what the psychotic cannot express, unless the analyst lets go into sleep. Dolto describes how she has experienced being with children who can only express themselves through play if the analyst is drowsily absent. It may be the case that the analyst has to become the infant in a fusional relationship with the child, who can now refind security in his identification with the mother he has introjected. After a session of this kind, she reports that a psychotic child becomes more peaceful.

Françoise Dolto was idiosyncratic, creative, and generous in her practice. She worked for no financial gain at the Hôpital Trousseau and, while teaching psychoanalysts at the Rue Cujas, she provided free child analysis for severely disturbed children from a local orphanage. In his conference paper, "Je suis Madame Dolto. Je suis psychanalyste et je dis la verité aux enfants" (2008), J.-D. Nasio spoke of his experience as a young analyst at these weekly sessions. Children were seen individually over a period of one to two years, in the presence of child analysts, whom Françoise Dolto encouraged to participate. The child analysands were treated with respect and were encouraged to speak to whomsoever they wished.

Dolto explained to the children that she was not there to love them, but to work with them, and that she could only work if she was paid. Each child was encouraged to bring a pebble as symbolic payment. Dolto sometimes asked the analysts to play. On one occasion, she asked the men to sing because that particular child needed to hear the voice of men. Singing brought them all to life. The analysts were brought into direct contact with the vibrations of the child's unconscious, giving the child a security it had never previously experienced.

Nasio recalled the case of a psychotic girl who wailed so pitifully it was unbearable. Having tried everything to enable her to emerge from regression, Dolto had to tell the child that she did not know what else to do.

In despair, she asked the analysts if they could help, but they, too, were impotent. But having asked from her despair, Dolto was able to put into words the child's experience as an infant. She explained to the girl that she cried so miserably because she was still a baby, just as her mother had been. The interpretation was transformative. The girl stopped crying and made contact with Françoise Dolto. She now knew she was not worthy of abandonment, but that her mother had been a baby and babies cannot care for other babies.

Dolto had an almost uncanny ability to speak to the child from the child's point of view, in a language, however mad it might appear to an adult, that was easily comprehensible to the child. She had considerable respect for the intelligence of babies, and realized how deeply troubled babies are by what they perceive. In addition, she had a tremendous desire to enter the child's anguish-ridden experience, so that it could be shared within a community.

Dolto demonstrates a remarkable sensitivity and imaginative capacity in her description of how one might have to be in order to function effectively as a therapist with a psychotic child. She says, again drawing on the most primitive womb imagery, that

> For many of them, we have to take on the role of the umbilical cord, the placenta, the circulation of the blood, things which do not have human appearance but which are essential to life. We are for them a partial object but we do not know which object. So we may feel

> quite lost without a reference point. We have to tell them of our confusion, verbalise it . . . If we put our state of mind into words they can make a start. If we do not tell them how we feel we do not represent a person to them. We are identified as a part object and because of this we are ill at ease. [1982, p. 82]

Conclusion

For Dolto, the causes of psychosis are complex; she examines everything that the individual is influenced by: innate predispositions, the wider culture, the family history over several generations, the significance of a particular family's structure, the effect of family secrets, and how the child is inscribed in the family's unconscious. She considers how the child may be caught in a web of unconscious identifications, prior to his having come into being as a subject, and before he has been able to find words of his own. She notes the nature of the body-to-body relationship between mother and baby, observing whether it lacks rhythm and structure. She considers whether the infant's needs are satisfied within a human relationship that may enable him to make sense of his perceptions. In some cases, she observes that psychosis arises out of the repeated and prolonged psychic or physical absence of the mother, so that this primitive experience of absence becomes part of the infant. For Françoise Dolto, more than any other factor, it is the rupture of communication between the nurturing parent and the baby that causes a traumatic discontinuity of being. As well as damage to a sense of continuity of being, there is a loss of the potential for the development of a "double", so that "I am not there for myself". The infant's cry into a void of communication and reassurance disturbs the basic body rhythm and damages the unconscious body image. The erogenous zones are deprived of pleasure and provoke massive regression. In some cases of childhood psychosis, the mother has been severely depressed; the infant puts its life into the mother in an attempt to bring her back to life, with the consequence that the child exhausts itself. The child is devitalized, but remains fusionally attached to the mother. The child feels guilty for having deprived the mother of her life, so that the mother becomes a persecutory figure within the child's unconscious. The child fears the mother's retaliation or collapse if he moves towards autonomy. Some mothers of psychotic children are omnipotent, treating their child as an object, loving their child only if he exists within the death drive. In such a dyad, the father is effaced. There is also a risk of psychosis for a child whose mother and father have suffered a breakdown of libidinal relationship, when the child becomes an object of fixation for the parents. Françoise Dolto also stressed the link between childhood psychosis and the transmission of trauma down the generations within the family unconscious, with the most damaging traumas being those that are not spoken about. Her observation was that it often takes three generations of severely neurotic parenting before a psychosis appears. Frequently, the two parents had experienced a trauma before they were five years old. Where there has been an acutely painful loss, the child may end up identifying, or being identified, with the person who is dead. Françoise Dolto was convinced that severe psychic pain experienced within a family, which was never talked about, could affect an unborn child to such an extent that it might later develop a psychosis.

A child with the potential for psychosis takes refuge in an imaginary world and regresses into a parasitic, foetal state. The lack of a language to make sense of his experience will lead such a child to inhabit a world of pure sensation, becoming a child of the cosmos, not of human intercourse. In his isolation, he regresses towards an archaic body image that precludes the potential for the development of symbolization. Regression is a defensive resort in the face of the terror of loss of continuity of being. Françoise Dolto is profoundly compassionate, perceiving the psychotic child as being an isolate, without solace. With great faith in humanity, Françoise Dolto healed by virtue of her capacity to communicate with consummate skill and with respect for the psychotic child as a subject of his own desire, listening carefully to the truth of his history spoken through words and symptoms.

I will let her have the last word, spoken in *Autoportrait d'une psychanalyste* (1989, pp. 167–168), in an interview in the last few months of her life. She says of the psychosis:

> When a person is seen as mad, he is seen as someone incapable of relationship with others . . . I think it is a disorder brought about by the deepest despair, of not having a relationship with a counterpart

who holds you in esteem, who can recognise himself in you . . . the person who is designated psychotic believes that he will not be allowed to be conscious of what he senses . . . to help him, I have to appreciate that his sensory reality may be different from mine.

References

Dolto, F. (1939). *Psychanalyse et pédiatrie.* Private publication, 1940 [reprinted Paris: editions de la parole, 1961].

Dolto, F. (1971). *Le cas Dominique.* Paris: Le Seuil.

Dolto, F. (1973). *Dominique: Analysis of an Adolescent Boy,* I. Kats (Trans.), New York: Outerbridge and Lazard.

Dolto, F. (1981). *Au jeu du désir.* Paris: Le Seuil, Coll. "Essais cliniques"; [reprinted Coll. "Points Essais", 1988].

Dolto, F. (1982). *Séminaire de psychanalyse d'Enfants I* (in collaboration with L. Caldaguès). Paris: Le Seuil. Coll. "Points Essais", 1992.

Dolto, F. (1984). *L'image inconsciente du corps.* Paris: Le Seuil, Coll. "Points Essais", 1992.

Dolto, F. (1985). *Séminaire de psychanalyse d'enfants, II* (in collaboration with J.-F. de Sauverzac). Paris: Le Seuil, Coll. "Points Essais", 1991.

Dolto, F. (1987). *Tout est langage.* Paris: Vertiges-Carrere [reprinted Paris: LGF, 1989].

Dolto, F. (1989). *Autoportrait d'une psychanalyste, 1934–1988.* Paris: Seuil, "Coll. Points", 1992.

Dolto, F., & Nasio, J.-D. (1987). *L'Enfant du miroir.* Paris: Rivages, Coll. "Petite Bibliothèque Payot" [reprinted Paris: Payot, 1992].

Lacan, J. (1977). The mirror stage as formative of the function of the I. In: *Ecrits. A Selection,* A. Sheridan (Trans.). London: Tavistock.

Laplanche, J., & Pontalis, J. B. (1988). *Institute of Psychoanalysis.* London: Karnac.

Ledoux, M. (1990). *Introduction à l'oeuvre de Françoise Dolto.* Paris: Editions Rivages.

Mannoni, M. (1970). *The Child, his "Illness" and the Others.* New York: Pantheon.

Nasio, J.-D. (2008). Je suis Madame Dolto. Je suis psychanalyste et je dis la verité de la vie aux enfants. Paper presented to the conference "Françoise Dolto: l'actualité d'une pensée 1908–2008". Maison de l'UNESCO, Paris, 12–14 December, 2008.

Tustin, F. (1981). *Autistic States in Children.* London: Routledge & Kegan Paul.

CHAPTER FOUR

Seeing the bigger picture

Guy Hall

> Lorsque l'enfant paraît, le cercle de famille
> Applaudit à grands cris. Son doux regard qui brille
> Fait briller tous les yeux,
> Et les plus tristes fronts, les plus souillés peut-être,
> Se dérident soudain à voir l'enfant paraître,
> Innocent et joyeux
>
> (Hugo, 2002)

Françoise Dolto is a more popular and better known psychoanalyst among the general public in France than Jacques Lacan. Outside of the English-speaking world, she is an eminent authority on child psychoanalysis and of similar stature to Anna Freud, Melanie Klein, and Donald Winnicott. In France, she is among the first sources that people turn to when it comes to the psychoanalytic understanding of childhood.

Challenging established boundaries and keeping her independence was one of the consistent features of her personality. While many people past the age of retirement seek a quiet life, Françoise Dolto chose to start a new career. Although she had for seven years been broadcasting on the radio as the anonymous Docteur X, it was in September 1976, that she joined France-Inter. The new programme was called *Lorsque l'enfant paraît*, a reference to Victor Hugo's poem. For this new radio programme, Françoise Dolto was able to use her own name and answered letters sent in by parents on issues relating to bringing up children. Many of the highlights, from over 375 hours of material, have been transcribed. They are now available as books and CDs. From the start, these programmes were very popular, and for the generation who have been influenced by them, they have become quite iconic. The programmes took the form of an interview, with Jacques Pradel reading letters and asking additional questions.

Lorsque l'enfant parait is also the title of a celebrated play by André Roussin, later adapted as a film. The play concerns a minister of religion who likes to take the high moral ground and is full of good intentions. In particular, he wishes the authorities to reduce the number of unmarried women having children. The drama of the play rises when the minister's wife admits that she is pregnant, in circumstances that suggest that her husband may not be the father of the child. Then, on the eve of her wedding, his daughter announces that she is pregnant, while the minister's son also declares that he is responsible for his father's secretary being pregnant.

Quite a few psychoanalysts were either jealous or aghast that a colleague should have such a high public profile. Some thought it diminished the standing and possibly the mystique of the profession. Others, along with some medical colleagues, feared that if she appeared to resolve difficulties through a four-minute exposition on the radio, they would lose patients, who might question the need for an extended analysis. She was also criticized for her willingness to actively work with educators and social services to improve how to understand in difficult situations. Françoise Dolto spoke simply and clearly. Her replies were a cocktail of good sense mixed with her experience as a paediatrician, psychoanalyst, and mother. The fact that what she said was not solely from a psychoanalytic perspective irritated others in the field. Françoise Dolto brought to her work with children the formative years of her own childhood (Dolto, 1986). She did not forget what it was like to be a child and the difficulties that could exist in understanding adults.

She would refer to the ideals of the 1959 United Nations *Declaration of the Rights of the Child*. UNICEF only adopted its *Convention on the Rights of a Child* in 1989, and many of the 190 countries that have since ratified it have included legal reservations that have the potential to undermine these same rights. In the UK, these rights came into force in 1992 and apply to all children and young people, without exception. They include, among others, the right to life, survival, and development, the right to have their views respected, and to have their best interests considered at all times, the right to a name and nationality, freedom of expression, and access to information concerning them, the right to live in a family environment or alternative care, and to have contact with both parents wherever possible, and welfare rights, including rights for disabled children, the right to health and health care and social security, the right to education, leisure, culture and the arts, special protection for refugee children, children in the juvenile justice system, children deprived of their liberty, and children suffering economic, sexual or other forms of exploitation.

While her theories inevitably appear to be dry and academic, her clinical examples are emotionally warmer and more dynamic. They show her capacity for empathy and intuitive understanding. This is revealed in examples of her works for clinicians, such as *Séminaire de psychanalyse d'enfants*, Vols 1–3 (Dolto 1982, 1988, 1991) as well as in her publications for parents such as *Lorsque l'enfant paraît* (Dolto, 1997a).

At the start of her career, the psychoanalytic treatment of children was virtually unheard of in France. Sigmund Freud saw mainly adults. It seems to have been left to women psychoanalysts in the early days to show how to work with children. Anna Freud extended her father's work in this direction. Melanie Klein founded a different, but no less important, school of thought. After her IPA-approved training, Françoise Dolto developed her theoretical ideas and pragmatic perspectives. It is not clear how much women psychoanalysts chose working with children, or were pushed into it out of their maternal nature, or because the male establishment directed them away from the more lucrative work available with adults.

At the time, from a Freudian perspective, it was considered better not to analyse children before the age of four at the earliest.

Even at that age, it was considered better to do so through the intermediary of a parent, often the father. Françoise Dolto accepted that parents could have an important role in the treatment of children.

> However small, a child for whom a mother, or father can speak about the reasons that they know, or that they suppose about his difficulties, is capable of overcoming these problems, while remaining confident of himself and his parents. [Dolto, 1997a, p. 27]

Kleinians pushed back the barriers with their insistence that understanding a child's unconscious could only be accessed directly without a go-between, and that such work could certainly be done with a three-year-old and, quite possibly, a two-year-old. Françoise Dolto did not follow either of these schools. She demonstrated that it was possible to work with children from any time after their birth, based on her ability to give meaning to, and understand the significance of, symbolic or imaginary words, sounds, gestures, acts, and creative representations. Françoise Dolto thought that, too often, Anna Freud favoured parents in her work. As to Melainie Klein, whom she had met, but whose works she had largely not read, she thought that asking a child to draw, or make a model was better then asking a child to play with toys. Françoise Dolto considered herself to be focused on the psychopathology of everyday life, while she viewed Melanie Klein's interests as being more in understanding psychosis. Françoise Dolto was impressed by Melanie Klein's personality and charisma, but considered that she was not doing psychoanalysis, but psychotherapy.

> It is a major distinction, so badly understood by so many people, between psychoanalysis, that is a concern for the kind of person one becomes as a result of the experience of a childhood history, and psychotherapy, that can take all sorts of means to directly help his actual difficulties. [Dolto, 1997b, p. 244]

For the psychoanalyst, ". . . our role is not to desire something for someone, but to be the one who can cause the other's desire to happen" (Dolto, 1982, p. 84).

In essence, she thought Melanie Klein's work lay in supporting a child's narcissism. For Françoise Dolto, there are no *good* or *bad* breasts, or *good enough* mothers (Roudinesco, 1988). Despite the simplicity that she used in her radio broadcasts, and even though Jacques Lacan had said she did not need a theory as she was intuitively gifted to hear what a child was saying, Françoise Dolto did develop a sophisticated, nuanced, and subtle theory. Some of her detractors have deformed and misrepresented much of what she said. The key to her understanding of children can be found in a childhood promise that she made to herself.

> And I used to wonder, having once been small and having grown up, how people could be so strange since they had been children. And I said to myself: "When I'm big, I'll try to remember what it's like to be small." [Dolto, 1986, p. 43]

Nowadays, work is being done to gain a better understanding of the pre-natal life of a child. Among others who are doing research in this field is Catherine Dolto, the daughter of Françoise. Her mother was curious as to what a foetus might experience before it is born. Her views reflect aspects of the Roman Catholic church's teaching on the sanctity of life from the moment of conception.

> During foetal life, a human being is never a part of the maternal body, he is already unique. It is he who through the mediation of the father and the mother takes life and allows himself to be born. He is life itself. He preserves during his development and his arrival at term, his desire to be born. [Dolto, 1997b, p. 285]

Foetuses who find themselves in unusual positions, or who might be at risk of being prematurely born, can be amenable to change through the careful choice of words spoken to the mother and the child. The conversation with the mother can result in changes in her muscles and blood vessels that encourage changes for the baby. Even at an early stage in its development, a baby is sensitive to the moods of its mother. One might wonder if there is a scope for having a centre run in a similar way to a Maison Verte, but open to pregnant mothers and their partners. For Françoise Dolto, the role of the father in cutting the umbilical cord is one of the first castrations that a child experiences.

One of the areas in which people have difficulty is in understanding what Françoise Dolto meant is in regard to *language*. The confusion arises because the normal model of childhood development suggest that verbal language skills start to be acquired between the ages of 7–10 months and that it will be 9–17 months before a child will be able to attribute meaning and sense to these words. How, then, can Françoise Dolto be talking about a child understanding language from birth, if not earlier, while still in the womb? The answer depends on being able to differentiate between a wide range of symbolic languages and only the spoken word. The physical development of the brain is such that it would appear that a baby is not able to immediately understand the spoken word, but a baby may well be able to appreciate the mood and feeling behind the words. Françoise Dolto made great claims about child development without always much supporting evidence. Furthermore, critics of psychoanalysis (Meyer, 2005, p. 487) say that the result is to engender in parents a sense of guilt.

Françoise Dolto's reply was, "Everything that is said becomes human (understandable). Everything that is not said for the child remains in an unusual state and is not integrated in the relationship that he has with its mother" (Dolto, 1997a, p. 27).

Having attributed to the child a profound need to communicate, Françoise Dolto explains childhood autism as having its origins in a lack of a dialogue between a baby and its main carer. It represents a lack of roots and sense of identity, for it is the carer who gives the baby this sense of security.

For Françoise Dolto, language is what differentiates human beings from other forms of life. In particular, it is the capacity to use language as a sophisticated symbolic structure to convey understanding. It is also the ability to attribute different representations to symbols so they convey more then their simple or obvious meaning that allows for the capacity for abstract thought. This ability to communicate between mother and child went beyond words. Françoise Dolto maintained that, "The child is in unconscious communication with the body of his mother" (Dolto, 1989, p. 68). At times, Françoise Dolto would consider other forms of communications, including, but not limited to, those from an inter-generational collective unconscious and psychosomatic conditions. Françoise Dolto could go past frontiers that other scientists would hesitate to cross. "Neuro-biologists smile and shrug their shoulders. They say, 'I don't believe in telepathy.' But the telepathy between the baby and mother is well known to all mums" (Dolto, 1997a, p. 244).

For Françoise Dolto, each child chooses to be born and to live in order to express its desires for and in life. This notion of *desires* and how to differentiate them from *needs* was vital for Françoise Dolto. It is the capacity of the child to be alive and to express itself through language that leads the child to the acknowledgement of its desires, otherwise there would only be objects and needs. Psychoanalysts know that life is only about our desires.

Needs play a less important role for Françoise Dolto than they did for Lacan. She sees them as material requirements for the physical body within the maternal dyad, which can be satisfied. *Desires* represent an insatiable tension found within an inter-psychic dialogue, and are more important then needs. It is the yearning to communicate, at first through mimicking and emoting, that establishes a relationship for the child and eventually leads to learning a symbolic code that is a formal language. The desires of a young child are a constant dynamic and express a vital search to be in communication with another. It begins for the foetus with exchanges within the placenta and an awareness of the mother's emotional states. After the birth, it is through smiles and cries that the continuity of the relationship is re-established, for the experience of the world is mediated through the body.

For Françoise Dolto, the analysis of children was essentially the same as the analysis of adults, even if the setting and technique required some minor modifications (Dolto, 1997a, p. 27). A person who had been trained to work with adults has the skills to work equally with children. It was the view of Françoise Dolto that all was played out before the age of four. This is not to say in some fatalistic way that the future of a child is fixed by such an age in a way that will determine its successes and failures in life, or in society, but that it has largely established the roots of its psychic identity and personality by that time.

In any given outline of the work of Françoise Dolto, there must be an acceptance that, rather like any iceberg, there is more than can immediately be seen. The indication for a clinical intervention is when a child feels caught in a painful interrelational conflict that spoils his existence, when otherwise there would be everything for it to be happy (Dolto, 1997b, p. 244). There is no minimum age before which a child should not be seen by a psychoanalyst. Special care should be with very young children who might be at the receiving end of parental projections. Françoise Dolto did evolve the idea of a symbolic payment that she expected from children. This may be in the form of a stone, a square of coloured paper, or even ten centimes. This represented a contract between the two of them, a debt felt by the child, as well as a sense of autonomy and separation of the desires of the child from the desires of the parents. The symbolic payment is a reminder that work is being done, in which the child adjusts its way of being. It is neither a partial object nor a gift, and does not need to be interpreted. A child who wishes to express a negative transference will feel increasingly anxious about bringing the symbolic payment. In the preliminary meetings, Françoise Dolto would see or, at the very least, have contact with both parents together, if the child had not reached puberty and was at least five years old. She would see the parents with the child and she would also see each parent alone, to establish their Oedipal history. An initial three sessions would be agreed to see if psychoanalysis would be of potential benefit. If that were the case, a more formal and longer term contract with the symbolic payment would be set out. If the child was upset by this, then the psychoanalyst would have to work out whether the child wished to stay in the situation in which it found itself, in which case treatment should not be offered, or whether it marked a rejection of the parents, in which case, it might be offered. The psychoanalyst should respect the child's desires and decisions (Ledoux, 1990, p. 169).

For Françoise Dolto, as for many other child psychoanalysts, it is words, drawings, and modelling that are the royal road to a child's unconscious and central to her work. The use of modelling is for children who feel inhibited, or lack confidence in drawing, although, for some children, working in three dimensions helps them express themselves more clearly. These drawings and models need to be talked about, rather than be interpreted in the classical manner. The child is not asked for its associations, but might be asked, "Where would you be in this drawing?" For Françoise Dolto, the drawings are the representation of a phantasy that is witness to some past experience as expressed in relationships with archaic objects. They can also be graphic illustrations that reveal the unconscious image of the child's body. They are an allegory for the real and imaginary representation of the child. Up to about the age of six or seven, these allegories are anthropomorphic expressions, so that a sofa can represent a grandfather, or a drawing of house can symbolize an image of security. A motif frequently drawn by children is the *maison-Dieu*, a square with a triangular roof, door, and windows. It is typical of certain constant themes and expressions that appear in children's drawings. Françoise Dolto saw a child who did a drawing of a *maison-Dieu* without any doors on it and who spoke in a very low voice. The absence of doors symbolized the child's inhibition from speaking out loud.

In time, a child evolves more skills and can draw sophisticated images that represent an evolutionary development of libidinal relationships with others. Windows tend to refer to sensory communications; curtains depict relationships with the external world. Françoise Dolto distinguishes between pre-oedipal drawings and post-oedipal drawings. The former tend to be more stereotypical, while the latter have the ego acting as a censor. They do not allow for the direct illustration of conflictual drives and sublimated phantasies. After the age of six or seven, they are more clearly metaphors and no longer of an anthropomorphic nature in the mind of the child, but, in each case, the child shows the nature of his difficulty. Even though nowadays men rarely wear hats, or smoke pipes, children often still draw these as a representation of their fathers, even if father is a non-smoker. There will be something that emphasizes the head that connects with the phallic person in their life, the one with the authoritative words. Women are often depicted as carrying bags, or cases, which may symbolize their femininity. Boys will draw belts with a large circle on them, or a button to represent their awareness of a lack of valued genitals (Winter & Dolto, 2002, p. 59).

Françoise Dolto was interested in the normal development of a child, as she was by unusual psychopathological manifestations. Her popularity was the result of showing parents how to support the psychic development of their children. The child has an unconscious image of its body and its identity that are established even as early as sixteen months after birth. Instead of making interpretations that bring phantasies into consciousness, Françoise Dolto is more directive in asking how the child links himself with the drawing. The drawings witness a transferential, if imaginary, life rooted in archiac objects and the body in the world. Like dreams, they reveal a metaphor by which a child's apprehensions about the image of the body and its relationship to others can be devined. They graphically reflect the Oedipal development of the child through anthropomorphic translations of objects within the drawings.

Sophie Morgenstern, who had been analysed by Freud and came to Paris from Vienna in 1924, introduced the idea of using drawings in child analysis while working for Professor Georges Heuyer. In 1927, she published a first paper that made drawings the central theme of her work. This was about a nine-year-old child called Jacques, who had remained mute since before the age of two. It was not clear whether Jacques was autistic, or hysterical. At their first meeting, she asked him if he was sad. He nodded in agreement, and then she asked him to draw his sadness. He drew a scene in which a boy with a terrified expression was next to an older man. Sophie Morgenstern asked about the drawing, but Jacques remained silent and grew hostile, but through both silently letting Jacques draw and through making some comments, but only about the drawings, by the end of four months of treatment he was able to speak. Ironically, it was in his final session that he could acknowledge that he had already revealed everything in this first drawing. Much of Sophie Morgenstern's work reflected a morality of the period that resulted in many interpretations being about childhood masturbation and that such sexual activity was then considered to be the main source of any neurosis. Sophie Morgenstern's technique evolved so that she would say nothing, or very little, during sessions, for up to a year when with children, while they worked on their drawings. After forty minutes into a session, she would announce that it was at an end, and the child would often say, "Already?" This was not an expression of disappointment, but a reflection of how much work the child had already done. Some of the children got better even without much having been said.

Sophie Morgenstern taught Françoise Dolto her technique. It was Françoise Dolto's view that a single painting was enough to create a relationship and establish the transference. She understood a drawing as something that needed to be heard through the observations of another. She appreciated that treatment is closely linked to the unconscious image of the body. It is the subjective identity of the child anchored in a body of sensations that are projected through the drawing in the immediacy of the clinical session. The child shows metaphorically where he is to the psychoanalyst. The task of the psychoanalyst is not only to decipher these cryptic representations of past bodily fixations, but, in the framework of transferral relationship, to allow a new space where desires can unfold and where the unconscious image of the body can be recognized. It is important to closely observe not only the contents of the drawings, but the sequence in which they are drawn, the colours used, and which elements, if any, are later discarded. It is also important to pay attention to the conduct and emotions of a child while it is drawing. Making a drawing should always be considered as work and not play, for both the child and the psychoanalyst. Elements in a drawing are not susceptible to a universal interpretation, so that a particular object in a drawing does not always symbolize the same thing for every child. However, they should be understood in the light of psychoanalytic theories about childhood development. The meanings of objects in a drawing will emerge as the child speaks about the significance that he attributes to the drawing of which he is the subject, while the analyst may be looking out for, among other things, unresolved Oedipal issues.

Understanding the meaning of illusion, mirrors, phantasy, and images of the body through the intermediary of words is central to the work of Françoise Dolto. The visual is a good starting place to get to the verbal. When a child is not able to articulate something verbally, another creative language is used, such as drawings and modelling with some form of plastic material. As a child psychoanalyst, Françoise Dolto followed the advice of her teacher in getting children to draw and to use this as a spur for understanding a child's mental state and situation. It is a technique that she also used sometimes with adults (Dolto, 1991, p. 33).

Françoise Dolto was well known for her clinical observations, and it seems appropriate to give some brief examples of the way in which she worked. Working with children is facilitated, by having a particular framework. There should be a table with paper and crayons as well as some material that a child can use to model. The psychoanalyst should remain outside the visual field of view of the child, but by his side. Interpretations in psychoanalysis, whether linked to free associations of adults or the drawings of children, are not expert declarations, but are words that allow the adult or child to become aware of new and different associations. The analyst says to the child who has accepted a contract to come and get better from that which he feels within himself as an obstacle in his path of development.

> You can say in words, drawings, or by making models, all that you think about, or feel while you are here, even if it is about other people that you know, and even if you think (or have been told), that you must not say it. [Dolto, 1981, p. 69]

Pierre, an intelligent child of six with a development more appropriate for an eight-year-old, drew a picture in which the sun was black, people's faces were black, but their clothes white. His mother confirmed that he had not seen a photographic negative, yet he had devised for himself a world in which everything was reversed. It transpired that the mother became pregnant three months after becoming engaged, although she had not wanted a physical relationship, and had even asked her fiancé for help in arranging an abortion. After the birth, the mother felt a wave of loving emotion towards both Pierre and his father, while Pierre resisted being held by his mother. Four years later, a second child was happily born, but Pierre says that he is indifferent to his brother. He is now able to speak, and says he feels claustrophobic when with his mother. She brought Pierre to see Françoise Dolto, complaining of her son's cold-heartedness. Dolto's understanding was that Pierre is expressing the mother's grief and mourning, without feeling in the least bit abandoned. Whatever negativity the mother had consciously carried while pregnant, she had physically looked after the foetus and produced milk when Pierre was born. A completely negative mother would not have been able to do so. The prognosis looked good in terms of Pierre adapting well to a social life with others, even if he is likely to be a distant with women. He took after his father in wanting to be in charge, but was not overly narcissistic in wanting to be the centre of attention, or in exploiting others (Dolto, 1995, pp. 105–107).

Christian was seen by another psychoanalyst, who brought the case to one of a series of seminars that took place while Françoise Dolto was in Quebec (Dolto, 1987, pp. 265–286). They were something between a master-class and group supervision. The child left the analyst and just about everyone else feeling perplexed by being almost mute, but with a great skill in being able to draw. His school had complained that he withdrew from any interaction with others. He never spoke to anyone, and refused to read out loud. At home, he would cry at night and say that he was upset by his own timidity. Christian was the youngest child, with five or six other siblings. He was born ten years after the second youngest, and his father died when he was three years old. The analyst had the impression that Christian's mother had not mourned for the death of her husband. There was some ambiguity as to how he had died. One version was from a car accident, but another option was from a cancer. The mother refused to confirm what was true. Christian spoke mainly to his mother and a little bit to his siblings, but not to other members of the family. He does not go anywhere and does not reply to telephone calls. In his solitude he watches television, reads books that are aimed at older children, and enjoys pottering about doing odd jobs. His mother is the main intermediary with the outside world. Despite his silence, he gains excellent marks at school. When producing a drawing, Christian works in an obsessional manner. Each crayon is carefully selected and when its use is finished, it is then slowly returned to the box containing all the others. In a first drawing there is a potato in the middle, then, to the left, a hat. To this he adds successively a butterfly, a flower, an aeroplane, a flying saucer, clouds, and the sun. When Christian is asked by his analyst to explain the picture he writes the word *potato.* (In French, *patate.*) The analyst expresses some consternation, and Christian draws a cake saying, "A hundred years for potato." When asked what he sees at the top of the picture, Christian draws fire. The analyst tries an interpretation suggesting that the flying saucer is angry with the plane and the cloud and is firing on them. Christian then draws a snail and adds an umbrella to it and the flower. When asked whether the butterfly is going up or down, Christian draws some spirals showing the path that the butterfly is taking is upwards. He then draws a bird, and, when prompted as to where it is going, Christian shows a nest and a tree. The analyst clarifies for Françoise Dolto that, in Quebec, the French expression *faire patate* means to miss out. Christian was seen once a week for a thirty-minute session, during which he did a drawing. In one of these sessions, Christian draws a butterfly, a caterpillar, grass, and a flower. When asked what is the relationship between all these objects, he drew eggs at the bottom of a tree and a cocoon on the trunk of the tree. The analyst says that the objects in the drawing reflect something about what he wants, or that things will change, that each thing becomes something else. Christian indicates that they show a life cycle, the butterfly lays the eggs, which hatch and become the caterpillar, that spins a cocoon and eventually another butterfly emerges. The analyst wonders if Christian has concerns about his origins and his birth. Some of his siblings are old enough to be his parents. After a few weeks, Christian's mother reported that he has started stuttering and that this was at the same time that he started the therapy. This is the third time in his life that he has stuttered while speaking. The first seemed to be linked to the death of his father, while the second coincided with his first day at school. In the next session, Christian draws a large single fish accompanied by four smaller fish, all of different sizes. The fish have no colour to them. He adds seaweed, a snail, and a crab. The analyst says to Christian that two of the fishes have their mouths open as if they wished to say something, but although he would like to listen to them, he hears nothing. Christian adds teeth to the biggest fish. The analyst says that this fish appears angry and might bite. For the first time in the therapy, Christian smiles, and then covers up his smile with his fingers. The analyst feels that for the first time there is a transferential and countertransferencial relationship between the two of them. The analyst admires Christian for his aggressiveness and feels attached to him. In a later session, the analyst tells Christian, in the presence of his mother, that the responsibility about whether he does or does not talk remains only with him.

The analyst feels that Christian's mother does not want to speak to him about the death of his father. Everything seems to revolve around Christian's origins. He feels that it would be inappropriate to comment while Christian is drawing, as it would be an interruption, like making a comment to someone who was dreaming about the meaning of their dream. The analyst acknowledges that it may be some resistance on his part, but he feels strongly that he does not want to rush in.

After a short break, the therapy starts again and the analyst asks for the symbolic payment. Christian brought a payment that was ten times greater then necessary, which was rejected by the analyst. He had asked for a black coin and Christian had brought a white one. Françoise Dolto observes that the coin is like the fish in the drawing, white with no colour. Some other objects in the drawings are not coloured and they symbolize a form, or idea, that has no affect for the child. In one of the pictures, Christian has drawn three and half moons, which links with the first drawing that also contained a cake with three and half candles on it. The analyst remarks that Christian always signs his drawings with his name and age, six and half. The halves are very important. Françoise Dolto points out that three and half was Christian's age when his father died. She points out that, with the death of his father, there was no man to support him. Instead of being a third with his parents, he entered into a new triangulation with his mother and one of his sisters. He knows that he is the real son of his father, but the father is dead and an imaginary father cannot carry the symbolic function required of that role. In the symbolic payment, he gave the analyst one coin, but the analyst gave him nine in change. He feels he has received nothing from his father. He needs to discover the powers that he feels have been taken away from him. She recommends that the analyst should ask Christian for a black stone. Christian's desire that he will receive more than he pays for should be unsatisfied, although he retains the right to ask for it, given his personal history.

Françoise Dolto looked at the pictures and she saw that the stomachs of the birds, otherwise coloured red, had a dark mass within them, except one bird coloured blue that had a head emerging from a neck that looked like a cross. She links this with the hope of the mother wanting Christian to be helped, but fearful that her son may grow up and become a virile man. Christian may feel ambiguous as to whether he wishes to remain a child, or become an adult. Mother may have wanted Christian to be a girl, or she may have incestual thoughts. Very traumatized children give an explanation about their pictures, in which the objects drawn seem to have no connection with the reality of the associations given. The necks of the birds, along with their tails, in Christian's drawing are green. Green is the colour of life. This suggests that, although Christian may appear obsessional in his outer reality, in his inner reality, he is more free spirited. A true obsessional would not do such a thing. One of the butterflies is coloured black and looks like a skeleton. This is a reference to the dead father. The snail is the first symbol used for the child's motor movement. In Christian's drawing, the shell is perfectly drawn and coloured purple. This means that it is without a gender. Christian feels guilty because he feels he has missed out. Through his magical thinking and Oedipal desire, he had killed his father. A child has a need to want the death of his father, without it becoming a reality. Christian is also wrestling with his sexual identity. The potato coloured blue is a colour favoured by pre-oedipal girls, yet he wrote *patate* in green and he has written *trois ans* in purple. *Cent ans* (a hundred years) may be a reference to a grandfather. It could also be a play on words meaning *sentant* (sensing), or *sans temps* (literally without time, but meaning without me). It could mean *s'entend,* to hear oneself, or possibly to understand each other, but Christian did not elucidate on its meaning.

In the first sessions, claims Françoise Dolto, it is better not to simply ask a child, as it were, out of the blue, "What do you have to say", but to treat him as an individual and to introduce yourself and explain why you have agreed to see him. It is also important, as in any analysis, to remind the child that it is not only the analyst, but the child who has to do the work. It is also important to make clear that what is said in the analysis will not be repeated outside and to tell the parents that they should not ask of their child to tell them what took place. If parents do not follow this guidance, then the child is right not to tell them.

In Françoise Dolto's theoretical view, a pre-superego exists. This is pre-Oedipal and begins when what is forbidden is internalized within the experience of a dyad, usually with the mother (Ledoux, 2006, p. 273). Children, who can go past the stage of drawing a very geometric representation of their house, believe they are the centre of the world. By lengthening their house they can make drawings of a church with a steeple, or reduce it to a dog's kennel, or even turn it into a sailing boat. The roof of the building represents this pre-superego. When the roof appears to be not aligned with the rest of the building, it indicates a missing connection with others. It is the result of a child being looked after by a succession of people with different internalized rules. The child then has a pre-superego that goes off in all directions and lacks consistency. Receiving a consistent direction enables the child to develop a positive narcissism. Without it, the child risks becoming capricious and hysterical, as the desire of others ceaselessly changes. Hysteria has its origins at that stage when a child is unable to establish a consistent code. Drawings will reflect this lack of consistency, as a child will be unable to represent himself within it. The distortion can be represented in this way as an expression of the unconscious image of his body. The distortion in the drawing will be repeated in other subsequent drawings of similar objects. Children who have difficulty in drawing upright trees are representing their own sense of mutilation, usually of a pre-verbal disavowed nature concerning childhood sexuality. The conflict is between their needs and desires at the oral stage of development. It usually is the result of their main carer disliking the gender of the child, such as mother who wishes that her son had been a daughter, or vice versa. The child will grow up with doubts and ambiguous feelings about their sexual identity, until they meet some other who can confirm what they are (Dolto, 1982, pp. 230–232).

The use of drawings can be very helpful when used in the children's wards in hospitals. Children in a cardiac surgery ward produce very different kinds of images to those in a general surgery ward.

A thirteen-year-old boy was sent to the Trousseau Hospital because he would spend all day tearing up pieces of paper while looking out of window. He was thrown out of school and remained at home. The first drawing that he did was of a church in a psychotic landscape. The drawing contained many crosses on the front of the church, no base line, lots of vertical lines, few horizontal lines showing a separation from the ground. Buildings appeared to have no foundations. When asked to describe the picture, the boy said that it was men ski-ing on the day that his father died. It appeared that father had been walking high in the mountains, and he fell into a crevasse. Françoise Dolto went to speak to the mother, who said that this took place when her son was four years old. A rescue party had gone to look for the father by torchlight, but he was not found and the search was abandoned. These lights figured in the next drawing done by the child. A memorial ceremony was held at the church, which many people attended. After a few months, the mother received a letter saying that her husband was still alive. He had broken his leg, but been discovered by a shepherd who carried him to his hut until he could be taken down the valley to the nearest town and a letter sent to his wife. In hospital, the bone was broken again, because it had healed badly and it took a few more months of recuperation before he could return home. For six months this child thought his father had died. He had either not been told, or not taken cognizance of the letter saying that his father was still alive. When the father returned, the child would not speak to him and would hide away from him. The mother said that she had completely forgotten about this day until Françoise Dolto asked about what had happened to her husband.

Ten days later, mother and child returned, and the child did another drawing of skiers. When asked to explain it, he said that it represented the day that he and his mother died. The boy says he was also injured and he has a deep scar on his hand. He says that he was the one who killed himself and his mother. In the drawing, mother has blood coming out of her mouth. Françoise Dolto asks if it was the same mother who brought him to the hospital and the boy confirms that it was. Françoise Dolto again asks for more details and the child responds that they were all on a tandem bike. The boy explains that father had hit a lorry that killed the boy and his mother. It was the child's fault because he had moved. While saying this, the child appears distant and only content to give an explanation because of the inherent contradictions in his picture. It later transpired that the family had indeed been riding, and the child had been told not to move otherwise they would all fall off. Father had been steering the bike. In conversation with Françoise Dolto, the boy acknowledged a difference between him then on the bike, who had died, and him being alive and in the consulting room. Again Françoise Dolto went to speak with the mother as to whether there had been another accident involving a tandem. The mother told of how two weeks before the accident in which her husband broke his leg, all three of them had been on a tandem on a mountain road hidden in fog, when they had hit a lorry. The mother had bitten her tongue, which then began to bleed, and she felt disorientated. The bike was damaged and could not be used. It was for this reason that, a couple of weeks later, father was walking when he fell into the crevasse. At the third meeting, Françoise Dolto placed both drawings in front of the boy and commented on them. He listened while pretending not to listen, and did not even look at her. He said that his father was not his father. This was a man who wore a hat; his father never wore a hat. Françoise Dolto responded by reminding the boy that he is not guilty of the accident because he moved. The accident occurred because his father had not seen the approaching lorry. The fourth session was due to take place four days later, but the child developed a serious inflammation of the knees and could not attend. In French, knees are *genoux.* Françoise Dolto sees this as an allusion to *je–nous,* or I–Us (Us = mother, father, and me) and the possible psychosomatic nature of the illness. Interestingly, while his knees were inflamed, the boy lost all his other autistic symptoms. When they met again, Françoise Dolto went over with him the significance of his symbolic illness. The boy said that he now wanted to return to school to learn how to read and write (Dolto, 1988, pp. 71–76)

One of the most interesting of Dolto's accounts of a psychoanalytic intervention occurred outside of a clinical situation and without the presence of the person most concerned. It was in regard to a boxer who was being treated by Boris Dolto for a damaged hand that would not heal completely when treated by others. A complicating factor was that the boxer would not be separated from his mistress. Boris challenged her, by saying that her behaviour was like someone who wanted her partner to fail. To the boxer he commented that, as much as his mistress loved him, if he failed to win the championship, she would think of him as an idiot. The boxer's trainer confided in Boris that they only succeeded when there was a good level of trust between them, but at the moment the boxer was feeling very angry towards him. Boris invited the trainer to supper to meet Françoise, so that he could explain the situation to her. That evening, the trainer gave details of how the boxer was the son of a very violent man, who had terrorized the little boy. In time the boy became an excellent street fighter. Soon, the father began to fear that the son might be able to reverse their roles and beat him. The son had a habit of not finishing what he had started. As a boxer, if he did not win a contest with an early knockout, which was usually well within his abilities, then he would win on points, but in doing so he took a lot of unnecessary punishment. The wife of the boxer had told the trainer that they were rich, but she became furiously jealous when he slept with other women. The trainer said that he no longer knew what to do so that the boxer was not distracted by his love life and could fight in the ring in a way that showed his real skills. Françoise advised him that the next time he was in the ring, when the trainer thought that the boxer was not able to deliver the knock-out blow, to give him permission to do what was necessary and remind him that he was not fighting his father. The result of the next bout was indeed speedily resolved. The boxer told his trainer that when during the match, the trainer had made the comment suggested by Françoise Dolto, the boxer had immediately felt released from any hesitation to deliver the knock-out blow (Dolto, 1989, pp. 199–200).

Françoise Dolto was interested in commenting on the drawings of children she did not know, during supervision, or in seminars. For this, she was criticized on the grounds that it was impossible to fully understand a drawing without the child being present to talk about it (Ledoux, 2006, pp. 93–96). She did believe that major issues that concerned the child are present in their first picture, if these can be understood. Subsequent drawings are refinements, either on the same themes, or they represent an evolution in understanding.

Such is the respect in which Françoise Dolto is held that her detractors joke that if someone showed her a drawing, even if she did not know the child, even if she did not know the child's history, and even if she did not know what the case is about, she would still be able to tell you ten thousand things from such a drawing (Winter & Dolto, 2002, p. 51). Another version says that she would look at it and after a few moments be able to tell you the first names of all the child's grandparents. The truth of the matter is that Françoise Dolto demonstrates that profound innovation in psychoanalytic understanding rarely comes from established institutions and is usually rejected at first by the establishment. Psychoanalysis started out because one individual thought about a problem in an original and radical way. In time, such thinking became tamed and rigid. Françoise Dolto hoped that her ideas might avoid such a fate, because she always acknowledged that what she was doing was not unique, or special, but that it was open to any psychoanalyst to work in this way. The application of this technique can be of special benefit to children and adults with eating disorders, cancer, those undergoing major surgery, or who have had a limb amputated, and who are showing psychological symptoms that are not alleviated by other methods.

References

Dolto, F. (1981). *Au subjet du désir*. Paris: Seuil.

Dolto, F. (1982). *Séminaire de psychanalyse d'enfants, Tome 1*. Paris: Seuil.

Dolto, F. (1986). *Enfances*. Paris: Seuil.

Dolto, F. (1987). *Dialogues Québécois*. Paris: Seuil.

Dolto, F. (1988). *Séminaire de psychanalyse d'enfants, Tome 3*. Paris: Seuil.

Dolto, F. (1989). *Autoportrait d'une psychanalyste 1934–1988*. Paris: Seuil.

Dolto, F. (1991). *Séminaire de psychanalyse d'enfants, Tome 2* (in collaboration with Jean-Françoise de Sauverzac), coll. "Points Essais". Paris.

Dolto, F. (1995). *La difficulté de vivre*. Paris: Gallimard.

Dolto, F. (1997a). *Lorsque l'enfant paraît, Tome 1*. Paris: Seuil.

Dolto, F. (1997b). *La cause des enfants*. Paris: Laffont.

Hugo, V. (2002). *Selected Poems* (p. 2), B. Haxton (Trans.). London: Penguin.

Ledoux, M. (1990). *Introduction à l'œuvre de Françoise Dolto*. Paris: Seuil.

Ledoux, M. (2006). *Dictionnaire raisonné de l'œuvre de F. Dolto*. Paris: Payot.

Meyer, C. (2005). *Le livre noir de la psych-analyse*. Paris: Les Arènnes.

Roudinesco, E. (1988). Des jalons pour une histoire—Entretien avec Françoise Dolto. In: *Quelques pas sur le chemin de Françoise Dolto*. Paris: Seuil.

Winter, J.-P., & Dolto, F. (2002). *Françoise Dolto, les images, les mots, le corps*. Paris: Gallimard.

CHAPTER FIVE

The unconscious image of the body[1]

Claude Boukobza

Françoise Dolto published *The Unconscious Image of the Body* in 1984, at a time when she was no longer seeing patients and had limited her activity to supervising analysts. Dolto considered this book, of which she was particularly fond, a kind of "last will and testament". It attests to a life spent in innovative clinical practice with psychotic and autistic children and adolescents, most of whom were labelled as "crazy". Her case studies, which punctuate the text, establish a new model for listening to children. She also thought of *The Unconscious Image of the Body* as a legacy for her students and a wider audience interested in the theories that she had forged and whose ramifications have undoubtedly yet to be exhausted.

Dolto's originality lies in the fact that, from the very outset, she placed the problem of the body at the core of her analytical practice, whether in the treatment of adults or children. What Dolto calls the unconscious image of the body—we will come back to this point later—is the living synthesis of the emotional, sensory, and language experiences of early infancy. For Dolto, such experiences make up the treasure trove of the unconscious that succumbs to repression after the mirror stage and the Oedipal complex.

Dolto's theory was elaborated over thirty years of clinical practice and theoretical work. A range of conferences and papers attest to her efforts (1956, 1957, 1961, 1967). After her death in 1988, manuscripts were found which reveal how often Dolto revised her conference papers of 1956 and 1957. These manuscripts, proof of her incessant reworking of her theories, were published in 1977 by Gérard Guillerault in *Le sentiment de soi, aux sources de l'image inconsciente du corps.*

Dolto's book, *L'Image inconsciente du corps* (The unconscious image of the body), which she worked on for over fifteen years with a number of colleagues and editors (she did not like to work alone), sums up and develops all these essays and adds to them an essential term: 'the unconscious'. The body image becomes thus the *unconscious* image of the body. It is interesting to note how Dolto's itinerary through institutions is rife with articles—from the Société Psychanalytique Française, which she founded with Lacan and other analysts in 1953, and finally to the Ecole Freudienne de Paris. After the dissolution of the Ecole Freudienne in 1981, Dolto did not belong to any institution.

What does this concept, hitherto unknown in psychoanalytic circles, add to our theoretical knowledge? It is noteworthy that Françoise Dolto begins her masterwork with a very "practical" comment about her clinical method: "I would give the child a sheet of paper and crayons. Later I started using putty".

The drawings and clay figures made by children play an important role in Dolto's practice because she considered them as so many "self-portraits". However, this does not mean that they were portraits in the traditional visual sense. In order to interpret the drawings and locate the projection of various instances of the Freudian psychic apparatus (the id, the ego, and the superego), Dolto relied solely on the verbal associations that the child makes when commenting on its drawings. To avoid the impression that she was providing a magic formula for the interpretation of drawings, much as one might provide a key to the interpretation of dreams, Françoise Dolto did not publish the sessions from her seminar on children's drawings. The body image is the representation of the organizational modes of these instances and the drawings, or clay figures, a representation of a representation.

Thus, Françoise Dolto posited a "metapsychology of infantile development" positioned before the Oedipal complex. To elaborate her theory, she forged her own concepts and at times even coined her own terms. Her use of the word "image" is, in itself, quite challenging, and does not correspond to what one means generally by "image", and still less to the *imago* of traditional psychoanalytical parlance. In the following pages, we shall take a closer look at Dolto's theory and how it was developed.

The body image and the body schema

Dolto distinguishes first of all the image of the body from the body schema. "The body schema" is a factual reality, which defines the individual in as much as he, or she, is a member of the species. The body schema is the same for all similarly aged people of the human species. It is, above all, both preconscious and conscious, and refers the body spatially to its immediate experience. It can be independent of language. It is, in fact, a conscious representation of the body itself.

The "image" of the body is, on the other hand, specific to each one of us and linked to the subject and the subject's history. It is the living synthesis of the emotional experiences of the desiring subject, the unconscious memory of lived relational experiences, both narcissistic and interrelational. The unconscious image of the body is always shaped in relation to the other—in particular to the caregiving mother—and refers the subject of desire to her *jouir.* In this respect, Dolto remains very faithful to Freud's *Three Essays on the Theory of Sexuality* (1905d). However, the *jouir* is always mediated by the language of communication with others, e.g., the words of the mother that articulate the baby's struggles and validates (valorizes) them or overrules them—"You are happy." "You like that, don't you?" "You're not comfortable." "Don't touch. It's dirty", etc.

We can cite the example of the little girl who, in her first session with Françoise Dolto, drew a beautiful bouquet of flowers in full bloom, whereas the same girl, in the presence of her mother, drew a bouquet of faded flowers. The unconscious image of the body was experienced differently depending on whether the child was with the mother, or alone with her own narcissism.

The body schema is connected with need as a source of drives; the unconscious image of the body is on the side of desire as a place where drives are represented. Neither the body schema nor the body image can exist without the other, except in certain cases of pathological defusion. Psychotic or autistic children seem to be absent from a body that functions flawlessly, like "a spaceship without an astronaut". On the other hand, a perturbed unconscious body image can cause serious functional difficulties, although no neurological lesion is evidenced.

Françoise Dolto writes of children with polio, whom she often treated when she began her practice. If the disease had not set in very early on, the handicapped children often had a healthy image of their body and dreamed, or drew, themselves as walking or running. However, if polio occurred before the child had begun to walk, the body schema was always affected. Dolto observed that the body image could at times remain undamaged, if the physical infirmity had been addressed without excessive anxiety and negativity on the part of the mother, or the father, or the child's entourage, and if the child was allowed to fantasize and express its desires. The case of little Iiro, who had congenitally webbed fingers, in Winnicott's (1971) *Therapeutic Consultations in Child Psychiatry,* can be read with this in mind. In such cases, the body image is symbolized through subject-to-subject exchanges despite the physical infirmity.

The unconscious image of the body is thus structured around intersubjective relationships. If there is no speech, no possibility of communication, the subject's symbolization remains "on hold". For Françoise Dolto, language—true language that conveys meaning for the subject—is always closely connected with the body. Understanding a word depends both on the body schema and on the unconscious image of the body linked to the real exchanges that accompanied the assimilation of the word. "To have meaning, words must first of all be embodied", as Dolto once wrote. We might refer here to a striking clinical case: Dolto began treating a five-year-old girl who, for two years, refused to do anything with her hands and kept them closed with her forearms folded over her chest. When Dolto noticed during the first session that the girl was looking intently at the modelling clay, she said to her, "You can pick it up with your *hand–mouth*". If Dolto had said "Pick it up with your hand", or "Do something", referring back to a long lost anal stage, the statement would have been meaningless for the girl.

For Dolto, the idea of an unconscious image of the body can overlap with the Freudian concept of the id, but it remains an id that is always "in relation".

The structure of the unconscious image of the body

The unconscious image of the body is constantly shaped and reshaped throughout the development of the child. In Dolto's opinion, the image comprises three modes, or dynamic aspects, all of which constitute the subject's narcissism at each stage of development.

1. *The base image*. This is what allows the child to feel that it is in a "sameness of being", a narcissistic continuity. It reminds us inevitably of Winnicott's "continuity of being". The feeling of being, or primitive narcissism, is the subject's narcissism in as much as it is the subject-of-the-desire-to-live which, for Dolto, exists before birth. This is why the child can be seen as the symbolic heir of the desire of its genitors. If the base image is damaged, a life-threatening phantasm emerges. Dolto saw here the source of phobic representations whose organization depends on the dominant erogenous zones.

   There is a base image at each stage (postnatal respiratory, olfactory, auditory stages), so many very early stages which Françoise Dolto was able to bring to light, as well as the oral and anal stages. All this demonstrates, it might be said in passing, that the unconscious image of the body is not scopic, or visible. These images participate in the construction of a "veritable relational architecture" centred on the erogenous zones and dependent on the way the mother responds to the child's expectations.
2. *The functional image*. This is the image of the subject striving for the fulfilment of his, or her, desire. It is regulated by the erogenous zones and brings about the enrichment of relational possibilities with others. Françoise Dolto rediscovered here the Freudian concept of *anaclisis*. Thus, the anal functional image

is an image of expulsive discharge, at first in relation to the need to defecate. It can be later displaced on to any partial object, including subtle "non-material" (as Dolto called them) objects—the expulsion of air from the lungs for sheer pleasure, or throwing an object. The example of the little girl with the "hand–mouth", who rediscovers the prehensile oral function of hands due to the analyst's words, provides us with a good illustration of this particular image of the body.

3. *The erogenous image*. This is where pleasure and displeasure are focused in the relationship with the other. Its representations are seen in circles, ovals, balls, tentacles, lines, and holes that the child imagines as being able to both send out and receive. Erogenous images open the subject up to a shared pleasure that can be expressed in words pronounced by others, thereby acquiring a symbolic and human dimension.

These three images are transformed and reshaped throughout the child's development and each image leaves behind its own trace and tonality. The unconscious image of the body is the living, and continually evolving, synthesis of these three components actualized by the subject in the *dynamic image*, which holds them together. The dynamic image is the "desire to be" and to persevere in a becoming. It is the very image of desire, what Françoise Dolto called the "towards–becoming" (in French, the *allant–devenant*, or the "towards–desiring", the *allant–désirant*). Dolto speaks of a subject "in longing desire" (in French, *en désirance*). This trajectory of meaningful desire, "moving towards" a goal, is represented in the dotted lines or arrows which we often find in children's drawing. In a similar way, the whirlpools or "snails" that are usually the first graphic representations of infants are the sign of a subject in a "desiring state".

Human subjects are defined by the fact that they interpose between the body and the self an image with which they identify. This is a fiction that is both of the "subject's body" and not the subject's body. The unconscious image of the body allows the body to tear itself away from raw carnality and gain access to the symbolic. The subject's body is not mere meat; it is always humanized and invested in a relationship with the other. The image is always shaped in relation to the adult care-taker who speaks and gives meaning to the child's emotions and feelings.

Images of the body and their destiny: "symboligenous" castrations

Each moment in the child's development takes place along the following schema: the satisfaction of an organic need and well-being of the child articulated around language and emotional exchanges with the mother; the separation and weaning from this state of pleasure, or *jouissance*, as soon as physical maturity allows for it; the abandonment of what has become excessive *jouissance*, and the promotion to another type of drive organization. At the centre of this is what Dolto calls "symboligenous castrations".

As Dolto observed, castrations make up the destiny of the unconscious images of the body much in the same way as Freud described the destiny of human drives. In contrast to traditional usage, Dolto employs the term "castration" in the plural. For Dolto, castrations are the trials that the child's desires come up against. These castrations allow for symbolization and shape the unconscious image of the body in its successive re-elaborations. Umbilical castration, oral castration, anal castration, the mirror stage (which holds a singular place), primary castration, Oedipal castration—all these "castrations" articulate the psychological development of the child and its "towards–becoming in the endowment of his/her sex" (in French, *l'allant–devenant dans le génie de son sexe*).

Castration is the radical prohibition of sought-after, previously experienced satisfaction. The craving for immediate satisfaction for the body leads down the route towards more and more—a route which one day must be cut off. This is a veritable operation in the mathematical sense of the word, the quotient of which is what Dolto calls the "fruits of castration". Thus, for example, the fruit of oral castration is access to language, which goes beyond the baby language understood by the mother alone.

Castrations are "symboligenous", a word Dolto coined to describe the process enacted in a human being when another human being signifies to him, or her, that the realization of desire is prohibited by the law. This brings about, at first, a reaction of rebellion in the child, and then a depression which leads to inhibition, and finally a shift towards a register of shared pleasure.

Castration is something that must be constantly re-enacted. It is the expression of the law promoting the subject. Drives, thus, are constantly undergoing a dynamic reshuffling.

Castration can lead to sublimation, but also to perversion, i.e., a symbolization that does not correspond to the law as it exists for everybody. A castration that brings about a desire to seek satisfaction in suffering, and not in pleasure, is perverse. Castration can also be understood as the prohibition of any desire whose goal is pleasure. Thus, the prohibition of the mother can be understood as the prohibition of all women, and lead to homosexuality. The positive, or negative, outcome of castration depends on the parents (or on those who raise the child) who "grant" castration and who must represent lived examples of it.

Through the operation of castration, the shortcut to pleasure becomes a longer path of communication from one psyche to another. Pleasure, which is given, becomes a dual creative act, a conjunction, via bodies, of the psyches of the mother and her newborn baby. This is not the disappearance of the maternal object, but, rather, the modification of the maternal presence. The mother, showing compassion, consoles the child and brings it to the attention of others. If the mother should disappear for good, castration is no longer the validation (valorization) of desire, or the bearer of something living and known. In time, we observe the exhaustion of desire and the end of its dynamism. This is what Dolto calls the mutilation of the unconscious image of the body. It becomes impossible to symbolize a link that has disappeared. The drives return to the child's body, which has become anonymous in terms of its desire. This is what happens in cases of autism or in cases of anaclitic depression.

There is a right time for each type of castration, a time when drives have brought the body schema to a stage of development in which body-to-body contact is no longer absolutely necessary.

The child accepts castration if it comes from an adult whom it loves, from an adult who bears a chaste love. The child feels valued and can hope that it will not always be little. It senses the danger of returning to the pre-castratory period as the danger of losing what it has gained. Many adults are incapable of granting "symboligenous" castration because they themselves regret not being children any more, or regret that their own child is growing up.

1. *Umbilical castration.* For Dolto, this castration takes place at birth with the cutting of the umbilical cord. The umbilical cord

and the loss of the placenta prefigure all the later castration trials. At birth, the child utters the first primal sound (the first audible version of its voice), hears the louder voices in its entourage, and no longer hears the sound of its own heartbeat. It begins to smell things and feel its body mass. The most striking auditory experience is the sound of its first name and the proclamation of its sex, coloured by the joy or reticence that this may have on the child's parents. Language, thus, symbolizes the castration of birth. Umbilical castration brings with it two symbolic sources of vitality: the organic impact of birth on the equilibrium of the mother's psychosomatic health, and the emotional impact that the birth of a healthy, or unhealthy, child brings to each parent in terms of increased, or decreased, narcissism. Here we have—and we will see this throughout the process—what can be called a "double-edged" castration: an umbilical castration of the child and an imaginary castration of the parents, evidenced by the signing of the birth certificate. This allows the baby to give up the illusion of vampirism, which characterizes foetal behaviour.

2. *Oral castration*. Oral castration prohibits the child from cannibalizing the mother. Oral castration occurs when the baby is weaned and prevented from eating anything unhealthy, or poisonous. It terminates—if all goes well—in the desire and ability to speak, i.e., with the discovery of new means of communication. Weaning also includes the oral castration of the mother. She must now communicate with the child through other means than feeding it, removing its excrements, and covering it with kisses and hugs. At this point, the mother begins allowing other people to feed the child. The mother's castration is demonstrated by the fact that she takes more pleasure in speaking to her child, in guiding the child's phonemes and its motricity (for example, in games involving taking back and throwing objects). The child notices the mother's pleasure and can symbolize oral and anal drives in language. It can identify with its mother in its relation to others and its surroundings. For the child, oral castration is a separation from milk, a part of itself. The child discovers a new type of sustenance, both solid and varied, and abandons the illusion of cannibalism. If weaning is gradual, the child often develops a

routine when it is alone and starts "talking" to itself, just as it heard the mother talk with it and with others. The memory of its mother is in words and her language becomes a symbol of the body-to-body relationship. Sensorial perceptions are "mamafied" by the voice of the mother. The assimilation of a mother tongue begins only after weaning. Between six and eight months, we witness the burgeoning of the symbolic fruits of oral castration. The child starts mimicking language and will continue to do so until the age of eighteen months. Next appear the first two-syllable words that, for Dolto, represent the "me-my mama".

3. *Anal castration*. For Dolto, anal castration goes far beyond the mere acquisition of cleanliness. It involves the separation of the child, who has become able to co-ordinate its movements, from the mother, in terms of "doing". It is the period of "me all alone, me, not you".

   The child is prohibited from doing anything harmful, of "doing" to another what it would not want the other to do to it. It is forbidden to hurt its own body, or harm the inanimate and animate world that surrounds the father–mother–child triangle. The prohibition of murder and vandalism forces the child to control its harmful motor functions. If the parents have not been castrated anally from the child, they convey in words the exact opposite of the example they give. They do not grant castration to the child, but rather raise an animal. Any human being, regardless of age, is capable of giving castration to a younger person through examples and words.

   Anal castration is granted gradually; it guides the child to the mastery of its motor functions, and does not just involve toilet training. It is the symbolization of useful, and playful, motricity. If "symboligenous" anal castration does not take place, the child returns to the initial, private communication with the inner mother and plays at retaining or displaying its faeces. Eventually, the child becomes bored. The mother remains an imaginary inner mother instead of being represented unconsciously by all the outer objects that she has named and thus "mamafied".

   Anal castration must be given by those who encourage the child's identification with its sex, but who also forbid actions incompatible with the laws of the group. However, if the child does something reckless but manages not to hurt itself or others, it should be congratulated and not made to feel guilty. Castration must thus be "given" in terms of words and support in favour of the child's narcissism. The child thereby discovers that prohibitions provide security. When we say, "Well done", the child believes that the adult is magically responsible for what happened to it. The parents should not be anxious for the child, or be made anxious by the child. They should know how to say no to the child's desire and at the same time be respectful of the child and its possessions.

Anal castration finds its source in the voluntary sphincter function, but goes beyond the simple acquisition of cleanliness. If this acquisition takes place at too early an age, it can be mutilating and not "symboligenous". An adult who seeks to control the child's needs will have a perverse effect on the child. The idea of a "poo gift" is peculiar to a certain type of upbringing. For Dolto, sadism is not anal, but oral. It is the adult's controlling behaviour that initiates the child to sadism. Oral and anal drives can be disciplined in a way that avoids "the bases of sadism".

Anal castration should be centred around the pleasure of doing and handling. It is the passageway to the sublimation of excremental practices, thus transforming them into industrious and creative activity.

The child needs the guidance of explanatory words as it makes new discoveries outside the comforting presence of the mother. In the face of failure, the child needs reassurance. The child must be made to understand that what is forbidden today can be done later. Gradually, by identifying with the admired adult, the child can begin to "mother" itself. Anal castration takes place over several months, or even over one or two years.

4. *The mirror*. Among all these castrations, the "mirror stage" holds a special place. More than a stage, the mirror is, for Dolto, a linchpin between anal and primary castration. It is the moment when the subject takes charge of his, or her, narcissism. Françoise Dolto speaks of it as being, above all, an experience.

Of course, the relational and symbolic aspect of the mirror stage is essential. "The subject needs a mirror of its being in the other, not just a mere flat mirror." The scopic image takes on meaning as a lived experience only with the presence of an adult next to the child—an adult with whom the child's unconscious image of the body and body schema can be recognized, while at the same time the child recognizes itself in the person in the mirror. Dolto writes of a little girl who became schizophrenic at the age of two and a half years, although up until then she had been perfectly normal. Her American parents, who were visiting Paris, left her all day with a young English woman whom the child did not know and who spoke English with an accent she did not recognize. The child spent her days in a hotel room where the walls and all the furniture were covered by mirrors. In such solitude, the girl had—as Dolto put it—"lost herself in the mirror", her body fractured into little pieces and scattered into multiple reflections.

For Dolto, unlike for Winnicott, the mirror does not include the mirror of the child in the mother's eyes. This is because the child is already individualized before the mirror stage, albeit more in terms of the rhythms of the maternal *habitus* than as a body. In the beginning, the child is the mother, and the mother the child. The first castrations will result in gradual separations and bring about a degree of individualization. However, the child must be reassured that its body cannot be divided up. This reassurance is given through the testimony of its mirror image. At the time of the mirror stage, the scopic image must superimpose itself on the experience of the merging of the body schema with the unconscious image of the body, thereby successfully repressing the unconscious image of the body. The moment when the mirror image is stronger than the body as felt is thus structurally necessary.

The child discovers itself in the form of a baby, just like the other babies it sees around it. If the mirror experience reassures the child that it cannot be cut into pieces, the child will observe itself also as if it were another, and "see itself" for the first time.

For Lacan the mirror stage is marked by the child's jubilation in front of its image. For Dolto, the same moment comes as a shock and leaves an "incurable wound": the child becomes aware that its unconscious image of the body does not correspond to what other people see. Thus, a "symbolic gap" will be formed. While Dolto acknowledged the determining and structural function of the mirror stage, she shows a degree of nostalgia for the authenticity of early childhood, since the mirror can be a trap.

In front of the mirror, the child learns to make faces, to change its expressions and enter into the realm of "make believe" and seeming. Dolto considered that only those who are blind from birth, and unable to see themselves in the mirror, keep the touching sincerity that one observes in children before the mirror stage.

In the mirror, the child discovers for the first time a face and a body henceforth inseparable. It also perceives the size of its body in respect to that of adults and other children. It can no longer confuse itself with the other, or with the fantasized image it had of itself.

This is the moment of the construction of primary narcissism, which, much like an onionskin, surrounds primitive narcissism and grafts itself on to it. Before this, the child's narcissism was informed by, and took the shape of, the mother's unconscious, modelling itself on the way the mother looked at the child. After the mirror experience, the child will break free of this dyadic dependence and begin to take possession of its own body and be deceived by its own narcissism: "Seeming begins to take precedence over the feeling of being".

It is also after the mirror experience that the nudity of other children will begin to interest the child much more and introduce it to primary castration. The mirror is indeed a turning point and a kind of "gearing up" for the question of sexual difference, and, later, for the Oedipal complex.

5. *Primary castration*. Primary castration is the result of the discovery of sexual difference associated with a human face. The child recognizes itself as a boy, or a girl, both in its present state and its potential future state. If the child's difference has been addressed and validated (valorized), it can integrate its sexual specificity proudly. Once it has gone through the mirror stage, the child experiences a feeling of shame, which will incite it to modesty. Feelings of shame and pride are expressed by

the way the child holds its head, by the look in its eyes, its gracefulness or awkwardness—all of these things tell us whether the little subject has assumed its desires without loss of face.

Once the mirror experience has been assimilated, the graphic representations of people will change. The child will start drawing figures to which it will add decorative clothing, partial objects, which designate the person as a king or a queen, a princess, warrior, etc., so many people on whom the child can project itself.

For both sexes, the acceptance of primary castration results in an initial validation (valorization) of the penis. Afterwards, the little girl will be consoled by the fact that she can have babies. Dolto insists on the importance of telling children that fecundation involves both the father and the mother. Children must be told about parenthood (carnal, emotional, and legal) and affiliation. Knowledge of sexual intercourse will allow the child to understand the vocabulary of parenthood. Dolto emphasizes the vital importance of formulating in words everything surrounding origins. Who is the child's father (if it never knew him)? What were the conditions of the child's birth? Only speech can humanize what the child has experienced and what it has survived, however painful the experience might have been. This observation may seem obvious to us today, but it was not obvious at all at the time when Dolto brought it to the fore.

6. *Oedipal castration*. Oedipal castration corresponds to the traditional Freudian castration complex, which is why we give only a brief description of the Oedipal castration. It is the prohibition of incestuous intercourse for the child. Until the Oedipal complex, the child is driven by its incestuous desire. With Oedipal castration, the child must identify itself with the "submission of the parent to the Law", and no longer simply with the mother or the father.

   Oedipal castration is the culminating moment of the repression of the unconscious image of the body and allows the subject to build a secondary narcissism—the third layer of the onionskin—which initiates the subject's interest in himself, or herself. The subject thus gains human dignity towards

> becoming a man, or a woman. In social life, for which Oedipal castration is the catalyst, sexual drives cannot exist without a humanizing law. The child learns to control desires and to make the difference between thinking and acting, and acting in its own name. Libidinal energies are liberated for life outside the family with the child's coevals, and for social life at school.

The concept of the unconscious image of the body allows for the organization of a veritable metapsychology for the construction of a human subject. Dolto's theory, while resolutely Freudian, allows us to deepen traditional theory.

Françoise Dolto does indeed use the idea of developmental stages, of which she said, in a discussion with Lacan, "she could not do without" (Lacan, 1973). However, Dolto always connects these stages with the language of the relationship between the child and the parents. The development is not, for Dolto, a linear development (as Abraham posits) but a series of moments, which interact and influence one another dialectically, much like musical variations. The oral function shapes the anal phase; what was inscribed at the time of umbilical castration informs the mirror stage. Primary castration determines the pride that the child may, or may not, feel about being itself, etc. None of these stages has a purely intrapsychic, autonomous logic, as Melanie Klein claims, but rather are always rooted intersubjectively in the unconscious of the parents and the way in which they interact, consciously or unconsciously, with the child. The child is included from the very outset in the unconscious of the parents, but removes itself gradually through the various castrations up until the Oedipal castration which, if successful, will allow it to "conquer human status", psychically autonomous and separate.

Thus are shaped the style and specificity of a human subject, always dynamically moving "towards–becoming in the endowment of his/her sex". The study of the pathologies of the unconscious image of the body, which always stem from the child's early relationship with its mother or parents, provides us with a rich and fruitful clinic for both the child and the adult. This clinic, which she transmitted to her many students, is Françoise Dolto's true legacy.

Note

1. Translation by John Monahan.

References

Dolto, F. (1956). A la recherche du dynamisme des images du corps et de leur investissement symbolique dans les stades primitifs du développement infantile. *Psychanalyse, 3*: 297–303, 1957.

Dolto, F. (1957). Cas cliniques de régression. *L'Evolution Psychiatrique, III*: 431–435.

Dolto, F. (1961). Personnologie et image du corps. *La Psychanalyse, 6*: 59–92.

Dolto, F. (1967). Débat à l'Ecole Freudienne de Paris en collaboration avec Irène Roublef et avec la participation de Maud Mannoni sur la notion d'image inconsciente du corps. *Les Lettres de l'Ecole Freudienne de Paris,* avril–mai: 55–98, 1967.

Freud, S. (1905d). *Three Essays on the Theory of Sexuality. S.E., 7*: 125–245. London: Hogarth.

Guillerault, G. (1997). *Françoise Dolto, le sentiment de soi. Aux sources de l'image du corps.* Paris: Gallimard.

Lacan, J. (1973). *Les quatre concepts fondamentaux de la psychanalyse. Le séminaire Livre XI.* Paris: Le Seuil.

Winnicott, D. W. (1971). *Therapeutic Consultations in Child Psychiatry.* London: Hogarth.

CHAPTER SIX

Gendering the libido: Françoise Dolto and female sexuality

Françoise Hivernel

For Françoise Dolto, it is education and not hormones that determines the genital and libidinal orientation of the subject. This is achieved through the interaction between the parents' desires for the child and through language, which leads to the symbolic determination of the infantile psychic structure. ". . . 'the' woman or 'the' girl in itself, doesn't exist, what there is, is libido in the feminine mode" (Dolto, 1996, p. 55).

Introduction

Before going any further, it is worth looking at the genesis of Dolto's book, *Sexualité féminine. La libido génitale et son destin feminin,* and the political context within psychoanalysis in which it developed. This I will summarize from the excellent preface to the 1996 edition, published after Dolto's death, and collated, annotated, and presented by M. Djeribi-Valentin and E. Kouki, which retraces the genesis of her text over twenty-five years. Neither this book nor any of its earlier versions has been translated into English.

Françoise Dolto was invited by Jacques Lacan to give a paper on the development of female libido, in its normal and pathological forms at the International Psychoanalytic Congress in Amsterdam (5–6 September 1960). This congress was organized by the Société Française de Psychanalyse (SFP) and Nederlands Psychoanalytisch Genootschap (NPG), both groups being dissidents from the International Psychoanalytical Association (IPA). For more details about the history of the differences and feuds between these organizations see Roudinesco (1986).

Dolto was foremost a child psychoanalyst and the task that Lacan gave her, to write on female libidinal development (from the early infant stages through to the menopause and old age), must have seemed quite daunting. She was also aware that the subject of female sexuality had split the Freudian analytic world between the Vienna and the London schools. Apparently Dolto hesitated, as she was not sure that she was ready to tackle such an enormous subject, but was eventually persuaded to do so. It was to be the first major written work since her 1939 thesis, *Psychanalyse et Pédiatrie*. She had hoped to write this paper with Marianne Lagache (a psychoanalyst) but eventually wrote her 118-page paper alone. Inauspiciously, the paper was lost in the post and another copy barely reached the Congress in time to be copied and pre-circulated.

Although the congress subject was female sexuality, Dolto was the only female asked to give a paper; all the other contributors were male. In addition, it appears that the congress had another agenda, the resolution of a difference in opinion about some current psychoanalytic trends summarized below. According to Granoff's interview on 29 March 1995:

> Matters in psychoanalysis were moving towards a total enveloping of the feminine in what was seen as maternal essence, through a theoretically extravagant promotion of the mother–baby couple so as to dominate the main coordinates of psychoanalysis. [Dolto, 1996, p. 11]

Responsibility for this controversy was attributed in some circles to Dolto and her extensive clinical work based on the observation of babies, children, and adolescents, which was yielding material which could not easily be accommodated within existing theories or which was difficult to incorporate into the more theoretical approach taken by other psychoanalysts, including Lacan. Her paper apparently made few waves among her male psychoanalyst colleagues, although Lacan is quoted (*ibid.*, p. 46) as having told her that she was *culottée*, in other words, that she had plenty of cheek, but refused to explain why he felt that way. *Culotte* means trousers in French and *culottée* (a feminine word), by extension, and applied to a woman, means to wear the trousers, to overstep the mark, to act as a surrogate male or as a phallic female. Several possible interpretations were put forward including that his interjection was in response to her proposition that: "some apparently happily married heterosexual women were in fact homosexual and that the husband was used as a maternal substitute" (*ibid.*, p. 26) The theme of homosexuality in women will be expanded in Chapter Seven.

The text of her conference paper was eventually published, with other contributions from the Amsterdam Congress, but in a much abridged version, in 1964, in Volume 7 of *La Psychanalyse*. Dolto agonized as to whether or not to publish the full version of her work, and it was Jean Rostand (a famous French biologist) who encouraged her to do so. She eventually reworked her paper between 1969 and 1970 in conversations with Pré-Laverrière, a French psychoanalyst, and it was later published in 1982, although not to her entire satisfaction.

Volume II of Dolto's *Correspondence* (2005), edited by Djeribi-Valentin, reveals that her original 1960 text was very much in demand, not from psychoanalysts, but from GPs, paediatricians, surgeons, and the clergy. These people were grateful to her for having produced a work which gave a thorough clinical description of how the female sexual body worked, how, from a baby, the little girl becomes what she is, how she develops her sensitivity to the other sex, and how her own sexuality develops. Vergote, a Belgian psychoanalyst with a background in philosophy and theology, wrote in one of his letters that:

> . . . your text offers an acceptation without prejudice of Freudian discoveries, as well as a constructive ethical attitude. You go beyond the biologism of some of the IPA, the nihilism of some Lacanians and the smug moralism of the Americans . . . [Dolto, 2005, p. 348]

Henri Van Camp, a theologian and professor of philosophy, wrote to her about her work on female sexuality (and her thesis): "You speak as the best interpreters do: philosophic technique receives its due to the same extent as the ontological evidence its own right" (2005, p. 368).

One cannot help wondering what it was that the more traditionally inclined psychoanalysts thought they knew about female sexuality that the "clinicians" obviously did not and were grateful for . . . She was apparently accused by some of drawing theories from her own observations of children rather than using Freud's. One can understand why Dolto chose to challenge such dogma and prejudice.

Her theoretical stance is very clear:

> The difficulty of a psychoanalyst's testimony is due to her own projections, resistances etc. and thus theorisation, which is a means of communication after observation, should be banned during observation, and this is one of the most difficult resistances to vanquish, because theory protects the analyst from the risks of a participative observation. [Dolto, 1996, p. 88]

She also warned that:

> There is a risk of endogenous induction of maternal components (from the female analyst to the female patient), which can induce an intertransferential regression, which will hamper the endogenous work. [*ibid.*, p. 89]

The clinical material used as examples in *Sexualité féminine* comes from her work with babies, children, and adolescents whom she saw during her consultations at l'Hôpital Trousseau in Paris or whom she had in analysis, as well as with their parents and sometimes grandparents—an early systemic approach. Françoise Dolto deemed that work done with children without the parent's participation/agreement was not conducive to change, as she saw the child's problems as a symptom of the parents' illness. This work formed the core of her 1939 thesis, *Psychanalyse et pédiatrie* published in 1940, by Amédée Legrand in Paris It is interesting to reflect that an article by Winnicott on the same topic and with an almost identical title—"Paediatrics and psychiatry"—was published in 1948, nearly ten years later, while his work entitled *Through Paediatrics to Psychoanalysis* was published in 1958, twenty years after Dolto's thesis. It would be fascinating to compare the parallel growth of Dolto's and Winnicott's ideas. However, that would perhaps be better left until such time as her work has been translated into English.

Some necessary definitions of key concepts as used by Françoise Dolto

A comment, already made on many occasions, regarding the translation of the French word *pulsion* into "drive" or "instinct", needs to be restated here. I chose to use "drive", but am aware that no more than "instinct" does it do justice to the dynamic tidal flux that is inherent to the word *pulsion*. A *pulsion* is never regular and gives a better image of the pulsating forces of life and death at work in the individual than either "drive" or "instinct" can.

The phallus, as signifier of desire

Dolto uses Lacan's theory of the symbolic order (1977) and acknowledges the importance of the phallus (as concerned with mastery and to be differentiated from the male penis). But the phallus in Françoise Dolto's writing seems to take the symbolic meaning of the power to stand upright (as seen through a child's eyes) and she speaks of the whole standing body, be it male or female, as a total phallic object. She illustrates this point with children's drawings, in which adults are drawn like phalluses with little feet. The partial phallic object is the object of partial satisfaction for the baby: nipples for the mouth; breast for the hands; faeces for the anus. This would seem to imply that it is the mother who introduces the baby to the notion of the phallus, but, for Françoise Dolto, the mother also represents, in parts, the father for the baby. All partial erogenous forms are referred to the phallus.

The first formal functional image of the phallus would then be the nipple, producing milk, and the first sensory–motor and imaginary perception would be the tongue in contact with the mucous membrane and the breast. The first mode of live relations (the sucking of the milk at mother's breast) is punctuated by rhythmic sensations as much for the satisfaction of a need as for pleasure.

Castrations

For Dolto, a series of chronological castrations is necessary to enable the infant to pass from one developmental phase to another. For example: the change from the parental bed to one's own bed, and the ability to separate and think. Each castration brings a sense of loss, which needs to be negotiated, but also a sense of achievement and greater independence. In this she differs from Freud, as for her a castration is not a castration of the unconscious pleasure principle, but that of conscious pleasure, administered by the parents, in order for the child to eventually reach her desire (see also Chapter Five). Dolto uses two terms: centripetal and centrifugal penis option (phases), which need to be clarified. The desire for a centrifugal penis (the seeking of a penis which she has not got) is associated with a narcissistic blow and with primary castration anxiety. The desire for a centripetal penis (a desire for the penis, once she has accepted that she has not got one) is associated with the valorization of her hollow sex and linked with procreation (Dolto, 1996, pp. 28–29).

Libido

Dolto stresses strongly that, although sexuality is a part of the libido, it is much more than just that. For her, the libido is a symbolic concept, which has a masculine or feminine incarnation. This is in opposition to Freud's views, which emphasized the sexual character of the libido and its masculine nature. For Dolto the libido starts to function right from the beginning of human life *in utero*. It is made up of the life drive, of the death drive that opposes the life drive's desires, and of the unifying tendency that the sexual drive carries through the release of tension (*ibid.*, p. 438). The libido is never inactive. She also sees the libido as the source of religious feelings, ethics, beauty, and joy. She points out that it seems to exist independently from the satisfaction of all needs (*ibid.*, p. 463).

Dolto believes that sexuality is never entirely genital, even in the adult, and that genital sexuality still includes pre-genital drives, oral (which symbolically means the perceiving); anal (which symbolically means the doing), as well as all the senses (sight, smell, taste, touch, hearing).

Françoise Dolto's view is Darwinian in that she says that it is the reproduction of the species which is at play when this initially genderless force becomes polarized between a female destiny, inclined towards taking in, and a male destiny, inclined towards emitting.

Sexualité féminine is an extremely dense work given the breadth of the subject, which is treated from early infant stages through to the menopause and old age, and I have had to make a selection between some of the themes developed in the book, as it would have been counter-productive to try to tackle them all.

Becoming erogenous

Dolto says that conception can be regarded as the first time that the child participates in the symbolic meaning of the parental libidinal couple, and daringly proposes that the narcissistic investment of the child's sexuality can be seen as an inheritance or a reflection of the surplus energy and emotions of the parents. In other words, the archaic pre-person (in the womb) is the "It" born from the primal scene and represents the total of libidinal energy with which that child will have to survive the numerous challenges of life (Dolto, 1996 p. 492).

The archaic

This is one of Dolto's main contributions; it is a phase covering the intra-uterine life of the foetus. It is marked by the absorption by the foetus of the mother's feelings and sensations, whether happy, sad, or indifferent, as well as by the impact on the foetus of traumatic events, which may have overwhelmed the mother. In other words, the foetus's own potential narcissism and life and death drive are being heavily inscribed by those of the mother. She stresses that it is impossible to know directly what the foetus feels *in utero*; it is only *a posteriori*, through the analysis of the mother or child, that it may be possible to reconstruct what happened *in utero*.

Her observations of early traumatized children, and of those who from birth onward present relational problems, confirm the existence of an archaic form of libido of a cannibalistic style (before oral and anal stages have developed, which are, for her, already very elaborate stages), which could account for a foetus which is not developing as it should and the possibility that: "The biological translations seem to be the symbolic effect of the emotional relation of the mother to her surroundings and to her child" (*ibid.*, p. 468).

It is worth linking this with some research done on schizophrenia (Khashan et al., 2008), in which it appears, statistically, that women who suffer severe stress early in pregnancy (during the first trimester) might be more likely to have children that go on to develop schizophrenia. It looks as if gestation is as much an affective incarnation as an organic one, and she illustrates this point through the case of a little Algerian boy who survived attempts at being aborted after the mother was rejected by her lover and who presented as a very backward psychotic child when he came to therapy. With the help of the mother, Françoise Dolto gave him back his history and his sanity. Several other examples are given.

Birth

Dolto sees birth as baby's first fight and its first castration in the sense that she has to exchange a total dependence and symbiosis with mother for an external world in which she has to breathe independently and start to individuate. The baby recognizes the mother by her smell straight after birth and, if left alone on the mother's stomach, the baby will slither towards the mother's breast and start sucking. There is a marked tropism of the baby to the mother. For a baby invigorated with love and voluptuous feelings, the mother is the first object felt as phallic. Where this is not the case (as when the mother is ill, or if the baby does not feel wanted), the baby will become anorexic, have digestive problems, and sometimes suffer from toxicosis.

Dolto gives the example of a baby who, having been left at home while her mother was taken to hospital, stopped feeding. However, when, on Dolto's advice, the mother's nightgown was wrapped around the bottle, the smell of mother allowed the baby to start feeding again.

Dolto proposes that the baby is "narcissized" or not, in her person and in her sex, through the unconscious attitudes of the father and mother:

> If the mother is "narcissised" by being female and happy to have a daughter then everything is in place for the child to invest her femininity and her sexuality in a positive way. When the child, through its psychological development and growth reaches the age to communicate emotions to an other, she will do this from the standpoint of what she has learnt from her surroundings to have value. This idea of what is valuable and what is not is delivered to the baby during her first year in an unconscious manner, unconscious as much for the parents as for herself. [*ibid.*, p. 212]

Dolto believes that, from the earliest stage of their conception, human beings are the products of language and, as such, infants understand much more than they are credited with. Their experience needs to be made sense of linguistically. She has been using this approach since her early 1939 work. She quotes Brazelton (1985), an American specialist of the newborn, as likewise saying that babies can understand what they are told and that they are born with this capacity. I cannot help wondering whether she was aware of Brazelton's earlier work (Brazelton, 1979; Brazelton, Scholl, & Robey, 1966; Brazelton, Young, & Bullowa, 1971), which was not available in French at the time.

For Dolto, the infant does not initially have a separate image of her body (see Chapter Five), or a notion of 'I', or of objects separate from that of her mother. Her budding narcissism is very much entwined with that of the mother, who supports and enables her structuring. One of the means by which this is conveyed is through a proto-language, an intimate mode of communication, between mother and child, which becomes the vector and the potentialities of her primary narcissism. Phonemes used by mother indicate a complicity of desire, which becomes the ever-extending field of the baby's language. Femininity is given through language, but not only verbal language; it comes also from what the child senses in her mother. Françoise Dolto also stresses the importance of giving the child a name straight away, which gives her a notion of who she is and that she was wanted, as well as explaining to her her consanguinity, her place in the extended family. She illustrates this with examples of observations of children between four months and eighteen months who were waiting to be adopted. She was able to settle them by giving them back the little history that was known about them (*ibid.*, p. 215).

This is a time (providing all goes well) that she describes as full of oral sensual pleasure. Sucking, chewing noises, gripping, and all these sensory–motor feelings are accompanied by erotic feelings, which can be localized or generalized all over the body, including the utero–vulval area, the nipples, and the anal area. But the little girl can only enjoy herself and learn about life fully as long as her mother is feeling well (physically and emotionally). For Dolto, this can only happen if mother is supported and valorized by father or by another usually supportive partner.

All pain at this age is felt like a breaking of the mother–child dyad, and leads to expulsive types of exchange, and she goes on to say that, for the baby, "The cry of the intestine is a sort of beginning of the death drive" (*ibid.*, p. 501).

Dolto speaks about a baby girl whose mother became anguished after her birth. The baby refused to suckle because she wanted to return to the *in utero* happiness and safety that she had felt within the mother. Dolto explained to the baby what was happening, and that if she did not suckle she would die, and the baby started suckling again (*ibid.*, p. 500).

The nursing mother is experienced by the baby as "multipalped" (sort of octopus-like, or like an Indian deity with fingers everywhere which touch the baby and give meaning to her body and a sense of continuity to her skin). She is protruding and spurting, full of warm liquid that is good to absorb, and produces in the baby a visual, auditory, and olfactory image, which Dolto will develop in her theory of *L'image inconsciente du corps* (1984) (see also Chapter Five in this book). There is, at this stage, a developing intuition of the "corporeal schema" of the other, even before the baby can see properly. She gives as an example a baby sticking out its tongue in imitation of the adult who is doing the same. Research done on children aged 4–8/9 months show *Gestalt* patterns present. A bald cranium worries them, if it puts a hat on, the baby smiles again. Babies do not like to see a face in profile; they prefer to be face to face.

A baby gets satisfactions even before her need for food has been satisfied, and her sensitivity to the mother's visage and odour is not a by-product of the satisfaction of her feeding needs. The little boy's pleasure is easily observed through his erectile penis, the little girl has got erectile nipples and it is possible that the same thing happens to the clitoris and vagina (orbicular vaginal turgidity and clitoral erectility), but this is not easily observed.

The passive oral and anal phase of the baby is influenced by the crossed desires of mother and daughter—it is good, it is bad, it is beautiful, it is dirty, etc. For example, a stool is described as good when mother takes it and congratulates her daughter for producing it, but labelled as dirty if the daughter plays with it. The child, therefore, discovers that she can produce a beautiful and good oral object and a well-made anal object, but also that it is not an object which is beautiful for everyone or good to eat, and that everyone may not desire it. If the object is associated with knowing that mother likes it and if the child feels loved, she can then feel love for herself and love the person who loves her (Dolto, 1996, p. 229). If mother reacts in a rejecting way, she is experienced as an orally devouring mother (a mother who shouts and sabotages the natural pride of the child and humiliates her). Dolto cites many other types of de-narcissizing mothers: the mother who is dentally castrating, the rejecting mother, the expulsing mother, and so on.

As soon as the hands become functional, a sadistic active oral (dental) and anal phase takes over from the previous phase. The "doing" with the mouth or the anus is now transferred to the hands. This is the phase of contradictions in which moral masochism may emerge. The child will forego her desire in order to please mother so as to remain in harmony with her parents.

Dolto also points out that the mode of propulsion of this phase is on all fours. Succeeding the bottom-shuffling phase, itself following a sort of snake-like wriggling, this, she suggests, leaves traces in a number of erogenous games in the adult associated with coitus, which display remnants of the archaic. Pleasure makes a little girl wriggle, and Dolto adapts Spitz's concept of "rooting" (1968). Spitz thought that this was a pattern of "saying no", but Dolto understands it as a pattern, in fact, of penetration, as a corkscrew, a helicoidal entrance. It is an erotization of the female sexual area.

Emergence of erogenous zones

Françoise Dolto gives the following description of the development of the erogenous areas: each area touched by mother in a loving way potentially becomes an area sensitive to pleasure. So the areas which receive the most attention from mother, such as the "nutritional" and the "toileting areas", will become the focus for sensations because of that sustained attention. In this she expands on Freud's theories (1905d).

However, for an area to become a true erogenous zone, it is necessary for it to feel a "lack", an absence of fulfilment, a theme developed by Lacan. Desire cannot emerge, or be felt, where there is permanent satisfaction. In other words, there is a need for a hiatus between mother and child for the erogenous zone to emerge. So, the place where the feeling of an unsatisfied desire begins is the erogenous zone and the place from which the satisfaction of the desires comes is the complementary erogenous zone.

In the game named *Fort Da* by Freud, the child learns in real life that the object of her desire will come back. She also learns to bear its absence. However, if the separation from mother is too long, the child eats herself up or rejects herself orally. Dolto notes that encopresy can be a way for the child to get mother to return, a regression to a time when mother was interested in her stools and toileting.

For Françoise Dolto, the notion of impossible desire comes during the oral stage with weaning from the breast. It contributes to the symbolization of language, in that the link to the other can continue and bring oral satisfactions through a longer circuit between child and adult, the circuit of spoken language. She observes that little girls can use their tongues in a way that boys cannot (well hung tongue—La langue bien pendue—*vs.* atrophied penis). She sees the role of the tongue in the mouth's hollow as the mediating organ of the sublimated symbolic oral power and of the sexual options derived from active and passive drives of the oral, clitoral, and vulvo–vaginal libido (Dolto, 1996, p. 128). However, things can go wrong, and, in the following example, Dolto introduces the notion of the "mouth of the hand".

> Some children who have problems with pronunciation leave one or two fingers of the hand sticking out, the thumb is not allowed to join the other fingers. It is as if, for them, the mouth of the hand is not complete and they can't enclose the column of air so as to be able to pronounce phonemes. It is as if they had a bit of nipple still

> attached to the mouth that prevents them from using the palate, labial muscles and the jaws correctly. This could possibly be due to a lack of freedom to explore imposed by the mother on the baby at an age of around four months. [*ibid.*, p. 511]

The mother is experienced as an additive or subtractive mother, or again as an ambivalent mother, depending on the ease and pleasure with which she tends her child. Because the child cannot explain it and just feels it, the mother's power, is experienced as "magic". If, for example, the mother attempts to force-feed her, it will provoke fantasies of "rape", for the lack of a better word (a breaking-in of the child's integrity) which will "de-narcissize" her.

The emergence of the erogenous zones is generally finished by the thirtieth month.

Gendering the libido

Dolto observed that, after having had her feed, the baby girl is attracted by the males around her. This attraction must be of an olfactory or auditory nature, as the baby cannot yet see well. The same happens for a boy, but in the reverse. If a man arrives in the environment of mother–baby, the baby boy turns away from the male and burrows into the mother, avoiding the rival male smell; however, if a woman appears, the baby boy immediately turns towards her.

> The attraction of the baby girl towards men is so marked that, for it not to happen means that there is something even at that early stage in her relationship to the mother which works against her desire or that her mother is affectively closed to that man. [*ibid.*, p. 507]

This is even noticeable in girls who are deaf and blind. Dolto states that some authors (not quoted, but we can safely infer that she means Melanie Klein) have taken this to be an indication of the onset of the Oedipal phase at a much earlier time than thought by Freud. For Dolto, the notion of an Oedipal situation needs to be reserved for a time when the girl wants to be her father's sexual object, to have his child and to defeat her mother.

She discovers her body

Subsequent to her muscular and neurological development, the child straightens up, walks, and notices the presence or absence of the penis. What Dolto names as "primary castration" for the little girl is the discovery that she does not have a penis like the boys. With this discovery comes a narcissistic disappointment for the girl, but it is something which is thinkable because mother does not have one either. However, it is only thinkable if mother allows this to be spoken and therefore known.

While it is possible for the boy with his penis to act towards it like a mother with her baby, the girl is obliged to hallucinate her "valuable" object. Just as the boy manipulates his penis, the girl manipulates language. Dolto believes that the formation of the ego is closely linked with language, and that the girl creates her own ego by saying "No" to an ego which is still enmeshed with her mother's ego. "The difference between boys and girls at that age is that the girl can say 'No' to the mother without reference to the father, but the boy says 'No' to the mother in order to feel more male (*ibid.*, p. 522).

According to Dolto, the father's and mother's physique also plays an important role in the representation of "force", and on the model offered to become like dad or mum. The little girl discovers the importance of the breast and thinks that a penis is a man's breast! Interesting fantasies develop and Françoise Dolto quotes a dialogue between two little girls that she overheard in a public garden:

> And then if the mother dies when there is a baby, it is the father who will suckle the baby . . . not with a bottle but with his "thing" which also produces milk. I have seen it and he has also told me. [*ibid.*, p. 126]

At this stage, the little girl enjoys the fact that women are attracted to father and males to mother (it is not yet the Oedipal phase and she is not in competition). In games with boys (3–6 years old), she is looking for a "centrifugal penis" similar to that of the boys and discovers its absence, but in so doing she also discovers what Dolto terms "the contagious emotions of pleasure" (*ibid.*, p. 124). For a while she hopes that the voluptuous feelings she gets from pulling/tugging at the clitoris means that it is a growing penis. In this way little girls discover their pleasure, through clitoral masturbation. The little girl expresses the discovery of her sex in a hysterical way over her whole body, undulations, simpering, and torsions, and in games by taking great pleasure in buttons and folds. It is through little details that she will attract the boys, because her sex is not clearly visible. In that way a boy "signifies" the sensation she has in her, which had previously no external signifier.

Dolto's observations led her to say that it is the little boy who may be more traumatized than the girl by her lack of a penis. The boy fears that if he identifies with the girl out of love, he will undergo an imaginary mutilation. Contrary to what Freud thought, providing that their mother has responded truthfully to their questions, and has valorized implicitly or explicitly their sex, little girls very quickly overcome their disappointment. Then the little girl can think that she will become a mother, and her mother will be her daughter and her father will be her husband.

> If she is certain that she has been desired as a girl by her father, in the image of the mother without penis, then she will very quickly accept her sexual characteristic of a button with a hole as a paternal gratification and maternal promotion. [*ibid.*, p. 123]

The ability to form object relations comes after the acquisition of walking, which allows the child to separate from her mother. At this age, objects allow the child a real transfer from her body to the world outside. A child learning how to walk generally carries an object, symbol of its newly acquired power (called a fetish by Dolto), and this makes her feel that she exists. When the child stands up she is identified with the mother, and this induces a change of position in which she becomes the adult towards the object she is carrying and the object becomes her (*ibid.*, p. 520) This is a particular example of a transitional object quite different from Winnicott's (1958) description. Dolto sees the fetish/transitional object as a medium on which the child projects its newly acquired power/skills, whereas Winnicott sees the transitional object as emanating from the parents and representing the parents and used as a comforter by the child.

Dolls as signifiers of erogenous areas and their different use by boys and girls

Dolls take the place of an oral or anal object in all sorts of interrelational games and emotions, phallic and narcissistic, which are transferred on to them. Girls play highly erogenous games with dolls, with the doll being used as a masturbatory object. If the little girl is identified with mother during that game, she feels that mother has a similar pleasure, oral, anal, and clitoro–vulval (*jouissance*) towards her. This is not sublimation after repression, but a fetishist erotic libidinal satisfaction (*ibid.*, p. 133).

Talk about excrement occurs more often in boys than girls, where the doll is the excrement substitute. Boys have aggressive games while girls have intimate games. "I don't love you any more, you are nasty!" is the first oral sublimation. The sadistic drives of little girls with dolls may indicate their need for a restriction/ boundary that they do not have in real life.

A doll is symbolic of father's penis and the girl is the mother of the dolls. Her father is their father. In her imaginary family, the girl will have girls who will belong to her and the boys will belong to dad. On the other hand, a boy mothers his toys, as his mother would do him, but from the position of the father. The boy imagines having a child (a son?) and more often than not he will see himself as both father and mother. The nature of games is different for boys and girls, with boys showing a preference for hiding keys and things which go into holes whereas girls put things in bags or boxes.

Entrance into the oedipal phase around the end of the third year

Dolto stresses time and time again that nothing which happens to a child is neutral. Everything has a meaning, either in terms of happiness or sadness, of increase or decrease in vitality. The little girl's starting point in the making of her persona and of gendering her libido is her mother. According to Françoise Dolto:

> All girls from 18 months up to 3 years, who have acquired the notion of a self, and outside the situation of the family threesome,

> have a notion of their hollow sex, with a hole so that the boys can put in it their sex in relief, the aim of which they see as a ludic pleasure, shared with the boys, but without any notion of procreation. [*ibid.*, p.140]

Little girls often say that their sex is hurting, which Françoise Dolto interprets as a pantomime of seduction in which they are really asking "who is going to come to where I feel a desire for penetration". Not the mother, because she does not have a penis, and because the daughter does not desire her. Because she has experienced the fact that desire has no location, despite being signified, illustrated, and represented by the specific body area where it manifests itself, she will try to master her body and all its conflicting emotions. But, because what is happening cannot be conceived in logical terms, she tries to explain it to herself in terms of magical happening. The imaginary presence of a selected person is so intensely sexually erogenous that it is as if something tangible is created by this imaginary act. This tangible product is linked with phallic body identification, with the passive/active behaviour of the mother (or her substitutes) and an introjection of her desires, which become the little girl's desires (*ibid.*, p. 135). The girl is creating a subjective image of herself, which is linked with the father identified with mother, or introjecting her, and this brings a release of tension (*ibid.*, p. 136). Dolto goes on to say that the structuring of the ego at the service of the genital libido will depend on the imaginary cultural behaviour allowed. It is those expressive or verbal gestures, authorized on a day-to-day basis explicitly or implicitly by the "real parents", which will give the right of existence, whether recognized, valorized or not, to everything about the genital area of the body, as well as the meaning of that meaning—desire (*ibid.*, p. 144).

The little girl plays verbally and in her fantasies everything she feels in her sex. She becomes a sort of mother to her own body as her mother was to her, and the permission given by her mother models her body care and ego ideal for her oral, anal, and genital libido. What the adult does not notice does not exist for the child, as no meaning is given to it. So she cannot express or valorize this thing or this subject. Aimless or aborted desires come back to the body as nothings, but, because they are dynamic forces, they act by provoking vegetative dysfunctions of the body. Nothing can exist without a signifier, e.g., a name. Dolto stresses how important it is that the signifier is not a derogatory word, and gives the example of a child who referred to his sex as his "sin", which was the name given to it by his mother (*ibid.*, p. 216).

What mother has not allowed is perceived as a castration for the girl's body, or an imminent rape, and the erotic becomes anxiety provoking instead of erogenous. The meeting of driving emotions with maternal emotional insecurity inhibits and "de-narcissizes" the girl. and this memory returns whenever the adult girl finds herself in that situation.

The female Oedipus complex. The anguish/fear of rape

According to Dolto, the falling of the milk teeth generally marks the onset of the Oedipus complex. During that phase, there is ambivalence towards the mother, and false accusations about her (which can start as early as the age of three). These are a projection of fantasies (the cruel mother) and the little girl tries to break up the parental couple.

Dolto observed that flirting provokes exciting sensations for the girl in the genital area, but the girl is not seeking penetration, but selective attention of the male and that at a safe distance. For example, the girl will accept sweets from a male who does not interest her but not from one who does (*ibid.*, p. 150).

The girl desires a child from father and father's penis. However, she will come to realize that father's penis is too big for her. Subsequently, she will fear all the penises she may have valorized and she will start fearing her desire. This will trigger dreams of rape and torture. The anxiety of rape by father in girls parallels the fear of castration in boys.

> If she imagines her father, his magic piercing potency is without limits, because she has over endowed him with the structuring option she has bestowed on him since her foetal life. He is the axis which gives her verticality, stimulates her feelings, moderates her nature and stabilises her drives in their polymorphous expressions, serving them as a representation of a symbolic phallus, desired but

> difficult to conquer, mainly because he is the castrating mother's exclusive possession. [*ibid.*, p. 159]

The little girl, in her ignorance of the erotic meaning of genital feelings, is afraid of being ill, and often attracts the inopportune attention of adults, which risks inducing psychosomatic illnesses. In fact, she is "lovesick". Dolto cites as an example the false appendicitis of a six-year-old. She also points out that "godmothering" or "godfathering" between siblings, instigated by the parents, is always harmful for the girl because of the inevitable emotional investment she will put in that child, and the unconscious substitution with the incestuous child she would have liked to have had with father. It could also be interesting to explore the impact this could have on the siblings' relationship (Mitchell, 2003). This is the age when neurosis with homosexual components (see Chapter Seven) begins to hamper the resolution of the Oedipus. This can block the little girl in a complex of virility, active or passive, which is to say, in a reactional attitude of obsessional type, which can evolve later into conversion hysteria. The little girl who is unable to distinguish between reality and the imaginary risks becoming a mythomaniac. This is often accompanied by false accusations of sexual abuse (*ibid.*, pp. 318–319).

Oedipal resolution and the primal scene

After six years old there is an avoidance of body-to-body games with adults. Games are felt as guilt provoking, and the Oedipal phase gets resolved around nine to ten years old.

For Dolto, the reliving of the primal scene—the scene in which the girl was conceived—should be lived imaginarily and verbally face to face with a parent in order to allow the child to effect a narcissistic reinvestment of her female body centred around the genital opening and her desire. This narcissistic reinvestment will happen through the renunciation of any further conjugal scene with the oedipal parent (or seduction of brothers) and the price will be her knowledge of herself in her pre-historic foetal genesis. It produces an emotional fusion between the narcissistic libido and the object libido. Dolto gives examples of how structuring this is for the psychic organization of a four- to nine-year-old. If (after her secondary teeth came in), the girl was never given an explanation as to why her desire cannot be satisfied, this incestuous desire may be rekindled and she may wait a very long time for the hoped-for manifestation of desire in her father, leading to a sterile genital repression.

> Not having received the oedipal castration, that is to say words from her father telling her about his non-desire and his non-love for a genito–genital meeting with her, the daughter may reach puberty and her desire for fecundity will reappear in that part of herself which is the death drive, which is the person without a story and without value . . . because the adult she "loved of love" and desired during the oedipal phase hasn't revealed to her the humanising aspects of her desire outside its incestuous enacting. [*ibid.*, p. 351]

Dolto thinks that it is necessary for the parents to give functional explanations to the girl about things such as penis erectility, and penetration of female sex by male sex, because of the possible traumatism that accidentally seeing parental intercourse or hearing about it from friends could cause to a six-year-old, at a time where her fear of rape acts as a stimulant to her genital sensual pleasure.

The absence of such explanations can lead to grave psychosocial accidents, such as marriage through narcissistic choice of a "perceived twin" or through transferential choice of fatherly love. Françoise Dolto feels that father's role during the Oedipal resolution can be positive if he valorizes women, but pathogenic if he goes against her genital superego (peeping tom type father, or jealous father).

Dolto writes movingly about tenderness, which she says can only truly exist between mother and daughter and father and daughter if the primal scene is assumed in a total sexual renunciation *vis à vis* the parents (*ibid.*, p. 163).

The resolution of the Oedipus complex is followed by a difficult phase in which the girl behaves hysterically at the least narcissistic wound. Eventually, the evolution of the libido will bring the resolution of the Oedipal conflict, with mourning for her dream of incestuous maternity being followed by the option of her own genitality in a mixed society.

Puberty

The onset of puberty, signified by physiological changes such as menstruation and the growing of the breasts, is accompanied by the arrival, according to Dolto, of the ego ideal and superego. This is a critical phase for the adolescent's narcissism—depending hugely on mother's response and pocket money, says Françoise Dolto! Mythical support of the ego ideal is found in identification with "stars", bands of youths are used as a medium for socializing their sexuality (rivalry, latent homosexuality, etc.), in order to attract the attention of boys, and is also used to confront their mothers more easily.

For Dolto, a girl's imaginary erotic life will not appear to her as normal nor as easy as it does for a boy, because her genital libido is concerned with the penis and her desire of a future intromission and her fantasies of rape. These fantasies of rape that have excited her femininity since she entered the phase of the Oedipal complex, are now confronted with the possible reality of rape by the young man she desires. She is believed to be neurotic, and Dolto says that in fact she just lacks information. Françoise Dolto makes an impassioned plea for media manipulation to be counterbalanced by an education to help girls to think for themselves. For a girl, to give her body in order to conform to peer pressure, without desire or love, or just out of the need to be something for someone, can lead to frigidity. The absence of ethical, aesthetical, or symbolic sense in the decision she makes leads to a narcissistic depreciation in the girl. However, Dolto also warns against the danger of an unconsummated relationship (chastity), which consumes the vital energies and is a form of masochism.

> Sometimes the oedipal renunciation can be perverse, and not only consist in the renunciation of the begetter, but also include, by the bias of the death drive, the voluptuous, narcissistic renunciation of all genital life. This is perceived as necessary for the acceptance of the girl by a certain group (seen as a maternal castrating entity). [*ibid.*, p. 175]

According to Dolto, these impersonal groups to which sexuality is sacrificed act to channel an infantile sadism which is the centre of projection of devouring and castrating drives of exalted adolescents and of young men whose fathers are not virile enough. It is also possible for the girl to retreat into romantic fantasies, which are easier than trying to seduce the man of her dreams, and to compensate for this with excessive masturbation.

Why is the non-resolution of the Oedipal conflict so widespread in women?

Françoise Dolto ponders (with examples) and places the origin of this problem around three to four years old, when desire for the "centrifugal penis" has been displaced on to a fetish doll, embarking on a relationship between a real and a fake person. Again, around six to seven years old, the game changes as the vulvo–vaginal region has been invested. The girl desires an imaginary live baby, coming from her father and, more rarely, from her mother, which can be transferred on to a brother or a sister who has just been born. These represent problematic areas for the resolution of the Oedipus complex in girls. Magical thinking and belief in the realization of their wishes (having got a real child from father) can make them feel incestuously guilty and can lead them to castrate themselves of their feminine genitality by repressing it, or trying to castrate their siblings. A woman who has not been frigid while not fecundated can become so after the birth of her half-incestuous child. The reality of the birth makes her realize that her partner is not the one she would have chosen outside of the Oedipal motivation (*ibid.*, p. 196).

Françoise Dolto ends her book with a series of reflections of a more or less philosophical and spiritual nature that address existential issues and the nature of relationships between men and women (see also Chapter Ten). She poignantly ponders on the impossibility of signifying oneself except through the other, and on our differences, and reflects on the mutations and progressive trials of the libido, accompanied by anguish. Narcissism makes us take our own selves as temporary objects in the absence of the other. But the death drive, tempting and consoling for the solitary subject, who exhausts himself with the desire to find the other, never leaves us in peace for long. For Dolto, the ultimate may be reached in:

> . . . the last phase of life, where at long last we have had our fill of the phallic illusion and we accept that our destiny is death. Then, perhaps, desire freed from all its conditioning . . . can turn the merely, a-sensorial a-spatial and a-temporal symbolic into a dynamic, without representation of desire, which may, for the sufferer, announce the longed for spiritual *jouissance*. [*ibid*., p. 306]

Conclusion

It would be nice, in conclusion, to be able to position Françoise Dolto on the Anglo-Saxon scene. She was, for France, what Winnicott was for the UK. However, her work has not yet been translated into English and is not known here. This is, of course, partly due to the exclusion from the IPA in 1953 of Lacan and Dolto and of their approach to psychoanalysis (Roudinesco, 1986, pp. 264–265). Gérard Guillerault (2007) attempted a comparison between Dolto and Winnicott, but his work has not yet been translated into English.

Another difficulty in undertaking such a comparison in the context of *Sexualité féminine* is that there is so little written by Winnicott about the subject. According to Bacon (2002), Winnicott, when writing on the infant, excludes most of the following from his writings: sexuality, gender identity, castration, Oedipus complex.

To evaluate what Françoise Dolto owes to the Anglo-Saxon literature is difficult, because she was not someone who tended to use references. I cannot help wondering whether this was part of a generous belief that once something has been published it becomes public domain, an integral part of everyone's culture. She freely did this with her own ideas through radio and television programmes, as well as during her consultations at l'Hôpital Trousseau in Paris over a very long period. However, according to Bacon (2002), Winnicott's texts show a similar lack of references; they hardly engage with anyone else. There is very little dialogue or argument. There is always the shadowy presence of Melanie Klein, but Winnicott rarely makes this overt and keeps it as a coded sub-text. The same feeling certainly applies to Dolto's present work as far as Klein is concerned, and she goes as far as to say that Klein taught us a lot on early object relations, but that there is a lack in her work of an ethical dimension, an ethics of the joy of life (Dolto, 1996, p. 462).

Françoise Dolto put herself firmly in the Freudian tradition, but keeps an open mind and is able to state very clearly her disagreements with Freud's theories, based on the viewpoint of her clinical work with children, as we have seen in the context of her work on female sexuality. She defines herself as "Pro-Lacan, but not a Lacanian" (Dolto, 2005, p. 655).

Throughout her work, she remains true to herself; there is no artifice in her writing, no attempt at a conscious seduction of the reader. She does not try to please or placate. This, of course, does not mean that she was not capable of using and elaborating theories, as her monumental work on *L'image inconsciente du corps* (1984) proves beyond any doubt (see Chapter Five). Françoise Dolto's style of writing is always engaged and passionate. It only becomes coldly clinical and factual while in descriptive mode. For example, in her illustration of the different types of female orgasms, her medical training comes to the fore and is reflected through the terminology used. However, she cannot remain for very long so detached and becomes lyrical and passionate in her elaborations. She is also a teacher; she wanted to be a "Doctor of Education" when she was young (Dolto, 2003), in order to teach parents to understand their children. This is abundantly obvious throughout the book, and can sometimes be slightly irritating. I believe that this didactic approach, which is so contrary to that taken in mainstream English psychoanalysis, comes from the pioneering work she did with children abandoned to institutionalized care, and her strong sense of social justice and militancy (see Chapters Eight and Nine). She also exudes in her writing an "appetite" for life, which is not often expressed in psychoanalytic literature.

The last words will have to be left to the editors of Françoise Dolto's book on *Sexualité féminine*:

> The text in its totality keeps a sharp profile. It doesn't cease to wrap itself around the same axis, always following the same direction from the start. It makes difficult reading because one has to abandon oneself to the vertigo produced by the apparent repetitions of a way of thinking which works in spirals *statu nascendi*. [Dolto, 1996, p. 38]

References

Bacon, R. (2002). Winnicott revisited. A point of view. *Free Associations, 9*(2)50: 250–270.

Brazelton, T. B. (1979). Behavioural competence of the newborn infant. *Seminars in Perinatology, 3*: 35–44.

Brazelton, T. B. (1985). *Trois bébés dans leur famille (Les différences du développement)*. Paris: Editions Stock.

Brazelton, T. B., Scholl, M. L., & Robey, J. S. (1966). Visual responses in the newborn. *Am. Acad. Pediatrics, 37*: 284–290.

Brazelton, T. B., Young, G. G., & Bullowa, M. (1971). Inception and resolution of early developmental pathology. *Journal of the American Academy of Child Psychiatry, 10*: 124–135.

Dolto, F. (1939). *Psychanalyse et Pédiatrie*. Private publication [reprinted Paris: Editions de la parole, 1961].

Dolto, F. (1964). La libido génitale et son destin féminin. Rapport pour le Congrès d'Amsterdam. *La Psychanalyse, 7*: 3–14.

Dolto, F. (1982). *Libido féminine*. Paris: Editions Carrère, 1987.

Dolto, F. (1984). *L'Image inconsciente du corps*. Paris: Le Seuil, Coll. "Points Essais", 1992.

Dolto, F. (1996). *Françoise Dolto. Séxualite féminine. La libido génitale et son destin feminin*. M. Djeribi-Valentin & E. Kouki (Eds.). Paris: Gallimard.

Dolto, F. (2003). Françoise Dolto. *Lettres de jeunesse. Correspondance 1913–1938*. C. Percheminier (Ed.). Paris: Gallimard.

Dolto, F. (2005). *Une vie de correspondances, 1938–1988*. M. Djeribi-Valentin (Ed.). Paris: Gallimard.

Freud, S. (1905d). *Three Essays on the Theory of Sexuality. S.E., 7*: 125–245. London: Hogarth.

Guillerault, G. (2007). *Dolto/Winnicott; Le bébé dans la psychanalyse*. Paris: Gallimard.

Khashan, A. S., Abel, K. M., McNamee, R., Perdersen, M. G., Webb, R. T., Baker, P. N., Kenny, L. C., & Mortensen, P. B. (2008). Higher risk of offspring's schizophrenia following antenatal maternal exposure to severe adverse life events. *Archives of General Psychiatry, 65*(2): 146–152.

Lacan, J. (1977). The signification of the phallus. In: *Ecrits*, A. Sheridan (Trans.) (pp. 281–291). London: Tavistock.

Mitchell, J. (2003). *Siblings*. Cambridge: Polity Press.

Roudinesco, E. (1986). *Histoire de la psychanalyse en France (1925–1985)*, 2. Paris: Fayard, 1994.

Spitz, R. A. (1968). *De la naissance à la parole, la première année de la vie.* Paris: PUF.

Winnicott, D. W. (1948). Paediatrics and psychiatry. *British Journal of Medical Psychology, XXI*(4): 229–240.

Winnicott, D. W. (1958). *Through Paediatrics to Psychoanalysis.* London: Hogarth.

CHAPTER SEVEN

Homosexuality in women

Françoise Hivernel

This chapter summarizes Françoise Dolto's theories on female homosexuality, and was "extracted" from her book *Sexualité féminine. La libido génitale et son destin féminin* (1996 edition), which is based on the paper she presented to the 1960 Amsterdam Congress. It needs to be read in conjunction with Chapter Six, on "Gendering the libido and female sexuality".

Introduction

When talking about female homosexuality, it would be very difficult not to consider Dolto's position (or absence of position) in the context of the French feminist movement. The French feminist movement originated as a result of the 1968 students' and workers' strikes. It was perhaps more of an intellectual debate than its sister movements in the rest of the world, and, in its early days, Simone De Beauvoir was its symbol. The Movement de Liberation de la Femme/Movement of Liberation of Woman (MLF) had different forms of feminism under its name, of which I will briefly name two branches. The first branch was more revolutionary, and concerned with bringing down the existing patriarchal order and with the sexual liberation of women. The second one turned towards psychoanalysis as a mean to interrogate gender construction and bring about political changes. I recently attended the Colloquium organized at the UNESCO in Paris (December 2008), in the context of "The international day of philosophy", to celebrate the centenary of Françoise Dolto's birth. During this Colloquium, papers were given about Dolto, but also extracts of her interventions (filmed by de Mezamat, 1994, 2008) on radio or television were shown, among which one particularly struck me because of its relevance to this chapter. In it, Dolto was very vociferous against the MLF, saying that its policies were leading to a mutilation of femininity and were conducive to hysteria and the emasculation of the male. She deemed the MLF to be an "annihilator of ovaries and testicles", in her highly truculent style. Françoise Dolto certainly thought and fought for her ideas that women had equal rights to men, in the certainty and pride of their sexual differences, and saw no reasons to join feminist movements. This could be one of the explanations as to why Dolto is not mentioned in feminist literature, despite her courageous stance on many issues, such as homosexuality, contraception, and abortion, but I suppose that she was too much of an individualist to feel at ease in groups. However, she is reported to have said about the 1960 Amsterdam Congress on female sexuality that "France wasn't yet ready to listen to a paper presented by a woman on women's sexuality . . ." (Dolto, 1996, p. 25).

In the first place, I would like to emphasize that Dolto is fundamentally a descriptive scientist and that the interpretation of her clinical observations are informed by a sound grounding in biology as well as psychoanalysis. She was a long-time friend of the famous French biologist Jean Rostand (1894–1977), who was also a philosopher, a deep humanist, a free thinker, and an atheist, very well known for popularizing biology to large audiences. He was especially known for his work on amphibian embryology, parthenogenesis, and teratogeny. It was he who encouraged Françoise Dolto to publish her book on *Sexualité féminine* in its totality (Dolto, 1996, p. 55) without editing out any parts of this book. Her ideas on homosexuality must have been thoroughly discussed between them.

From the biological standpoint, Dolto is convinced of a complementarity of the sexes, which is essential from a reproductive perspective, and of the innate attraction to the other sex from the earliest stages of life. The latter is based on her clinical observations of babies and their reaction to mother and father. She points out that none of the girl's cells are identical to those of a boy. All cells are genetically either male or female and this is bound to have an influence on human affectivity and the seeking of the complementary other (*ibid.*, p. 422). Her clinical and psychoanalytic observations had also led her to agree with Freud (1933a) that the human being is fundamentally bi-sexual. Although the body is biologically mono-sexed, emotionally, it is bi-sexed, implying a libidinal oscillation between male and female objects.

She firmly contends that homosexuality is not the by-product of some physical or biological dysfunction, no more than is the absence of orgasm in women who are apparently functioning sexually, or their incapacity to produce children with fertile men (Dolto, 1996, p. 433). She stresses that homosexual females are definitely female in their somatic characteristics and those of their genital organs. Their chromosomal make up and their chemistry are also typically female, and no gene has yet been found which could account for homosexuality (*ibid.*, p. 95).

She speaks about some women with "male bodies", or women whose genital organs have anomalies (no vagina, or internal testes), but, in the cases mentioned, she also stresses that these women have the sensitivities and desires of physically functioning women, and, although they cannot produce children or, in some cases, be penetrated (*ibid.*, p. 467), these women are not homosexual and can be happily married.

Dolto has always put a strong emphasis on the emotional and spiritual aspects of life and on the ability of the individual to transcend and symbolize, seeing this as a sign of emotional maturity, so it is not surprising to hear what she has to say in the following quote:

> ... when homosexual relationships between adults are fully conscious, they are often more emotionally involved and erotic and are more symbolically and culturally fruitful than the heterosexual relationship . . . to affirm one's homosexuality and live it as a sexual option in a society for which it is not the norm and according to which the masquerade of bodies apparently coupled according to

> their complementary sex is enough to reassure the "crowds" . . . pushes two people of the same sex to love each other, without possibility of procreation, to create . . . on an abstract level, to give each other joy, in brief to bear fruit on a symbolic level, which is often genitally conceived in a more authentic way than many children are who are born from indifferent or sadomasochistic coitus. [*ibid.*, p.402]

The making of an homosexual woman

Freud (1931b) sees two different ways in which the choice of a sexual object is made. The first springs from the way the child relates to her mother during early infancy, while the second is of a narcissistic nature, whereby the girl later on seeks the image of herself in the other person, unable to relate to the other as different from herself, and therefore falling into the realm of psychopathology. For Freud, the relationship of a wife to her husband will be modelled in all cases on her relationship with her mother, and not on that with her father.

Dolto's position on the issue of female homosexuality closely follows the Freudian view (Freud, 1920a) as far as the basics are concerned, but she also elaborates on it. For her, too, the foundations for the emergence of homosexuality or heterosexuality are laid down during the early period of infancy. Her observations of mothers and children showed that a child can differentiate between a male and a female at a very early stage (see Chapter Six), and that the sense of belonging to one sex or the other and the idea of gender is likewise introduced and may be voiced to the child very early on, by her principal carer, who, more often than not, is the mother.

Infancy

Dolto contends that, for a girl's desire to awaken to the opposite sex, it is necessary to be brought up in close proximity to a significant male who plays a positive role during the period of early infancy. But it is not only the access to a male that guarantees heterosexual development. Although, at this stage, it is the father who is her instinctual complement and responds to her genital drives, this male must play a significant and positive role in her mother's life, so that the little girl will want to be like mother and have what she has (*ibid.*, p. 291).

Dolto posits that a baby girl brought up entirely in a female world would not be able to access her sexual desire for a male. This poses an interesting question as to whether, in that case, the little girl's desire would be turned towards the same sex object and become fixed there with no possibility of a later reawakening to her heterosexuality. Dolto does not entertain this hypothesis, but its implications are fascinating for lesbian couples with daughters. This question would not arise for a boy raised in an entirely female world, as his sexuality is instinctually (according to Dolto) turned towards the opposite object. However, it would arise if a male homosexual couple raised a male child. As an extension to Dolto's point, in the case of both girls and boys, and assuming that they were brought up in an entirely single-sexed world, it might be impossible to negotiate the Oedipal complex, as it would not exist as we traditionally understand it. Additionally, it would be interesting to analyse the role of language in these relationship which either have two mothers or two fathers (terminology often used by children for their two parents of the same sex).

Dolto introduces a further element as likely to determine whether a girl or a boy is going to become homosexual, and that is the gender of the parents and the point of fixation of their desire. She remarks that experience shows that "Homosexual girls, just like homosexual boys, are those who have been the unique point of libidinal *jouissance* of the person who looked after them" (*ibid.*, p. 424).

A word is needed here about the meaning of *jouissance* in French. It implies "pleasure" which, in the context of sexual libido, is too much to bear, hence the saying in French of *mourir de plaisir* (to die from pleasure), and it is in that small death that *jouissance* is located. However, it can also indicate energy which cannot be fully incorporated into the symbolic order and which is then identified with a self-eroticism centred on the body of the mother.

Because of the early emergence of the erogenous zones and because of their repeated toileting needs, these zones are likely to become erotically imprinted by the way the mother habitually cares for them. This will also shape the way in which the girl's desires and their satisfaction will exist in her immature ego. What happens during this imprinting phase can change the course of "becoming" for a future female or a future male, leading them to seek the arousing object in a body similar to hers or his. This erotic future is determined, prepared at the phase in which oral erogenous zones are dominant, through the interplay of all the senses: hearing, seeing, touch, and smell (*ibid.*, p. 424).

Dolto says that some little girls who have not been stimulated, but have been obliged to become passive objects abandoned by the parents in the nursery, develop an excessive tendency to masturbation, which is generally an expression of their boredom and the need to mother and entertain themselves if there is no one there for them. This situation may lead to a virility complex, which is described by Freud as a refusal to access vaginal sexuality. Some types of frigidity can also arise from devaluation, around 25–30 months, by parents of the erotic value of the erogenous zones, with injunctions not to touch or not to speak about them. Such parents, according to Dolto, are people for whom frustration has become a way of living.

What happens during the negotiation of the Oedipal complex that can lead to homosexuality?

Dolto says that this is a phase during which several things can happen and makes the point that

> After puberty, if the Oedipus complex and the primal scene have not been lived through, and if there was difficulty in passing through primary castration to the centripetal penis option as in the case of a girl who has an infantile or phobic mother . . . then the girl is likely to develop an array of neurotic symptoms and to repress her genital puberty drives. [Dolto, 1996, p. 178]

Dolto uses the two terms, centripetal and centrifugal penis option (phases), in the following sense. The desire for a centrifugal penis (the seeking of the penis she has not got) is associated with a narcissistic blow and with primary castration anxiety. The desire for a centripetal penis (a desire for the penis once she has accepted that she has not got one) is associated with the valorization of her hollow sex and linked with procreation (*ibid.*, pp. 28–29).

As exemplified in Chapter Six, the acceptance by a girl of her femininity is based on an identification with her mother, supported by her father. So, if both sexes are psychologically bi-sexual, what does it mean for a girl to negotiate the Oedipal complex? It means a renunciation of father for a male of her own, but does not it also mean a renunciation of mother too . . . and for what? The perennial question has been: "Can a girl ever renounce her mother as a primary love object to turn towards a man, why does she do it? Does she do it fully or half-heartedly?". Dolto's answer to this question (*ibid.*, p. 142) is that latent homosexuality is, for a girl, a guarantee of the safety of her genital body base image (see Chapter Five). However, if the "body base image" is damaged, it can lead to phobic representations. These phobias Dolto thinks are the representations of a pathologically repressed desire for the penis and its eroticized fear, which means that the Oedipus complex cannot be negotiated as the penis is rejected. Several different phobias can establish themselves at this stage, e.g., phobias of mice, rats, cats, for example, which can represent, according to Dolto, a repressed desire for caresses of the vulva and can also lead to vaginismus. This could be linked to a memory of mother's toileting of the infant, reactivated by the young girl's desire for men, a desire the expression of which is forbidden by the parents. The forbidden expression of erotic feelings could also be paralleled with, and/or lead to, a fear of rape. This could, according to Dolto, lead to an over-investment in passivity, resulting in aboulia, asthenia, constipation, melancholia, hypochondria, a host of problems linked with the oral and respiratory system, and a repression of the genital drives at puberty. A repression of the clitoral–anal drives and an over-investment in the body areas that have not been made the object of guilt could lead to a virility complex.

During the Oedipal phase, when the little girl may wish to reject mother in her desire for father, or men in general, the "potential rejection" of mother triggers guilt feelings and the fear that mother may lose interest in her. Because the image she has of herself is not yet strong enough, it pushes her to submit and/or to seek mother's attention as a passive object. It is through homosexual relating to the mother that the little girl can introject the image of a "violated female" that, though perhaps symbolically castrated, is still alive and still phallic (powerful), standing by father, whom the little girl has over-endowed both in his person and genitality (*ibid.*, p. 143).

Dolto says (*ibid.*, p. 180) that this phase of latent homosexuality in which mother is the structuring person is only healthy if female sexuality organizes itself around heterosexuality. This is one of Dolto's value statements, which seems to contradict her position adopted about homosexuality elsewhere. Perhaps the word "healthy" here should be read from a Freudian psychoanalytic perspective with regard to the structuring of human sexuality.

A girl may become homosexual when the castrations relating to the Oedipal complex are imposed by mother alone, instead of being administered jointly by mother and father. The interdiction of *jouissance* with father, expressed solely by mother, can sometimes lead to the feeling in the little girl that *jouissance* is not only forbidden to her with father, but also with all males. Castrations affect the place where pleasure is focalized. Castration during the Oedipal phase can lead to sublimation, but also to perversion (see Chapter Five).

Dolto wrote at an early date about the possibility of female perversion, when classically this was a domain reserved for males; women, and especially mothers, could only be neurotic (Welldon, 1988)! For example, the daughter's fantasy that the mother has seduced her often comes from the fact that the mother cleans her on her own and that it excites her. In fact, the mother may become seduced by her own obsessionality *vis à vis* her daughter's cleanliness (Dolto, 1996, p. 431). Dolto also cites as an example the fact that maternal encouragements to a daughter to make herself up can be traumatic. The daughter can experience this as an attempted seduction by mother; in other words, make yourself beautiful so that I can desire you. Dolto thinks that this encouragement can be the result of the homosexuality of the mother turned towards her daughter, combined with a projection of her adulterous desires. Dolto refers to her hypothesis about some women who, although married (coupled with men, as she puts it), are in fact homosexuals, transforming their husbands into a maternal substitute (*ibid.*, p. 26, n. 3), and the damage that these "paedophile" women inflict on their children. This is the hypothesis that led Lacan to his famous comment after the 1960 Amsterdam Congress that Dolto was *culottée* (*ibid.*, p. 46) (see Chapter Six). Other types of pathological mothering will be examined later.

Homosexuality and the unconscious image of the body

If the unconscious image of the body (see Chapter Five) is the "living synthesis of the emotional experiences of the desiring subject, the unconscious memory of lived relational experiences, both narcissistic and inter-relational", which is mediated through language from earliest infancy, then the libido can, at different stages, be hemmed in. This hemmed in libido can affect the image of the genital body (such as in gynaecological pathology) as well as that of the kinetic body (the body in movement) in the pathology of the metabolic life. It would be interesting to pursue this line of research applied to homosexuality, especially as Dolto underlines that heterosexuality is itself linked to a secure image of the body, kinetic and phallic, in contact with a body of the other sex and based in intimacy and authentic exchange. In the *Sentiment de soi* (Guillerault, 1997), Dolto is reported to have said that "Homosexuality doesn't make sense for the subject of desire, it only makes sense for the body, that is to say for the individual as desire's part objects, but not for the inter-psychic relation" (*ibid.*, p. 231).

Does it imply that only a secure body image can match the biological reproductive imperatives, and that homosexuals do not have a secure body image? Or that homosexuality is limited to desiring only part objects? This is not clear to me from my reading of *Sexualité feminine*, and may be due to my incomprehension or else indicate a possible internal inconsistency or contradiction in Dolto's thoughts (see Dolto, 1996, p. 402). There is here a whole field of possible research and interpretations

Different types of homosexuality

Dolto examines different types of female homosexuality (*ibid.*, pp. 197–201), some of which are compatible with heterosexuality. In all cases, she observed a dissociation between emotional and erotic desires, which happens when the object relation of the person and her erotic fixation do not concur in a creative unity specific to the reproductive genital structure of that person.

According to Dolto, two types of virility complex can be established. The first virility complex consists of a total negation of identification with girls or women. The little girl will refuse to see herself as anything other than a boy and will be looking for fights with others; she will display little or no masturbation. In boarding schools she has the reputation of being homosexual when, in fact, she very rarely is. However, this can lead later on to "true homosexuality", often brought about by feelings of disappointment in males (either because father is absent for a variety of reasons—physically or psychologically—or because he is dead). She can also become homosexual if a lesbian female who will "whip", in a metaphorical way, her narcissism in a domineering, passionate or ascetic way seduces her.

The second virility complex consists of the girl becoming totally engrossed in a world in which the other is a pure fantasy. Therefore, the girl's desire is aiming for an object without corporeal materiality, which is a reflection of her fantasies and a narcissistic involvement with herself. The over-excitement of the sexual areas mean that the little girl lives in a masturbatory dream and there is therefore little sublimation of oral or anal phallicism as everything is imaginary. There is a serious risk of narcissistic neurosis, because these girls are not interested in pragmatic life. They may later on become intellectually successful, but remain prisoners of a non-resolved Oedipus complex (*ibid.*, p. 156).

For Dolto, masochistic perversions (when an orgasm is obtained out of pain, without penetration) seem to be typical of latent homosexual females. She explains this by the fact that their body was invested narcissistically as a partial phallus (foetal or anal) of their mother. Their body then submits to an erotic object playing the role of the phallic mother or father, with erotic fantasies of being devoured. What is done to the body (as phallic) is enough to satisfy the female's *jouissance* and their partners are often impotent. According to Dolto, these girls are often marked by a delay in emotional maturation and an absence of narcissistic interest in their bodies (*ibid.*, p. 276).

Types of homosexuality coexisting with heterosexuality

Dolto noted that the occurrence of homosexuality with heterosexuality follows on from a non-resolution of the Oedipal conflict and that the "vicious circle" can only be broken through psychoanalysis. There seems to be an inconsistency here, as later on Dolto seems to think that some types of homosexuality and heterosexuality can coexist quite happily and healthily. This is a rather dry part of Dolto's work, as there are no case studies mentioned to illustrate her points. Some of the different types of homosexuality are not that clear-cut, and one would have to go back to her case studies to extract information about the mothers and fathers of the children she treated, and then other adults, in order to form an educated opinion.

1. Dolto described how some women brought their children to her consulting room saying that they were worried about their behaviour, when they should, in fact, be worried about their own, implying the presence of some violence, be it emotional or physical, towards the children. Although these women were in a consummated heterosexual relationship, they were often frigid and harboured a latent homosexuality, but, because they were psychically "pre-genital", their genitality was unconscious (latent) and coexisted with their heterosexuality without being expressed. What was projected on to the children were these passionate and violent unconscious homosexual feelings. Dolto referred to these women during the 1960 Amsterdam Congress on female sexuality as women, coupled with men, but in fact homosexuals, transforming their husbands into a maternal substitute. She pointed out the damage that these "paedophile" women could inflict on their children (*ibid*., p. 26, n. 3).
2. The second type described by Dolto has its source in a morbid fixation to the narcissistic dyadic relationship with mother. This can lead to psychosis and child abuse, and to unconscious moral delinquency. The homosexuality of these women is genitally conscious and assumed, but not always orgasmic, and is often accompanied by a repression of emotional and genital heterosexuality. According to Dolto, this type is sometimes found in people working in the caring professions, in some young single mothers, or in single mothers of adopted children. The desire of which they repress the genital satisfaction,

to abduct a child, is linked to their social activity and erotized in an all-encompassing obsessional mode.

3. The third type of homosexuality described by Dolto is called "sublimated", and allows a relationship of a genital type with female persons (but without body contact) as well as a heterosexual relationship consummated genitally but in which the woman is generally frigid. These women are unconsciously stuck in the fantasy of being "raped" by their husband, perceived as a pseudo-father, admired in his persona for his social aura, but ignored as a real being. The latent heterosexuality is genital and the sublimated heterosexuality is without any erotic genital desires. According to Dolto, this is the most compatible form for living in a mixed society and does not seem to affect the mental or physiological health of the woman. These women are often encountered when they bring their children with Oedipal difficulties. They do not valorize their male children's erotic desires and these children often become aboulic at puberty (it refers to a lack of will or initiative). Their daughters tend to become hysterics and homosexuals with spectacular symptoms because, for them, their father is the only desirable person, but their mother does not allow them any access to him, as the mothers want themselves to be their husband's only daughters, requiring the children to remain passive and non-threatening.
4. According to Dolto, the fourth type of homosexuality is stuck in the pre-genital. She calls this type "polyandric" heterosexuality. It is consummated genitally with or without any repression of homosexuality. It stems from a lack of structuring due to the fact that the girl was not ethically or culturally valorized during the anal and phallic pre-genital phase of her development. The result of this is a body that lacks coherence and is made of fragments, each with its desire. The more partners (or consumers, according to the oral logic), the more valorized she feels. Dolto adds that social and affective "debility" are always present, especially if the woman is married to an indulgent and rich husband who gives her social standing. These women can only exist if they can seduce, whatever the seduced object is. They are not frigid, but only have clitoral and vulval orgasms of a nymphomaniac nature. These women can be characterized

by masochism through the evolution of their passive oral and anal tendencies, over-compensating with "dipsomania", or with an addiction to pharmaceutical products, or an obsession with diets.

5. The fifth type of homosexuality is originally latent but becomes consummated following an emotional or sexual failure with heterosexuality. This leads the woman to renounce all heterosexuality. It is the result of an Oedipus complex impossible to face because of the emotional fragility of the father, sometimes complicated by an overwhelming infantilism in the mother. The desire for the penis is unconsciously repressed and is fetishistically represented by children. This is not a stable genital state, and there can be an evolution towards psychosis and criminality, when the imaginary necessity to act out in the sensory and social domain the killing of the Oedipal child is carried out. Often, the child is the result of an affair, or of artificial insemination, or of an incestuous relationship. According to Dolto, the obstetric services see a number of these cases: children admitted for accidents that represent *actes manqués* of the mother—in other words, which have been indirectly inflicted or triggered by the mother.
6. The last type of homosexuality recognized by Dolto is, paradoxically, a heterosexuality of total dependency. It stems from a morbid fixation, and a dependent regression of the woman towards her mother, which is then transferred on to the marriage. It leads the woman who has this fixation on her partner, generally of an erotomaniac type, to reject any other possible attachments or sexual attraction to anyone else, whichever sex they are, and to deny them all erotic value. Such women will also renounce their desire for maternity in order to please their partner. Of course, all these renunciations rapidly become a source of huge anxiety and of psychosomatic regression and illness, which is then used as a secondary defence mechanism against phobic anxiety.

Conclusion

According to Dolto, a total resolution of emotional Oedipal residues in female sexuality can only be reached after the woman has had a child. The mourning of the phallic narcissism, of her body and sex, and the abandonment of her homosexual dependency (via guilt) on her mother (Dolto, 1996, p. 206) can only happen then. It seems as if this is due to the fact that the reliving of the primal scene is often delayed until the birth of her first child. This birth will allow the daughter to relive narcissistically the centrifugal rape of her mother, via her foetus, who is a part of herself identified with her mother. This, of course, leaves open the question of those women who have not had children. Is it impossible for them to reach a total resolution of Oedipal issues? And what is the destiny of homosexual mothers, or of those who have been artificially inseminated? These again are interesting social issues of our century.

Françoise Dolto, however, points out that maternity can also bring to a woman the risk of homosexual regression to a pre-Oedipal stage. Her mother can become like a twin, or a big sister, or a servant to her daughter, and a latent homosexual couple becomes established between them. This "relationship" is sacred, and if they live close by each other, and if the grandmother is genitally frustrated, this can enable chain regressions and the formation of neurotic families. The woman's father becomes like a big/little brother, and there is no possible return to the Oedipal situation, as there is no possible seduction left. The Oedipus complex has imploded and become unsolvable (*ibid.*, pp. 209–210).

It is difficult to conclude this chapter without wondering why a Colloquium on female homosexuality, organized by the Société Psychanalytique de Paris (SPP) in 1964, is only mentioned as a footnote in the 1996 edition (p. 13) of Françoise Dolto's *Sexualité féminine*. The colloquium took place four years after the 1960 Amsterdam Congress, and led to a series of interesting articles which were published in 1964, under the title of *Nouvelles recherches sur la sexualité féminine*, under the direction of Janine Chasseguet-Smirgel, with the participation of Christian David, Bela Grunberger, C. J. Luquet-Parat, Maria Torok, and J. McDougall (whose paper is entitled "Homosexuality in women"). Conversely, the 1970 translation of Chasseguet-Smirgel's book is striking for its absence of references to Dolto's paper on *Sexualité féminine*; Lacan does not feature either, and there is no mention of the 1960 Amsterdam Congress on female sexuality. A possible explanation may be found in Roudinesco's book (1994, p. 520). Roudinesco suggests that, because of the political climate between the SPP and the Société Française de Psychanalyse (SFP), there was no communication between the therapists of the two groups. Chasseguet-Smirgel (SPP) did not seem to have been aware of the 1960 Amsterdam Congress, where Françoise Dolto had presented her work on female sexuality, nor that this work had been published in *La Psychanalyse* in January 1964. And, vice versa, Françoise Dolto (SFP, subsequently dissolved) did not seem aware of the work undertaken by the women of the SPP.

It seems to me that this sad state of affairs was in part a consequence of Dolto and Lacan's excommunication from the IPA in 1953 and the ensuing splitting of the various French psychoanalytic schools. It will be left to others to contrast and compare these two approaches to female sexuality and to female homosexuality.

References

Chasseguet-Smirgel, J. (Ed.) (1964). *La sexualité féminine. Nouvelles recherches*. Paris: Payot. English edition: *Female Sexuality—New Psychoanalytic Views*. Ann Arbor, MI: University of Michigan Press, 1970.

de Mezamat, A. (1994). *Coffret*. DVD, Abacaris Films. Paris: Gallimard.

de Mezamat, A. (2008). *Francoise Dolto parle*. Abacaris Films: France 5.

Dolto, F. (1964). La libido génitale et son destin féminin. Rapport pour le Congrès d'Amsterdam. *La Psychanalyse, 7*: 3–14.

Dolto, F. (1996). *Françoise Dolto. Séxualite féminine. La libido génitale et son destin feminin*. M. Djeribi-Valentin & E. Kouki (Eds.). Paris: Gallimard.

Freud, S. (1920a). The psychogenesis of a case of homosexuality in a woman. *S.E., 18*: 145–172. London: Hogarth.

Freud, S. (1931b). Female sexuality. *S.E., 21*:225–244. London: Hogarth.

Freud, S. (1933a). *New Introductory Lectures on Psycho-analysis* (Femininity), *S.E., 22*: 112–135. London: Hogarth.

Guillerault, G. (1997). *Françoise Dolto. Le sentiment de soi. Aux sources de l'image du corps*. Paris: Gallimard.

McDougall, J. (1970). Homosexuality in women. In: J. Chasseguet-Smirgel (Ed.). *Female Sexuality* (pp. 171–212). Ann Arbor, MI: University of Michigan Press.

Roudinesco, E. (1986). *Histoire de la psychanalyse en France (1925–1985), 2.* Paris: Fayard, 1994.

Welldon, E. (1988). *Mother, Madonna, Whore—The Idealization of Motherhood.* London: Karnac, 2004.

CHAPTER EIGHT

La Maison Verte: a place for words. Personal reflections on working with Françoise Dolto

Anne-Marie Canu

On the 6th January 1979, on the door of a little blue shop, the following notice appeared.

> A place has opened for children and parents at
> *57 Place Saint Charles.*
>
> Why?
>
> Because we know the importance for young children, from the first day of their life, of preparation with their parents to enter into society.
>
> And because parents are sometimes very much alone as they face the daily difficulties they have with their young children.
>
> This place is not a day-care, not a *crèche,* not a *kindergarten,* nor a child health or welfare centre. It is place of words, of relaxation, where mothers and fathers, grandparents, nannies and babysitters, are welcomed with the child they have in charge and sometimes are worried about. Little ones will be able to make friends.

> Expectant mothers and their companions, as well as young siblings, can also come, because the arrival of a new baby is very important and sometimes a very difficult time in the family.
>
> We will be open, starting January 1979, every morning at 9.30, except Monday mornings, and every afternoon from 3.00 to 6.00 p.m.
>
> You may meet, on different days: Pierre Benoit, Josée Boone, Gérard Guillerault, Colette Langignon, Marie-Hélène Malandrin, Marie-Noëlle Rebois, Claude This, Bernard This.

This notice, to a casual passer-by, could simply have appeared to be completely banal and unimportant. One could easily believe it to be just one more place for children, or isolated mothers, to spend a pleasant afternoon. If, for Françoise Dolto, the *L'image inconsciente du corps* was her most important theoretical work, then it was, I believe, La Maison Verte that was her most practical contribution. She would bring to it everything she had learnt in the course of forty years, listening to patients, adults, children, and babies. La Maison Verte was the place where she worked most actively. It was both the work of her life and, truly, the life of her work. Here it would all come together, be transmitted, and would be carried on after her. Her aim had been to put the findings of psychoanalysis at the service of very young children. She was going to find, in return, that La Maison Verte would bring new developments, previously unknown to psychoanalysis. As she said, "Psychoanalysts should pay to come to La Maison Verte, they would be taught their trade". From this new experience, she would continue to be taught by, as she called them, "my colleagues, the children" and to teach.

Nothing of the sort had previously existed. Nobody really believed in it. Certainly not Social Services. They thought France already had all it needed, with its *crèches*, *garderies*, or *halte-garderies*, and the *école maternelle*. All of these were supposedly meant for children, but in reality they were for the convenience of adults, parents and employers. They made for "good" social organization. "Besides," asked Social Services, "what do psychoanalysts have to do with babies?"

It took all of Dolto's determination and enthusiasm to make it happen. She was by then seventy years old. A year earlier, she had decided to put an end to her practice, both private and public, including her work at l'Hôpital Trousseau, that had, up to then, been so important to her, where she had in her own words, "forged her instruments".

The foundation was a small group of friends, colleagues, some analysts, some not, some for various reasons of their own sharing in her enthusiasm, and some just not wanting her to sink alone in what could only be, or so they thought, a catastrophic venture.

She herself said, "I don't know. I have been thinking about this for a very long time. I think our society needs it. If it fails, it fails. It will only mean that I was wrong. Never mind."

A few years later, she would write,

> It took us two years to form our group. Then two years working on the project, meeting every two weeks, discussing what it was we did not want without being able to ascertain what we could do. A place to be oneself, where with no pre-established programme every person present would find and develop who he is in contact with. This is not something easy to understand for those who are in charge of social affairs, welfare and the like. They need to "do" things, or have people "do" things, according to their norms. And doctors, they are always "searching for", or "fighting" a symptom."

While writing to someone who had experienced La Maison Verte as a mother and was later struggling to establish their own version, Françoise Dolto said, "Do not let yourself be discouraged. This is something people need. So it will happen." The very same authorities that had been so hard to convince that this was a worthwhile project were now begging Dolto to open more Maisons Vertes around the country.

She had said, "There should be one in every arrondissement, people need it." But she answered,

> No, I opened la Maison Verte; it is not a chain of restaurants. The idea belongs to everyone. If people are interested, let them form their own team, build their own project, find themselves a name and get on with it.

When, for example, the Jardin Couvert in Lyon was starting, they asked Françoise Dolto to come and help. She refused. It was lucky that she did. They are still talking about it and they are still working hard to build on their own experience and to learn from it. They did later thank her for saying "no". Now such centres exist all over the world.

Donald Winnicott, who had interviewed Françoise Dolto in 1963, had found her to be thirty years ahead of everybody else, but also too charismatic to be allowed as a teacher within the International Psychoanalytic Association (IPA). This resulted in her following Jacques Lacan when he was excluded from the IPA, and, as a consequence, her work has remained for too long unavailable in the English-speaking world. Paradoxically, she was probably closer to Winnicott and to other Anglo-Saxon psychoanalysts, such as Frances Tustin, than too many of her French colleagues. If these two ladies had met, I feel there would now be Maisons Vertes all over the UK. It has been a loss for both countries. I remember mentioning this to Dolto on one occasion while deploring the fact. She thought so too, but with her typical attitude of not wasting time crying over spilt milk, her only comment was to say, "Maybe some day . . ."

Two years after the opening at Place St Charles, La Maison Verte (now green, and taking shape as it went along) moved and settled at 13 Rue Meilhac, where it remains to this day. The change from one venue to the other allowed for much of the practical experience and theoretical understanding gained at Place Saint Charles to be carefully considered when planning for setting up the Rue Meilhac. At one point, the powers that be, those who give the money, suggested that we could open an hour later.

"Certainly not," said Françoise Dolto. "Would you open a department store only at peak time? Mothers who choose that time to come need it for themselves, and that's just fine. They will relax. People can be so terribly lonely sometimes in our society."

Parents, who have heard a lot about it through the radio, television, talks, and books, are sometimes astonished to find it so simple a place. It is not big. If you wish to come, you could take the metro, get off at Cambronne, walk along the Rue de la Croix Nivert, turn off at Rue de l'Amiral Roussin, which is easier to find than Rue Meilhac. In a few minutes you will reach a small pedestrianized square, where you will have no trouble finding a small wooden gate painted green. So easy, yet obviously even this first step is going to mean something very different according to whether you are a child living in the neighbourhood, or within walking distance, when it is already familiar to you. If you are a child coming from afar, taking the bus or metro, then it is a different experience. For the adult, it demonstrates a commitment in time and effort, but for the child it can be an exciting and exotic journey.

Inside, there are two rooms and they are not very big. They are on the ground floor of an HLM (*habitation à loyer modéré*) in the 15th district of Paris. It is unpretentious. Anybody can come here and feel at home, whatever their social status. Drawing a plan of it would not help you much as you enter it. This crosses my mind because so many times, during the first years, we have seen would-be Maisons Vertes teams come and visit us with a pen, pencil, and measuring tape. Their intention is to faithfully reproduce what they saw at the, so-called, Maison-Mère. There have been changes in the light of our experiences. For instance, opening hours are now every afternoon, from 2.00 to 7.00, and on Saturday afternoons from 3.00 to 6.30. We do not open in the mornings any more, because people simply do not come. Opening later in the evenings and on Saturday afternoons makes it possible for fathers to attend. Each person enters la Maison Verte as they wish. One can arrive without a problem or issue. Some come with a variety of different concerns. What is important is to watch and listen to the interactions that take place in the rooms. For example, some parents bring biscuits to give to their child and some bring cake. When a child becomes upset that it cannot have what is being offered to another child, Dolto would say, "You can have the biscuit (or cake), but you also have to swop mothers. Do you want to change mothers?" The child then understands that teatime is not the same for everybody and that not all parents act in an identical manner. It gives rise to all sorts of interactions, envy, cravings, exchanges of different kinds between parents and between children and other parents. Differences become accepted, a new way of being social comes up, and words can be put on every feeling that arises.

At the Rue Meilhac, a red line separates the two rooms, and little pedal-cars and tricycles are not allowed to cross over it. This is one of the two rules that cannot be infringed. It introduces the sense of limits, boundaries, and transgression. It is the notion that there are laws in every society. There is a lot of interplay between adult and child that takes place over it. The red line has become something like a dogma for many new Maison Vertes. Yet, it never came from any preconceived theoretical idea. What happened was simply that, at the Place St Charles, there was no room inside for the pedal cars and they were allowed to run freely on the wide pavement outside. Then, the nearby shops complained that it bothered their customers. So, we took a piece of chalk and traced a line on the pavement limiting the space within which pedal cars were allowed. It was a very practical solution to a very practical problem. It also demonstrated respecting the rights of other citizens.

The other absolute rule is that aprons must be worn when playing with water. Françoise Dolto believed little children need to play with water; it reflected her experience as a therapist. So there was, even at Place St Charles, a place to play around with water, and children loved it. But French mothers said: *Il va prendre froid, mon petit, il va se mouiller, je ne veux pas.* "My little one is going to get wet and will catch cold. I don't want that." Françoise Dolto was not one to interfere in the way parents chose to bring up their children. She was not going to stand in between, at the risk of making the child believe someone knew better than its mother. Dolto did not want to be the cause of separation for a child when it still needed unity. Later, the child would face the necessary separations without losing the security in its own identity. So, what did she say? "Of course, you are perfectly right. Why didn't I think of it before? We will have waterproof aprons, and no child will be allowed near the water if it refuses to wear one." Parents were respected in their parenthood, the child encouraged in its "going-on-being", in its right to make its own decisions, within the limits set by adults in giving it security. The child learnt that there were laws in every society, but that these were not the same as those at home, or elsewhere. Children could learn about entering into another society and have fun at the same time.

Dolto was acutely aware of the traumas caused by early, unprepared, or unanticipated mother–child separations and the repercussions that would follow in later life. These would take a long time to heal and La Maison Verte was designed to prepare a child to have a social life without losing the security of its identity, which it receives through the presence of its mother. It is meant for children who are at the age that Dolto calls *Moi–Maman*. If a child is cut off from its mother, at that age, they are, as it were, also cut off from themselves. They are maimed, and become aggressive or depressed. They find it hard to enter into relationships with others and difficult to enter into society.

I am going to try to take you to see a place that you are not normally allowed to enter unless you are accompanied by a child. I want to describe something that defies description, precisely because it is, in the end, neither a concept nor an idea, but a concrete location, a place that means what it means only to the children for whom it is destined. I do not mean children in general, but the one child who is here, now, and no other. Even this one is not the same as he was yesterday, or will be to-morrow. It is a moment-by-moment experience. It is always in movement, always changing. It is only because of the presence of all the others that this child will be aided to become fully who he is, forever son or daughter of this mother and this father, but different from them both. He will become completely himself only when he is able to share that same reality together with others.

As a child, maybe, your parents know all about la Maison Verte, and wish you to find friends to play with in a social context. Maybe they are displeased with you for some reason and are dragging you there to talk about it. Maybe your parent thinks you will meet "specialists" who know and will give them good advice on how to deal with you. Well, they will be disappointed. We try not to do that sort of thing. Maybe you have already been to some other place where children go to, such as *crèches*, *garderies*, or *halte-garderies*, maybe even *l'école maternelle.* In France today, children as young as two years old can enter such places, even while they are still babies in nappies. Some feel that is much too soon, but then they think that later, when you are much older, these children will enter a *polytechnique*, or one of the *grandes écoles*, and do brilliantly. The *école maternelle* is free, while the *crèche* is not. Maybe things did not go too well with you at one of these places. Maybe there was an adult there, such as the director, intelligent enough and caring enough to take notice, to warn your parents, and suggest to them, "Why don't you take your child to La Maison Verte for a while. It might help". And maybe no one noticed and you started developing what those "specialists" call "symptoms". There is a whole gamut of them to be assigned to children. Let me name just a few: sleep disturbances, biting, scratching, howling all day long, or the opposite, refusing to eat, losing weight, refusing to play, being negative about everything, or clinging to mother, or turning away from her, there is no end to the list. You will normally pick what hurts your parents most, because that is how you feel you can reach them. Maybe your parents are experiencing real difficulties in their own life, and you so much want to help them, but you have not been told how to do it and it hurts. Of course, they do not know that you are trying to help them. They just feel irritated by you; and eventually everybody gets more and more unhappy. Misunderstandings, that is "missed understandings", can be resolved with just the need of an interpreter, or a go-between.

Maybe you have already started building for yourself a little protective shell, which is very useful at times, but, if left to harden, can be quite a nuisance, as it cuts you off from so many of the pleasures of life. Or, maybe life was just so blissfully happy with a loving mother and father and then another human being comes along whom you did not need or want and your whole world collapses. For you, the child, this human being is just a "little thing", but it takes up so much of your mother's time and is so often in her arms that you start to think that maybe your mother does not love you any more, and you feel so desperately lonely. Or, you might be going through what the specialists know as one of these violent transitions, so painful to you and to your parents who just do not know what to do. Maybe, when you were born, your parents wanted a boy and you turn out to be a girl, and now what are they going to do? Again, maybe your parents want the very best for you and to give you the best education ever, and although you want to please them, really all you want to do is play with water and sand and stuff and get your clothes dirty, because that is what you like, but, sadly, they do not know it. Maybe your parents had read some of Dolto's books, or maybe your grandmother had listened in the 1970s to her radio broadcasts, when all of France heard her famous voice. Whatever the case, whatever you and your parent had in mind, what you are going to find here will be quite different. That much we know.

Maybe . . ., maybe . . ., maybe. All these and many more experiences, however trivial they may seem, can cause real distress to a child, which adults tend to dismiss with a smile and by saying, "Nothing to make a fuss about, really". Sometimes, with a bit of luck, it can lead you to the door of La Maison Verte, where words could be used that would begin to let you know that you can deal with these things, and find your own way of doing so. You just needed the words and to be heard.

We are now at the little green gate. There is a latch, a little high up, out of reach of children's hands. Your parents will release it, push open the door, and close it behind them. You then enter a space like a covered porch, where prams can stay. Then you come to a glass-panelled door, opening on to a first room, where you might see other children already playing, and some adults, too. That room opens on to still another one, where there will be more adults and children. If it is not raining, there is a tiny outdoor playground with a couple of swings and slides, where you can have fun.

After the outside porch, where prams are kept, you enter a relatively small first room slightly triangular; on your right hand, a little play house, like a hut, child size, green, of course, as are the doors and all the woodwork! Walls are painted white. The wall on the right is a glass panel that reaches almost to the floor, so that a child standing inside is able to see what is going on outside in the square. There are trees; the wind is blowing, families walk by, other children, dogs, birds, all sorts of interesting things. On the wall opposite, there are hangers, where you can leave your coat. Remember to take your purse; this place is open. On your left there are stairs leading to a first floor, to which children normally do not have access. There is a small gate signifying that it is all grown-up stuff, offices, nothing much for little explorers who try to find their way up there. For the bigger ones, eighteen months and over, there are several baby tricycles and pedal cars available, and just enough space to run around. An open doorway leads to the second room. There you find sofas for mothers to sit down and relax. In between the two rooms, the famous red line that the pedal cars and such are not allowed to cross. There are young babies crawling around in the second room, and, however much you might like to run them over, it really is not such a good idea. And, of course, it is so much fun trying to pass, pretending you have not heard, or you do not understand, the rule about the red line and testing the adults. When this happened, Dolto would say, "Ah, where are your good little eyes?" The child would raise a finger, pointing to them. "Ah! So they are there?" Dolto would reply. "And the red line, can they see it?" The child laughs. Complicity in the transgression is there. There is lots of fun for both the child and Dolto who would go on to say: "You don't want to, I know, but it's the rule of la Maison Verte, I work here, and I have to give you the rules." For my part, at this point, I usually add, "My name is Anne-Marie and I work here." I bend down and put myself at the same height as the child. I am always amazed at the difference it makes, in the way the child listens, and all of a sudden the child is interested. We are in a relationship. The *interdit* becomes the *inter dit*. Something is said between us, and good communications are established between two equal humans and not between an adult and child. The child's work is to be who he will be. My work is to explain the regulations. The child may still try to pass by again, stealthily, or flagrantly, and we laugh knowingly. The child is aware that the car, or the truck, and I are not the same. He discovers that he is the one with power over his own self and, in accepting the law, he is allowed to live together with others. The child asks, "But if my daddy came?" I reply, "Even your daddy wouldn't be allowed to cross the line with his car." That is a matter for some thought! And on and on, and again at his next visit. Sometimes another child interrupts, saying, "Red line, no go." A dialogue starts between the two. It is all that simple.

It is the same thing around the water play area, with the no less famous apron. Some children, very few, absolutely refuse, and they so much want to play with water, but we remain adamant. Tantrums and rages follow. I say, "You don't have to play with water. There are lots of other things to do. I know you are very angry and certainly you have good reason to be." And maybe from this conversation we will go on to other things that make the child angry. Words are given, words concerning emotions that the child is experiencing, sometimes so violently. And he is listened to and taken seriously, at the same time as the law is enforced. He exists, as a human being, responsible for his own life, and not a thing just to be ordered around. We are really talking to him, and not about him to his mother, as is so often the case.

La Maison Verte is small enough and big enough for children to wander around and still be within sight of their mothers, and for their mothers not to have to trot behind them to make sure they are safe. For some, this is a new experience. Also, the place has to be independent and not enclosed by such structures as Social Services, or together with a medical clinic. Françoise Dolto wanted above all to remain independent from state regulations and administrative controls. No files would be kept, no accounting of what was going on, no records of who came, what social, medical, or other category that they belonged to. There are few statistics and no evaluation of results.

Now, in October 2008, almost thirty years later, we are still very happy and would not want it to be any different. It is still the same little Maison Verte, and maybe that is how its influence continues. It is, in our experience, a place where psychoanalysis is alive. It does not need the privacy of a consulting room, where two people are in an enclosed area, away from the reality of a social space and time. A mother and child discover their reality much more easily through sharing time in a social space with others. It is a reality in which there are others who are similar, but different to them, and in which a psychoanalyst is also present. Dolto thought that psychoanalysis for children worked better in a group offering the opportunity for some sort of social life for the child, with mother and other mothers and children present along with other Maison Verte people. The interaction is not like anywhere else. What takes place here opens up new and unexplored dimensions, widening the scope for psychoanalysis to dimensions we are far from having fully understood. All this is happening at this little Maison Verte, invented by Françoise Dolto, for and by little children.

Françoise Dolto was there, at the Place Saint Charles, every Monday afternoon. She would continue to come to la Maison Verte until almost her last days. The telephone would ring. If she were the one who picked it up, she would ask,

> How old is your child? Under three? Good! This is a place where you can come together with your baby and you can stay with him. He and you will meet other children under the age of three and other parents. We will be there to greet him and you, and talk with both of you about whatever you wish. There are lots of toys around and there is place to play with water, children love it.

She would not hold a long conversation. In her brisk and warm manner, she would say,

> What else can I tell you? Come and see for yourself. That would be for the best. Then you will know whether it answers your questions, whether it fulfils your needs. We are open from 2.00 until 7.00, every day of the working week, and on Saturdays from 3.00 to 6.30. You can come any day, stay as long or as little as you like, five minutes, or five hours. *A bientôt, mais quand vous voulez.*

To journalists, who, as time went by, often wanted to interview her and ask, what was this Maison Verte that she was always talking about and that seemed to have such an amazing importance in her life, in her mind and heart, she would say, "It's so simple, what can I tell you, I wouldn't know where to start." Then she would start and she would go on, trying to share something of the new insight brought to her by the experience of La Maison Verte. She was fascinated by it, like an explorer discovering passages on a new continent.

I have even heard Françoise Dolto, on the phone, saying, "Well, if you absolutely must, if you want to come and see what this is all about, find yourself a baby somewhere, pick one up off the street, then come, but it's not a zoo. This is the Children's House."

That is the name she had in her mind all those years ago. One does not quite know how it became verte, green; there are various versions. Some say that as the children were walking by the Place St Charles it was closed, and, pulling their mothers towards it, they would hear their mothers say, *Non, c'est fermé*, and when it opened, *Ah, la maison c'est ouverte*, and in they went. The child would not say *ouverte*, but *verte*. Françoise Dolto commented, "Well, I don't know, but anyway it is my favourite colour."

No outsiders are allowed in; children are not here to be observed, even with the best of intentions. It is a place for a child to be who he is, the way he is, with his differences, and thus become a member of a society that can be alive and creative. As Tustin might put it: "He enters into the enjoyment of belonging to the human race".

In the first years, when it was still so new, many people wanted to open a Maison Verte. Surprisingly, it was social workers that were the first, long before most psychoanalysts, to catch on to how this would help them in their practice. About twice a month, and sometimes more, information sessions were offered to those who were interested. Nowadays, we offer them on request. They are held at La Maison Verte in the mornings, when no children are yet there. Two of us in turn talk about the place and answer questions. Françoise would take her turn at these sessions. For those who were fortunate enough to hear her, they would appreciate how she made evidence evident.

What was it they heard? Something like this:

Come in. During the information session you will also visit the place. I remember this lovely little girl with big brown eyes, coming in one day with her young and beautiful mother, who said with great resentment, "I can't understand, she is two months old now, she should be reasonable, but she just never stops crying." The baby was clearly in perfect health. After a little while I asked, "Would you let me carry her a little while, so you can rest?" To the little girl in my arms I just started talking, simple things, her name, where she was, my name, just like that. She instantly stopped crying. It wasn't the words; it was that I was talking to her as a person. The mother watched, in awe and said, "When I talk to her this doesn't happen." When she talked to her it was to only say "Stop crying." I remember the intensity of the little girl's eyes, looking at me while we were talking.

In the second room there is the water play area; a sort of large double sink at a child's level is in the far left-hand corner. The aprons are hung close by, and it forms a sort of special place, a little bit apart from the rest. The room is slightly irregular in shape, giving room for little nooks and crannies for privacy. There are seven or eight sofas, a thick carpet in the middle for tiny babies to lie, or sit, on. Toys all around, for all ages. On the right-hand wall is the support for a large white board on which children can draw as they wish, with big felt pens that are always lying around and much coveted. There is also a double-sided ladder. You can climb when you are big enough to be able to do so on your own to the top. When you get there, quite an accomplishment, something to be proud of! "Regarde, Maman—Look, Mummy." Now you are as high as an adult, you can triumphantly look around the room. There is a mirror up there and you can discover your own face, isn't that something? Having seen you up there, of course, other children are trying to achieve the same feat. You are not always ready to let them take your place. Same thing with toys: the toy you are having fun with comes alive in your hands and here comes someone else, suddenly vividly interested. So what happens: encounters can be quite violent, and mothers sometimes feel we don't interfere enough. An interesting dialogue can start around the water play area, or putting on the red aprons, as with the famous red line.

What is important at *La Maison Verte* is not the walls, toys, or the rooms, but the people and what happens between them. Inside there are three people who will welcome you. Any child from birth to the age of three can come with their parent, for any length of time, without making an appointment, subscription, or anything of the sort. There is no need of a pretext, like having a "symptom", or "disorder". They can come as often as they please. It is totally open. Dolto said,

> We should feel honoured that a child consents to come and spend some time with us. If only we adults would consent to be with him, as with a citizen as important as any adult, if that were done in very early childhood, everything would be changed in human society.

If this is a first visit, we will introduce ourselves. "What is your name? I am Anne-Marie and I work here." Our question goes to the baby. Of course, the answer will come from the parent, a bit taken aback that we would talk first to the child and only then to her. "And is this your mummy?" Sometimes it will be a nanny, or grandma, or a friend, or an aunt. Couples sometimes visit during the week and fathers, too, but more often it is on Saturdays. The child is greeted with whoever has him in charge on that day. For the adult, the greeting touches her as an individual adult, but it also connects to the child within herself. Simultaneously, the relationship of this parent to her own parents is revealed in the model and image of parenting that she has. This is an endless chain that we see unfolding here more than once, much to a parent's surprise, who had thought that she was coming to just another play-space and to entertain for a while a child who at home seemed a bit at a loose end.

"What do you do in real life?" asked one parent the other day. We all have different trainings, but they are linked by a concern for children and parents. When, in 1979, La Maison Verte opened, there was one nurse, two or three social workers who had experience in the field of early childhood, one housewife, and one or two trained psychologists. In time, probably everyone underwent an analysis and indeed, much later, many, although not all, became practising psychoanalysts. Among those who are present, there will always be one man. We find this very important nowadays in the domain of early childhood. In the early days there were always two educators and one psychoanalyst. Dolto suspected that some mothers were frightened of psychoanalysis and would not come when such a person was present. I was recently in another town in the French provinces and was told that this is still the case! Also, from her practice with children and adults, she had acquired the conviction that for a child, especially a young child, psychoanalysis was not enough, there was the need for education, by which she meant, in her own words,

> Giving the child the laws of life in society, in respect of himself as well as of others. The psychoanalyst is not the one who will teach the child how to behave with others in his social life. He is there to suffer with him and be the resonator of his failing to master things immediately and the consequence of being hindered by others.

As it is, at La Maison Verte, both functions overlap each other and are carried out by every Maison Verte person, at one time or another. So much so that, in the course of time, we decided to make no difference in denomination, status, or function. We all call ourselves *Accueillants,* for which I can find no satisfactory English equivalent. I will be content to use the term Maison Verte person. The experience of La Maison Verte changed the lives of everyone of us, and in more ways than one. Indeed, whenever Dolto was invited to a conference or seminar, she would always find a moment to refer to La Maison Verte and to say what she had recently learnt from being there.

I should explain how it came about, this idea of there being three people at La Maison Verte every day. Each Maison Verte person is only there one afternoon a week. Not knowing how her project would fare, Françoise Dolto did not want any of those she was leading into it to lose too much if it failed. In practice, it is very useful. It allows a child and parent a lot more freedom to come on the day they prefer. Every day has a different atmosphere. There is no transference on to any one person. If some day a disagreement arises between children and/or parents, or with me, well, the next day is altogether different. We do not tell each other from one day to the next what happened. No two days are ever alike. Never the same children either; even those who come regularly come at different times. The group is constantly changing. It is the start of a child's social world. A child meets other children, other adults. When a child is with its mother, it feels if she likes it too, and is happy to see her child with friends, in the same way as the child is happy to make contact with other adults. It is now that the child can safely leave its mother and discover the world. She does not have the child around her all the time, the way it often is at home.

The child will see another baby in its mother's arms, and suddenly realize there are two of them, and it might register that it could be the same way with it and its mother. While in mother's arms a child will start taking an interest in this other baby, itself in its mother's arms. New bonds start forming, without ever losing that first and essential one in a child's life. La Maison Verte does not teach about separation, as has too often been preached. Quite the contrary! The child will learn that one never loses one's mother; she will always be with and be inside her child. This experience will only deepen and widen as it extends to others.

La Maison Verte is a place meant for children, very young children. The only requisite to be here is precisely to be a child with a parent. Deprived of his parent, a child simply is not there: you can see it in their eyes. If you pay attention you will see it; when their mother leaves, they retire to some place within themselves where there is a sort of retreat, they draw the curtains. You could also say that when she leaves they leave with her, and when she comes back, they come back. Even with the best of nannies you can see it happening.

In the end, it all adds up to this. La Maison Verte is a place where analysts and non- analysts can work together, under the same status, with the one and only condition: to be really there, at a time of life when the child is going through various pre-oedipal stages. The mother, through her child, is drawn back to the same time in her own life where her child is now. Maybe at this point we could venture, tentatively, to say that a Maison Verte person, to be there really, should at least have integrated her own personal story enough so as not to obstruct that of the mother and child at a time when the mother is being so deeply questioned about her own childhood and the child is learning to clear a path within his own life.

La Maison Verte is a social place, and open on the outside world. There is a door, meaning that there is an outside and an inside. This door is not always easy to open. One father recently said, "We often walk in backwards, we adults, although it helps us a lot." This is where the presence of psychoanalysis is seemingly just taken for granted. That presence, together with the rules of the place, brings to life things that would not happen elsewhere. A place meant for children, but where adults can find themselves questioned to the very core of their being. It is a place that is meant for children, but that can be very helpful for parents. Françoise Dolto explained at a conference in the 1950s:

> When I started psychoanalysis with children, this is what I did. The child sat across from me at a table, with pencil and paper. Parents had first come and told me what they deplored in their child's behaviour. I had no clinical experience except from my personal analysis with Laforgue and supervision with other Freudian psychoanalysts. I listened to the child, I asked for a drawing. I let him talk about the drawing and themes around it. I took in his gestures, his explanations, or confabulations, the way he behaved all the while, keeping in my mind also what the parents, or the teachers had to say about him during the past week. I never provided advice. I kept my intervention down to a minimum. You might say I was present, very present and very attentive. I listened and I encouraged the child to find his own associations, his own answers to his own questions. Since that time I have pursued my work as an analyst, but I never saw any significant difference between child and adult analysis. All this still remains essential to La Maison Verte.

It is a venue that allows for the exploration of a space that is larger than a therapeutic space. It has no therapeutic goal, but we see therapeutic results, because it is a listening space. What we hear is spoken through the body, drawings, and gestures. It is a space for hearing and words. Then the child will find its own way. For adults, it is always the child within themselves, whether at a foetal, oral, or whatever stage. The only thing is to be there with them. This experience affects psychoanalysts in an unexpected way. They develop the ability to hear the child within their adult clients. Words go around and listening goes around. If someone, somewhere, having been listened to, can listen in their turn to words, then words appear that have been stifled and which have become unutterable. But when such listening and words connect for a mother or child, the other mothers in the room at La Maison Verte hear something that they recognize about themselves. Then what has been repressed because it is too painful to bear can return through this life-giving relationship between mother, child, and the mother's own childhood.

At five o'clock it is rush hour, and other children gradually appear. Soon the place is fairly full. All of a sudden a little toddler, barely steady on his two legs, finds that he has lost his mother. He is a little babe in the wood. A moving forest of adult legs is all around him. He becomes distressed. I happen to see him and I know his mother is there, not far away. I tell him and he grabs my hand. We find our way to his mother who is sitting peacefully on the sofa in the second room. Along the way I tell him, "You know that here mothers never leave their babies. You are going to see her right away." Back on his mother's lap, he is instantly recomposed, reassured in just fifteen seconds. He wiggles away, a jolly little fellow. I just sit there with her, just a short while, thinking of something to say. But I do not say a word, because I suddenly realize she is weeping; tears flowing down her cheeks, she sobs uncontrollably. So I just remain silently. And now I hear her saying these extraordinary words: "You spoke to him." And after a long while she goes on, "You spoke to him. All of a sudden it came back to me how no one had talked to me when I was a child." And her whole life poured out. All the unspoken words, pent up in her for so long. It would have taken years, and with what difficulties, using classic psychoanalytic sessions, even to get to that point. It does happen that a mother seeing us talk to her baby and seeing the effect will say, "Could I do this for myself?"

Sometimes whoever speaks and is heard becomes like a first link in a chain, weaving a web where words at last become true. Sometimes, the ones who are best at listening are not Maison Verte people, the ones who are supposed to know. Instead it is another mother, and sometimes also another child. Maybe it is the presence of a third party, listening to both of them, whereas in other circumstances it might feel too dangerous. The child is the analyst. That is how, at La Maison Verte, what Dolto had practised, what we called her genius, what some called her magic, surprisingly keeps happening, even today when this magical analyst is no longer here in flesh and blood. When Freud started listening to his patients, he did not know where it would take him. When Dolto started listening to babies, she did not know how far it would go. Like the great explorers, they know something is there and they do not know what, but they still go forward. She went forward in a region she called "the archaic".

On the day that children go back to school, several babies who have been to the *crèche*, or *garderie* will also come to La Maison Verte. When they look through the glass doors and see babies on the floor, they refuse to enter, throwing themselves back in tears on to their mothers. To the child who is afraid to enter, I will say, "Here your mother will stay. She will not leave you, not even for one minute, not even to feed the parking meter or to buy a croissant. If she has to leave she will take you along and come back with you afterwards." A sort of calm sets in and we see the baby relaxing, confidence is restored, and the child can start enjoying all that this place has to offer. It will take a few visits to La Maison Verte before they discover the pleasure that can exist in the company of other children. Dolto always focused on the child's *allant–devenant* "going and becoming".

Today, however, the first little girl we see coming in is Emma. She is eighteen months old and is a very happy little person who instantly takes possession of the place as if she had never done anything else in her life. Her mother is a very charming young woman, all smiles. She has travelled quite a distance, at least an hour and a half, taking a bus, a train and three metros. This is their first visit. She found the name Maison Verte on the Internet in answer to her search: "Where to go in Paris with a small child?" She had no idea what it was and came out of curiosity, just to see. Mother and daughter are perfectly happy and content together, and really Emma is amazingly grown up. You would think she could easily go to school right now. Mother is a happy to stay at home. Father works late hours, but they are planning to move south, *en province*, in six months time. She has only vaguely heard about Françoise Dolto. She speaks easily, freely, while Emma is exploring with glee everything around her. It is a sunny day and there is no other child there yet. She does not seem to mind, but when they start arriving she is delighted and makes friends instantly. *Bisous*—kisses, all round, but only when she feels the other one agrees. All perfectly natural, free and easy. Just like the mother, in whose conversation there is just one little moment of shyness. "My husband and I wish for another child; I have decided to wait until Emma is three and a half." Well, that seems to leave time enough.

They will stay all afternoon, until closing time, Emma alternately playing, nursing, and, at times, sleeping in her mother's arms as there had not been time for a nap before leaving home. She is still being breast-fed, day and night. We will see Emma's mother, in the course of the afternoon, talking to other mothers, mostly, it seems, to those expecting a baby. Maybe she wants another baby sooner then she says.

One lovely moment: Philippe, four months old, his first visit, and he cries non-stop from the moment he arrives. His poor mother cannot do a thing about it and none of us can even come near. She heroically resists for over fifteen minutes and then finally gives up and decides to get up and leave. I feel sorry for her, she had come with great expectations, and we had had a little chat at the door when she arrived. As she is on her way out, I notice there is Pierre, same age, in his mother's lap, a regular visitor. It just crosses my mind they could be introduced to each other. All I do is say, "Philippe, this is Pierre and Pierre, this is Philippe." Believe it or not, Philippe stopped crying instantly, looked at Pierre, and they started talking to each other. It was so spectacular that everybody in the room, starting with the mothers, stopped talking and we all stood there, in a sort of incredibly amazed silence. Of their own accord, the two mothers laid both boys down side by side on the baby's carpet in the middle of the room. They turned to face each other, and talked for something like twenty minutes, after which Philippe's mother picked him up and left, with a big smile on her face. We will never know what they talked about, but it doesn't matter—they know.

CHAPTER NINE

La Casa Verde: speech, listening, welcoming in Françoise Dolto's work

Bice Benvenuto

> "The shop where it was set up was painted 'bluish-green', that's why it was called the Maison Verte. The pompous name 'Association for young children and their parents' was too long . . . No need to stick to this name though"
>
> (Dolto, 1986)

When Françoise Dolto wrote these words in 1985, she did not yet know that the contingency of the colour of some green paint in her house had given the name to what I would call "a new impact of psychoanalysis in the social". She presents herself as a psychoanalyst for today's discontent, as someone offering some oxygen to the lungs of the contemporary mind. When she created La Maison Verte in 1979, a place on the street where anyone could drop in, if accompanied by a child, she marked, in my opinion, a passage for psychoanalysis: from nineteenth century bourgeois rituals and posh consulting rooms to the streets, to meet people and their children. If Mohammed (the man in the street) will not go to the Mountain (of psychoanalysis) then the Mountain must come to Mohammed. This entails quite a shift of the analyst's position when working with the unconscious, something that has not repaid her with too much consideration from the psychoanalytical establishment. This includes most Lacanians, although she was, theoretically, very close to French psychoanalyst Jacques Lacan.

But Françoise Dolto was an original and a solitary thinker. Similarly to Winnicott, in the UK, she never established a school of her own and her name, like his, is a benchmark for analysts from different schools. If her fame was hardly recognized among her colleagues, it certainly was by the general public. Her radio programmes, during which she engaged in a dialogue with the audience, were such a success that she had to interrupt her practice for a while, as this media popularity was not compatible with her private analytical work. Many of her books were addressed to parents, and even children. In other words, she was a psychoanalyst who decided to speak to people outside orthodox analytical settings, and the creation of La Maison Verte is still a pioneering work, even though it is emulated all over the world, as far as the Far East. Her work is well rooted in the twentieth century's variegated psychoanalytical thought, especially her relation to, as well as her divergence from, Melanie Klein's object relations theory, Lacanian theory, and anti-psychiatry's social engagement.

The social

The link between the psychic and the social that Dolto emphasized may remind some of the anti-psychiatry movements of the 1960s, led by psychiatrists such as Laing in the UK, Guattari in France, or Basaglia in Italy. They produced a critique of the pathogenic family and, therefore, of society at large, as the ultimate cause of mental disturbance. This implied both a militant struggle with society and a libertarian approach to treatment in psychiatric hospitals and therapeutic communities. Although Dolto's sensitivity towards the social may have some family resemblance with that of anti-psychiatry, she did not hold a condemning position towards a malignant society. She saw both society and culture as holding the seeds of illness within itself; what Freud called the discontent of civilization. However, she also saw the social as a main source of its cure. There is no dichotomy between society and the individual, even for a social outcast. Being social animals, we cannot but find a way through this source of repression and of psychic enrichment at the same time. The social, of which each one of us is made, is not condemned, but welcome in La Maison Verte, in the form of people who drop in, children or grown-ups, the ill and the apparently healthy.

The earliest seed of the idea of La Maison Verte was set, I think, when she visited London during an internship in the Psychology Department of Great Ormond Street Hospital. She was struck by its Day Centre and the work they did with seriously ill children and their families. In the UK, she was also exposed to Kleinian thought, still little known in France. Later, her encounter with Jacques Lacan and his thought allowed her to re-elaborate the Kleinian theory of object relations. By questioning the fundamental role of the object in that theory, Dolto was instead to highlight the importance of the relation to the fundamental humanity of others, right from the start of life, even from the moment of conception. The psychic dimension is, for Dolto, a human and, therefore, social dimension, from the very beginning, as the genesis of the subject resides in their relation with that human being who takes care of them. The mother is not an anonymous carrier of a series of objects (breasts, nipples, etc.), but the real addressee of her baby's relation to her body. Objects in themselves cannot be relational; an object is defined by the fact that you cannot relate to it. We use things, even in order to hurt ourselves, but they do not relate to us. If we believe they do, they stop being objects and become representatives of some human involvement, as in fairy-tales, where animals, objects, and monsters act in the place of people. It is rarely the other way round. Maybe Kleinian objects, too (breast, nipples, penis, the inside of the body, etc.), take on a life of their own on the stage of the baby's phantasies because of a human mother who is the very flesh of those objects; it is not that she simply has them.

Dolto takes Freud's fundamental principle of the human psyche, the pleasure principle, seriously. In fact, she points out that we are marked by an original coexistence *in utero* with the mother, whose placenta is the source of nourishment and, therefore, of pleasure. She cannot see the foetus, or the baby who takes in mother's nourishment, as moved primarily by a will to destroy her breast, even if envy, greed, or any human feeling may later enter the scene. First of all, babies are moved by their desire to live, driven towards the mother, as towards their source of pleasure. Here, we have a radical turn away from Kleinian thought, even more than Lacan's. Indeed, at first Lacan had chosen Klein as an interlocutor in his new elaborations about both the imaginary and the status of the body in pieces, that is, lacking a primary cohesion.

The drives in Klein and Dolto

For Klein, the body of the infant has no cohesion, it does not "feel" whole. Such a fragmented body is dominated by the death drive, which reverberates in the infant's delirious "phantasies" of a destructive and sadistic nature. The only feeble counterpart to these feelings and phantasies is a still potential and shapeless ego, which is developing very slowly. Still, only this weak ego will be the vehicle towards the life drive. For Klein, the life drive, which strives for cohesion, coincides also with what is good, in an always uneven struggle with the evil of the death drive. There is an explicit Manichaeism of the drives in Klein, especially at the beginning of life, when the undisputed master is death.

Françoise Dolto's psychoanalytical ethics takes a different turn by turning again to Freud and his theory of the drives. According to him, the death drive is not an independent and active force that wants to annihilate the object with greed and envy, it rather works as a limit, a brake, on the cohesive activity of Eros; it is inertia, pleasure's mortification. The death drive gathers its force from what Freud called "dams", the rocks of repression tied to traumatic events, which block the flow of libido, that is, of pleasure. In this perspective, where Klein sees cannibalism, even in the foetus feeding on the maternal placenta, Dolto sees a self-nourishing activity, the foetus's drive to live. In the same way, the baby sucking at the breast is, for Dolto, primarily a vital and sensual necessity, while for Klein, sucking is primarily a vampire activity, an expression of omnipotent will over the object. Are children who play with guns driven by a death drive, or are they practising their life drive instead, that is, their capacity to aim at a target, to go for it. From Dolto we learn that a certain degree of aggressiveness is not a prerogative of the death drive alone, it is needed by life itself in order to subsist in the face of all kinds of threats to our existence. That is why most of us eat animals and fight against what resists our will, and so on. The life drive runs on beyond the good and the evil of our relative human morality. If there is an ethical stance in Dolto, it is her swinging the scales towards a desire to live and fighting for it, rather than a peaceful, obedient giving up, which is indeed closer to death, a stance that is starting to be recognized, at an empirical and clinical level, by a number of analysts, who seem to realize that destructive, guilt-provoking interpretations do not lead very far therapeutically.

Feeling and sensing

Yet there is a subtle common thread between Klein and Dolto that I would like to highlight. Klein recognized the evidence of an original "sensitivity" of the infant's mind that she called "feelings". The newborn "feels" the experiences which come either from outside or from inside their bodies. The Anglo-Saxon term "feeling", which has no correspondence in Romance languages, covers many meanings, such as affects, sentiments, and even love, as when you say, "I have feelings for you", and, in a more concrete way, it can mean "sensing". This is the term Dolto chooses to describe the baby's early perceptions.

Sensing, besides being the activity of the senses, is also a "making sense" of them. If, according to Lacan, we are born into language, we are also born into the discourse of the flesh and its senses. We cannot exile the body from our mind and consider it, or parts of it, an object, neutral matter to be moulded by our minds. The living body can never be an object, or just a series of objects. According to Lacanian theory, there are, in fact, two kinds of body: a visible one, the image of the body that a mirror returns to us, and an invisible body, made up of the parts of the body that are excluded by the narcissistic mirror image. The infant's body, even though still a premature and fragmented one, is not neutral matter. It is endowed with the senses that give it a sensorial cohesion and a way of communication through sensorial body codes exchanged with the mother. Messages are exchanged through touching, gazing, her voice, their smell. If the infant's body is plunged from the beginning in the water of language, its new amniotic liquid which places it in a larger background, it would be an empty concept if we did not take into account that, beside language with its universal system of signifiers, there is a sensual order with its universal codes pertaining to living "matter". We could call it the sensual language of the living, which has nothing to do with either the inert body of medicine, or the objectifying discourse of science. We could infer a homology between language and sensual codes, as Teresa Brennan did in her *The Transmission of Affect*, as they both pre-exist and inhabit the subject.

In her most theoretical book, *L'image inconsciente du corps*, Dolto gives us an example of the importance of sensual attachment in relation to the mother and breast-feeding in the case of little Agnes. After five days of breast-feeding Agnes's mother is taken ill and goes to hospital. From then on the girl stops feeding and drinking and starts losing weight. Dolto suggested to the father, who consulted her, that he should take one of the mother's garments from the hospital and put it around the baby's neck. In this way she would be able to smell her mother's shirt before being given the bottle. In fact, little Agnes was starving herself to death not so much because of her mother's absence, but because of the lack of her mother's smell, which Agnes had attached to the pleasure of feeding. With the smell of her mother's shirt, she was able to resume her vital functions. Together with the mother, she had lost her primary narcissism, which could not yet mirror the imaginary unity of the body, or a sense of *sameness* given by the consistency of her sensual relation with the mother. The baby senses the body as rooted in the repetitive relation with another, which accompanies her breathing, nutrition, touch, hearing. These more or less subtle perceptions have the property of counterbalancing the trauma of separation by assuring continuity with the sensorial universe the baby experienced in the womb.

The image

Long before the encounter with the mirror, the child has already gained a sense of cohesiveness thanks to mother's gaze. This is the baby's first mirror, according to Winnicott. Most analysts give an undue priority to the sense of sight, the sense closest to consciousness. Dolto's thought is that an imaginary cohesion of the infant's body is offered by "sensing" rather than by "appearing". The most important organizer of primary narcissism, the image, is, for Dolto, an unconscious image of the body. It does not belong to a self-reflective subject; it appears before the baby can say *I*. Not being the ego image, it is, rather, linked to the individual's unconscious history, to the forms of her libidinal relation with relevant others. Dolto defines the unconscious image of the body as a living synthesis of our erogenous experiences, the incarnation of the memory of our relational life. When she defines it as, "a symbolic incarnation of the desiring subject", she seems to conceive the unconscious image as a space where the symbolic can meet the real of the body, the flesh, that is also always an outcast, in psychoanalysis. It is not to be confused with a scheme of the human body that is common to the human species as a *gestalt*, but it is a developing image. It changes according to a psychic progression of narcissistic events, as well as traumatic ones, such as weaning, separations, and disappointments.

Dolto adopts the Lacanian concept of desire as being the motor of the dynamics of life, but she links it also to a dynamics of the image. For example, the foetus that, according to Klein, is like a vampire sucking mother's nourishment, is acting according to a "base image", linked to the basic desire to live, whereas the suckling who actively searches for the breast and sticks eagerly to the nipple is under the sway of a "functional image", linked to the accomplishment of pleasure in her nourishment. And when, later, the well-fed baby looks for the mother's face, or other people's smiles, they are giving evidence of a "sthenic image", which is pushing them towards the others in order to achieve pleasure beyond the need for food. Notwithstanding the dynamic and composite nature of this image, one of its components is a rather fixed one, the "base image", the most archaic image concerning the foetus and, later, the baby's breathing and feeding. This basic image resists change while at the same time allowing the child to perceive her body in a continuity of being. Even though illusory, this sense of continuity is the basis for our perception of existence. A body filled with narcissism is an eroticized, enjoying body, therefore existent.

But, as we do not just exist in a pure erotic state of being (for Heidegger, this is the poor world of animals such as the tick, only absorbed in its blood sucking), humanization starts with a desire to go beyond one's own body, ever in search of new objects, of a richer world. Such a desire is reflected in a dynamic image that opens on to a shared pleasure with some other who can add words to their exchange. Dolto saw a little girl of four who had stopped using her hands and would eat and take things only straight from her mouth. One day Dolto handed her some plasticine and said, "Take it with the mouth of your hand." And the girl seized it with her hand and put the plasticine into her mouth, as if Dolto had appealed to that erogenic part of the body, the mouth, which the girl had saved out of her mutilated body image, in order to eat and survive. Dolto had appealed to her desire to live, which was still active in her mouth, by lending it to her hands with her words. The hands, which grasp and reach out for things, had stopped being part of a functioning image of her body that had regressed instead to a *basic* image of oral survival.

It is evident that this kind of image is neither the Freudian image of the body's surface nor the Lacanian mirror image, both being similarly the origin of the ego. The Doltonian image constitutes not an exterior unity of the body, but a "sense" of existing. It would, thus, belong to the id, to be considered not a cauldron of chaotic drives, but marked, from the very beginning, by the presence of others, a "relational id", as it were, not at all alien to a symbolic universe. Said and unsaid words get incarnated in the body and offer new elements of organization of the image by changing it. But words also contribute to splitting the image further and further from its sensual source. As much as the image splits from the real original body, those parts of body that are left out become matter without an image, a body as good as an object which one possesses, but one is not. These discarded parts of the body resemble what Kristeva calls "abject" in her semiotics, unimaginable and unnameable parts of one's own and of mother's body, some living matter which gets lost in the construction of the image.

This appears rather clearly in the case of a patient of mine. Elisa suffers from obsessional indecisions; among these, the indecision between two men and the one between two jobs. Both indecisions reflect an impossible choice between the calming and reassuring presence of her mother and the judging presence of her father, who demands maximum sacrifices to achieve success. Her mother survived a particularly aggressive breast cancer she developed ten months after Elisa's birth. The cancer returned, and can still return, while many surgical operations to scrape the tumour out of her breast, shoulder, and arm have left her mutilated. The Sword of Damocles of her mother's death still accompanies her today. Elisa is her doctor and nurse, completely devoted to her. She calls her mother's warm body "my hidden light", but a light that hides her mutilation and always on the verge of dying out. In the end, between the two young men, she chose to marry the motherly one and started to burn with the desire for a child. After a further excruciating indecision between having a child or her career, she decided not to have a child and keep her job. However, she became pregnant anyway. After three months, she discovered that the child was dead inside her and had to be "scraped" out. She used this word that is used in Italian to mean an abortion. It was scraped out of her body, in the same way as the cancer had been scraped out of her mother's body. In the end, her body's demand for a child had succumbed to the demands for her career. The demand of her "stupid" pregnant woman's body was shut up with an operation. It was a final sacrifice to the altar of her father's intelligence. The career took the upper hand only until a few months later, when she got pregnant again with a little girl whom she was very happy to keep. Her previous abortion had functioned as a realized castration, something that had never taken place before for her, because her mother's body was mutilated in the real, traumatically taken away from her and then shamefully hidden. Her own body could not go through the time scansions of weaning and of accepting the alienation as well as the narcissism of separated bodies, because, to her, separation is a danger of real mutilation and even death.

This case throws some light on the logic of the flesh that, not being an object of inert and thoughtless matter, can speak for her much more quickly than her endless doubting would allow. There is a sensual mind in the flesh that requires an ear and a reply that recognizes it; otherwise it will carry out its outcast's discourse in the form of a somatic catastrophe. Body and language spring from the same cause, yet their vicissitudes make them divert in a different timing, or converge in unexpected ways at certain points, which

Lacan called *points de capiton*. Elisa's pathological doubting emphasizes a subject fuelled by different systems, different logics: the discourse of the flesh, of the image, and of language are hardly aligned with each other; they mingle or set themselves apart in odd oppositions and conflicts. It was not easy in Elisa's analysis to know which was saying what.

After a brief but intense sensual relation Elisa had with her mother, the cancer disfigured the image of her mother's body, which was hidden away from her ever since. There was never a name for her mother's mutilated body, nor for her own: a no entry zone for linguistic signifiers. The safety net of language did not cover her mother's hidden mutilation; language got stuck and became inoperative at the level of the body's wound. No words, no edifying names for the feminine body. The woman is stupid and shameful, as was signified by her father's insults. Her unconscious body image was a mortified and sacrificial one that contributed to turn Elisa's first pregnancy into a deadly activity. But, even though hidden and forbidden, her body had maintained the original integrity of her "base" image that she had constructed as a baby with her mother before the cancer. In analysis, she had to go through a process of mourning of that "perfect" time of her early infancy and to begin producing revised images of it. As there no words to describe her mother's deadly experience, it was left to her pregnant body to give voice to her death drive with the dead baby, as well as to her life drive, with the birth of a daughter. Her body was literally acting (and speaking) for her.

The death drive thrives on repression and exclusions from unconscious images, by transforming the logic of our primordial appetites and pleasures into somatic symptoms and illnesses. Very often the death drive finds refuge in devastating "phantasies", which replace the "abject" parts of the body with statements of mortification and aggressive, or masochistic, perversities. This is evident in those cases where a real threat against our primary narcissism forces the production of fantasies of bowels, breath, and urethral persecutions.

Francesca, for example, still complained of night enuresis at the age of forty. A memory was recollected during analysis, when once, aged six, she had been seduced by her father. Since then Francesca had always been expecting a sequel to the interrupted seduction, having interpreted it as a love-affair with her father, even though the event was put away in a secret drawer; deeply buried as if down a mine, in her own words. Something about it only leaks from her urethra. Still now her life is kept in a hysterical suspension as she had been for most of her childhood, waiting for her father to make a choice between mother and herself. Her conscious construction of the trauma is not about an experience of child abuse, but about having been abandoned after seduction. The intrusion of her father's fingers in her vagina had provoked an imaginary dislocation between her genital and urethral image in her chronic enuresis. She is now in a relationship with a married man who, like her father, never leaves his wife, while keeping her as a "concubine". She had a child from him, and even if he recognized the child, he could not tell his family and friends. One day she came to the session saying, "A name has been given to the devil." In fact, the child's father had told his family about his newborn, thus accepting responsibility for his act, something her father had never done in relation to the abuse. Once she felt that her child's father had given a recognized existence, both to the child and to his relation with Francesca, she was able to tell her mother about what she now saw as her father's abuse, for the first time after nearly forty years. Calling things with their names is not the same as stating a name, it is rather giving that name a place in the family history, whether on a straight genealogical line, or on more complex lines. Although this father had given her daughter a bureaucratic recognition, only when he could tell his family about his newborn could he allow Francesca and the child to realign the axis of language with their existence.

Another case described by Dolto is one where the proper name was in question. Armand was taken away from an orphanage, adopted when he was eleven months old, and had his name changed to Frederic. Later, the child was unable to learn at school and could only write the letter "A". When Dolto learned about his original name she told him about it, but with no evident result. In one session Dolto started to call out his original name, "Armand, Armand", as if from afar and looking away from him. The child followed her gaze, which was moving about until their two gazes met. Only then was Dolto able to interpret his name change effectively. Frederic was able to recognize Armand only when the name was called out in an anonymous way, from a "voice over" and without a gaze that could reflect him. This was the same situation as in the orphanage from which he came. Frederic and Armand could meet when the two gazes met. Frederic could find his lost archaic identity not when he was simply informed of it by Dolto herself, but only when his name had been called out from the place to which his previous identity had belonged.

This is true not only of Armand, as there was no archaic state of nature, or original trauma over which culture has not laid its net of names, or failed to do so. Dolto applies the Freudian term "castration", the Oedipal process of giving up the mother as an erotic object, to the gradual loss of original previous enjoyments, from the oral to the genital stage. These "castrations", in the plural, are not painless, but the child can be allowed to express the pain, to cry or fight with the "castrator", rather than locking it up in a drawer, as Francesca had done. We have to negotiate our relation to the world's chaos and can, of course, choose neurotic solutions. The three cases above show a failure in negotiation which relegates lost, or disappointing, parts of their world, such as mother's mutilated breast for Elisa, the loss of the father because of incest for Francesca, his own original name and identity for Frederic, to the world of those Kleinian phantasies where inert objects are in the way of our ever changing relation with the living.

If we are marked from the beginning by those who welcome us (or not) into the world, the primordial relation to the mother is already the core of a social link, a link that can easily degenerate into a loop-knot, a seducing as well as an oppressive enclosure. What to do? Dolto would say, "Go to the Maison Verte with your child and . . . socialize".

Beyond the threshold: La Maison Verte

First of all, La Maison Verte offers a place to enter. Once you have crossed its threshold, you find yourself in a familiar, intimate place, but, like "the other place" of the unconscious, it feels foreign at the same time. You are unlikely to cross it unless you have some sort of demand, or suffering, but you do not necessarily have to be conscious of it. If some may already have a precise demand, or necessity for it, others come across it accidentally and make the first step towards its threshold, just out of curiosity. The offer will have created a demand. As in a street market, you look around in case you find something you stopped looking for, or you had not looked for yet. A certain disengagement is the peculiarity of contemporary attitudes to any psychic approach. Even those who have been sent there by a doctor, or school, may not have a personal demand for it. They have not chosen the place, one among many other therapeutic possibilities on the market. The objects today's market culture imposes as desirable have created a sort of obstruction in the freedom of desire. This obstruction constitutes the first resistance to any therapeutic venture, and La Maison Verte makes no exception, apart from the fact that it requires no such an engagement; it does not rely on a conscious engagement, or idealization of psychoanalysis. It would rather offer the possibility of crossing the threshold. In fact, beyond the threshold there is nothing but an opening, finding oneself is just an option on the other side.

This sense of entering a different space was somehow confirmed by the children who would come to the Casa Verde, a Maison Verte-like space that the Dolto Association had set up for a few years in a nursery school in Rome two afternoons per week after school hours. You could see those children, who, until then, had been all day inside their nursery school, running into the Casa Verde room rather than running towards their parents who had come to pick them up. Instead, the parents had to chase them into the Casa Verde, which consisted of a very big room with no windows, but with trees and skies painted on the walls. The children, all from a rather well-to-do neighbourhood, would keep running around the room for a while, excited by the many simple toys scattered around, laughing and asking questions as if thrilled by such a place, lacking in expensive toys, high tech gadgets, or nice food. Mothers also found it extraordinary that, after a whole school day, the children wanted to stay in yet another classroom rather than to go outside, go swimming, or do any other physical activity. The park became our rival on fine days when some mothers had to make the decision whether to give in and stay in an enclosed room (what the Casa Verde ultimately was), or insist and take their children out into the open. But the children seemed to have immediately sensed the threshold effect of La Maison Verte, wonderland does not need parks and swimming pools, but the freedom to play with one's own fantasies, to speak "non-sense" and be responded to. They sensed permission, not to some kind of entertainment, but to another kind of pleasure, which the parents were slower to accept.

The claustrophobic mother

Once Marc, aged about four, broke into the Casa Verde room like a rocket, and his mother, who was chasing him, stopped abruptly outside the threshold, calling him back. As the child ignored her, I went over to her, on the other side of the door to where she was standing, and invited her to come in and fetch her child if she wanted to. She explained in a gracious way that she could not, as she was claustrophobic and could not stand crowded enclosed places. In the meantime, Marc was running around clumsily and falling dangerously over other children. He was really the one who was filling up the room with his anxiety-provoking actions. Eventually, someone managed to bring him over to his mother, who remained outside the threshold, and they left . . . and returned the next time.

Initially, their second visit was similar to the first: mother at the threshold, Marc rampaging about inside the room. There were desperate attempts on the mother's part to catch him when he was nearer the door, but to no avail. Eventually, she seemed resigned to waiting for Marc until he might be ready to go. At one point I went up to her with a cup of tea, which she gladly accepted and drank, and, while chatting to me, she made a step over the threshold and stood there. After this step, each time she came, this mother started to make a step further into the room. She could enter the room as much as we had accepted her outsider position (in relation to the Casa Verde as to her child). The Casa Verde had to make an extension outside its threshold in order to include her; we turned ourselves into go-betweens through that phobic space dividing mother and child. After a couple of weeks, she was sitting in the middle of the room chatting to other parents, and became one of the Casa Verde's most regular frequenters that year.

No one mentioned her claustrophobia again, not until the Casa Verde's last day before the summer holidays. She came over to me to say good-bye and thank me for what we had done for her child. Marc had become much more manageable, she said, since he had started coming here. Maybe thanks to her having bravely managed to be inside the Casa Verde with him, I said. Startled she replied, "True, I forgot my claustrophobia. Has it gone, then?" I replied with a question. "Do you remember when it started?" She grew thoughtful, and then had a start. "Since Marc was born." We said no more, but smiled at each other and said good-bye.

Isn't it strange that this exchange of words took place at the end of the process and after the symptom had gone, without this mother even realizing it herself? Was it a cure? She wondered, so do we. From our perspective, each new step she had been making on this side of the threshold was also a step inside an unconscious space where she was kept roped to her child, a no-breathing space. When this child had run into the Casa Verde room he was possibly taking refuge in it and, with his dangerous behaviour, was asking for help. Probably the Casa Verde was also standing for the child's desire to have the mother at that safe distance, but, with his behaviour, he was forcing his mother gradually to come closer to him by her own will and to overcome her fear, helped by the mediation of the Casa Verde's people. She could be with him as long as she was free of being in company of other people at the same time. I think that the Casa Verde had provided a breathing space for their survival via a silent speech, by putting into action their quest: our cups of tea, brought to her outside the door, had made an extension of the room up to the threshold in order to welcome her claustrophobia.

If we define cure by the disappearance of the symptom, this mother seemed cured of her phobia. From an orthodox psychoanalytical point of view, as there were neither interpretations nor working through of the causes of her symptom, it could not be an analytical treatment. This view is challenged in the Maison Verte. Interpretations can be a means, among others, to facilitate a psychic working through, or to help lessen the anxiety and the resistance that goes with it, but do not cause the opening of the unconscious by themselves, although their conscious and often standard speech form cannot but be addressed to the patient's consciousness. Lacan went closer to this problem when he identified in the analytical "act" the spring of psychoanalysis: constructed interpretations leave their place to "interventions", free-floating responses to the other's unconscious questions. La Maison Verte takes on the idea of a space where to allow the unconscious of anyone who drops in, through La Maison Verte "hosts" and, most of all, of the psychoanalysts themselves, to live and express their questions. The general rule is that there are three people welcoming the children and their parents, called *Acceuillantes*, in English, literally "welcomers or greeters". La Maison Verte "hosts" can be voluntary workers, teachers, trainees, paediatricians, etc. There is always at least one psychoanalyst and one male Maison Verte host. More than well formulated verbal interpretations, the unconscious needs the living immediate response of the other. False responses, commonplace chat, and power abuses happen here as anywhere else, but not being a one-to-one therapy, abuses and suggestions can always be challenged by someone else. One is in the public square of one's own mind, and the working through is the effect of transference to such a place, *agora*—a place of open assembly and at the same time, closed *cloister*.

Still, La Maison Verte is officially designed simply as a means of prevention against children's mental disturbance by way of socialization. Even if the use of the words "prevention" and "socialization" do not mean much in psychoanalytical jargon, they nevertheless function as a message for the guests: that anyone, whether they consider themselves ill or not, has a chance to drop in. Contemporary civilization does not spare anyone, and anyone can freely attend and benefit from it in different, individual ways. If civilization holds the seed of illness, the strategy of socialization aims at the seed by dealing with primary relations. But the seeds have already their more or less evident symptoms, so that we could say that prevention is already therapy as far as one intervenes in a non-invasive way at the root of the pathogenic knot. And, in this sense, La Maison Verte cures.

Even if it was found to be particularly effective for an easier inclusion into schools of children from immigrant or socially disadvantaged families, psycho-social problems do by no means stop at the less privileged cases in society. We need to reflect on transformations of family ties that have deep effects on the psychic development of children in contemporary society. The phenomenon of a growing isolation of the nuclear family, and more often of single parents, highlights a form of decline of the paternal function, along with a transformation of the maternal one, as well as an instability of sexual identities. The timing and the forms of the formative experiences children encounter in their relation with others are rapidly changing. While we are losing many of the rites of passage which once marked our psychic and social life, new ones are either too uncertain, or not emerging at all. What is replacing the order of the traditional family that, in its own debatable way, built a protective system for children when facing traumatic experiences linked to inevitable losses and separations? Is there a new structure supporting both the working mothers, who lack the safety net of the extended family, and children and babies who have to face their primary separation from these mothers? Is there any form of thought-out process (both psychically and legally) of caring for all those children, now mostly left to themselves, who undergo that most painful but frequent rite of passage, the process of their parents' divorce? Is there any kind of safety-net for the neglect and marginalization of immigrant families and their children? There are gaps in the structure of today's family and society that make the child's need for adaptation more and more onerous for the human psyche. This is fertile ground, even for standard or well-to-do families, because of the suffering caused by new silent symptoms spreading in the contemporary era: depressive syndromes, feeding problems, addictions, juvenile delinquency.

La Maison Verte was set up as an intermediate environment between the family and the nursery school, and intermediate to any other form of forced separation of children from their family (e.g., hospitalization, parents' divorce, mourning, etc.). Its preventative function consists in its providing an environment in which to prepare for these inevitable moments of separation, during which psychic disorders in children most commonly manifest themselves. *Psychosomatic illnesses, enuresis, phobias, and personality changes are often signals of distress* the child sends, and, if they go unnoticed, they will follow their course towards more serious illnesses, both psychic and somatic.

In over two decades of experience, La Maison Verte has proved the effectiveness of a phase of *primary socialization*, consisting in the inevitable introduction of the child to a broader social context than the fusion–relationship with the mother or the small family circle. It is called "primary" socialization because it still takes place in presence of the mother. This is why her presence, or that of any other adult family member representing her, is the crucial condition for participation in La Maison Verte activities. Even in cases of a brief attendance, at the time of an inevitable separation, there is none of the traumatic anxiety-inducing effects so common in the majority of children. Separation from the mother or from the family with no preparation is a brutal passage for the child, a trauma, in other words, and, as such, can lead to malfunctions in biological rhythms, sleep, and/or digestion. Malfunctions that, if not understood in time, will develop into more serious pathogenic effects.

What is a Maison Verte?

It is not a place of treatment, counselling, or re-education, but one for play and meeting people. Through an experience of conviviality, the child is included in a gradual socialization process respectful of his family identity. Children, even at a very early age, manage to tolerate separation on the basis of a process of becoming more autonomous from their mothers, a process that gradually develops from the day of birth. But this delicate process of independence inevitably generates in children the anxiety of a loss of the integration of their body image, which is still linked to the presence of the mother, to a sensual relation to her. Separation from the mother causes in children the anguish of losing their original resource, therefore of losing themselves. The presence of others is crucial to encouraging children's separation process, as they gradually develop an unconscious image of the body more independent from the mother's image, with a gender of their own and a place in the family group. Through the mother–child–Maison Verte host dialogue, starting from the degree of independence children have already acquired, they are made ready for contact with other children and adults and to freely experiment in that small outside world La Maison Verte can represent for them.

Dolto's bet was that an ethical and analytical position before the child's words and knowledge can be maintained also in a setting which is not an individual psychoanalytic session. Here, those others who surround the child in their daily life, parents, siblings, grandparents, nannies, among whom words are not flowing well, are invited to speak, too. It is not a family therapy; it is not their behaviour or family dynamics that is the object of interest or of interpretation. Speech is entrusted to the guests, both children and adults, but there is a third party who is listening, not only a Maison Verte host, but also other mothers and children. One speaks to another, but is also addressing a third. La Maison Verte hosts are often a medium for an otherwise impossible dialogue; by lending their ears to those who do not want to hear, they turn themselves into means by which to elaborate and act on what is happening. The most hurt or hurting feelings, family stories, or even a temper tantrum, may acquire new meanings if there are others involved in the action, by either challenging or reassuring comments or just listening. If a certain degree of anxiety gets released by articulating what bothers you, the presence of a listener can challenge and change a pathogenic perspective. Speech can be addressed to the daughter or the father, but for a transference effect it passes through the Maison Verte host, who has the function of holding the message-words by making themselves means of access to one's own words and the other's. A Maison Verte host embodies somehow the threshold effect, of a hole through which words pass. This is equivalent, in a different setting, to the state of mind typical of the psychoanalyst, their "floating attention" to true and lying words (lies are only the other side of truth) that float, too; pieces of truth that appear and then vanish. Perhaps truth is this very floating, its own becoming (what was true yesterday is no longer true today). We can get stuck in an anachronistic fixed truth and the neurotic child or family are characterized by a fixation to a dogmatic and inexorable truth. The neurotic is not Heraclitian.

Words are not necessarily meant by Dolto as vocal messages, but as what can be communicated also in silence, in between the lines, while playing with the Maison Verte host, in a fight, or in the absence of a dialogue. The guest knows that the absence of words or the excesses of their behaviour will be registered by the host as well as by other guests, that some pieces of truth have been lodged there to be found again when they return. Perhaps just the time of a visit, of a chat. This is how Dolto wanted to engage the unconscious in an informal, disengaged setting. It might not work for some, for others it may work as the courtyard of the therapeutic palace, but for many it can be the right place of elaboration, their therapeutic workshop.

Words and listening

To listen without bias or prejudice to the messages that children and adults exchange during play activities and conversation is at the heart of psychoanalytic intervention in La Maison Verte. A Maison Verte host becomes the "obstetrician" of those small truths that escape the guests, whether adults or children, by participating in their activities and responding verbally or with actions within the immediacy of the situations as they present themselves. A Maison Verte host's intervention should aim at clarifying the sense of the affective or verbal messages that the guests will send during their interaction. There will be no interpretative intervention in the classical sense, or any verbal descriptions of psychic conflicts, but there will be a verbalization opening new non-pathogenic possibilities in the communication of conflicts. With, for example, a boy who is afraid of falling off a tricycle, there will be no interpretation of his separation phobia or birth trauma, but he will be told, "Even if you do fall off, I'll be there to hold you, together with your mum. Have a go if you feel like it." This type of discourse is not an interpretation, but a form of verbal intervention that speaks directly to the unconscious of the boy who is afraid of being abandoned by, or of abandoning, his mother. It implicitly communicates: (1) that the message of his being afraid of falling off if he has no support, if his mother should be absent, has been received; (2) that his mother is still there to support him, even if she delegates someone else to do so: nanny, dad, or even a Maison Verte host, for example; (3) that he has all the time he wants to prepare to do it on his own. It is a type of apparently very simple response that acknowledges the boy's anxiety and that works as a stimulus towards action and that can, at the right moment, restart a previously inhibited motor blockage. The inhibition of motility due to separation anxiety already traces a pathologic trajectory on which it is possible to intervene before it proceeds undisturbed into chronicity.

Listening is not only a Maison Verte host's prerogative: "A child who plays is a child who listens," says Dolto. So, as children play with water, sand, or whatever, they will be included in the conversation if its subject matter has anything to do with their stories, their conception, or the projects their parents have for them. Thus, children are given the opportunity to give their opinion. It is by taking their wishes and sufferings into consideration, and by verbalizing them without reprimand, that these can be given a sense that is not humiliating but humanizing (to use a term dear to Dolto).

For example, if a mother talks about her difficulties during her boy's birth, even in accepting him, a Maison Verte host could say to him, while he is playing and listening, "Did you hear how ill your mum was after your birth, and how she feels much better now because she's so fond of you?" Assuming that children discover their identity through their mothers' affective messages and words, a Maison Verte host will be able to take in these messages and try to clarify them with both child and adult. "It is the attempt to give words to what is forbidden or impossible to say," said Françoise Dolto. To offer words and accept them, even when they express unspeakable hidden truths for the person, because they cause punishment and abandonment anxieties (what is forbidden), or because the words to say something are not yet known (impossible to say).

This was the case with Mathew, who was only three months old when he first came to the Casa Verde with his mum. The mother was anxious about having to raise the baby by herself—her husband was working in the north of Italy and her family living in another town. Her big problem was the baby's sleeping habits: he slept mostly during the day, when his mother was out at work, and was awake at night demanding his mother's presence. Because of her lack of sleep her manners were hasty; she would often let him cry throughout whole parts of the night, already wondering when to start weaning him. But what about Mathew? What kind of work can you do with such a young baby? I talked to him while he was in his mother's arms, explaining to him what she was telling me about his sleep. "Of course, you want your mum with you at night, as she has to be away most of the day. Maybe she could be with you before you sleep and then she can go to sleep in a bed very near you all night. If you wake up you can see her and don't need to cry. She is so tired; she has to sleep, but near you.". His sleep got better and his mother got into the habit of spending some time near his bed, talking to him and reassuring him.

A couple of months later the mother came up to me with a tired face and said that his sleep had got suddenly much worse, nothing could calm him down, and she was exhausted from lack of sleep. "Has anything happened recently?" I asked impulsively. Some silence, then, embarrassed, she "confessed" that she had started weaning him from her breast. While she was telling me this Mathew, who was in mother's arms, threw his arms at me for the first time (I had never taken him in my arms before, although many others did). His mother begged: "He wants to come to you." I took him and, incredibly, he put his head on my shoulder and started to sob and sob like a grown-up in despair. Startled and moved, his mother said, "He really wanted to tell you how he feels. He's never sobbed like that before." With these words she had given me permission to communicate to him my understanding of his suffering, a suffering we all go through: the loss of the breast. "It feels so terrible now, but later you will enjoy the new food, growing bigger and playing with dad at the Casa Verde." He fell asleep on my shoulder, his new object of pleasure and communication. My words were simply acknowledging his distress at not being able to appeal to his senses, which were suddenly deprived of their object of smell and taste. I was trying to help him to make sense of his experience of loss, because words help making sense of the sensual gap.

What about the parents?

Separation is not only a problem for the child. In fact, it is often the mother, too, who finds this separation, or at least recognizing her child's independence, difficult. The mother, or whoever acts in her place, will take advantage of the environment in various ways: like the children with the games, adults will find time to relax and take their minds off their everyday problems together with other parents and *La Maison Verte* hosts themselves, who will welcome them warmly with a hot drink, for example, or a slice of a cake brought by another parent. I was struck by the fact that all children, even the youngest who never drank tea, could not wait for their cup at teatime (a ritual I have imported from England). They drink it eagerly, not because they like its bitter taste; tea, in this case, is not like a demand for food or sugared dummies, but for that sweet–bitter taste that is part and parcel of the process of losing primordial sweet pleasures for new, bitter, but exciting, ones.

This is not a place where psychotherapists, doctors, or trainees begin a treatment, or one where they act as guardians of law and order, but simply one where they make their competencies, both professional and human, available to those who want to make use of them. The Maison Verte host's discreet participation, with no prescriptive or interpretative function, will consist in making parents feel free to chat about "frivolous matters" while giving them the opportunity to talk about themselves, to be truthful in their relationship, whether difficult or not, with their child. The effect of the conversations will be that some hidden truths will unintentionally be set free. Once they are uttered, even the most unpleasant truths change their anxiety-inducing and painful quality, taking not only the children, but the parents, too, on a search for new, less pathogenic solutions.

Most symptoms and disturbances suffered by very small children, those still in osmosis with their mothers, echo the difficulties suffered by the mother or the parents as a couple: they are, therefore, extremely vulnerable to others' moods and to any imbalances in the environment immediately surrounding them, and these may mark them for a long time. As they are at an age when one's table of reference is being formed and one that will inform all future experience, it is easy to see how important this work of support and clarification is for the parents themselves, because it is through an improvement of the adult's conditions that a child can often be helped. A relaxed environment lends itself to the expression of everyday suffering and to its being played down to the advantage not only of the adult, but especially of the child, who will feel freed from the maternal anguish until then unexpressed, but painfully felt. A vicious circle is thus broken, a tacit complicity of the mother–child couple, where each absorbs and makes their own the other's anguish. Once this potentially pathological bond of dependence is undone, the pair tends to open up to others and is thus ready to be introduced gently and not brutally, as is usually the case, into the community and is made ready for future separations.

Tom, two and half years old, stopped going to the nursery where both Tom and his mother had been unable to separate. He is an exceptionally articulate child, but speaks only to his mother and other adults. Sometimes, when some other child manages to involve him in a game, just when he seems about to let go and enjoy playing, he stops and goes to mother, asking if it is time to go home. At first, the mother would obey with no delay and state, "Tom wants to go." But they kept coming regularly, both trying to negotiate the possibility of untying from each other in each other's presence. Gradually, the mother stopped the habit of springing up and leaving as soon as Tom showed anxiety by asking to go home. She started asking him to wait, because she was enjoying talking to other mothers and did not want to leave right then. They took their time to overcome the anxiety arising at any attempt of being freer from each other, of enjoying relating to others, of opening up their enclosed circle. Unlike their experience in the nursery, where it was decided when the time was right for them to physically separate, the Casa Verde simply allowed them to separate while being together. The presence of others who welcome you and your child without judgement or prescriptions, changes the pathogenic perspective within which that relation is imprisoned.

The freedom to speak does not include the freedom to do whatever one likes. Inflicting pain on the other, on one's child or on oneself, can happen in La Maison Verte; in fact, for some, it can be the reason why they come. The message which gradually gets through is that one may feel bad and say so, but not intentionally hurt someone else, even if only out of fear or because of unexpressed frustrations. Failed communications, failing to understand one another, especially between mother and child, are part of life. Words on what is being experienced at a particular moment, in the present, is a characteristic of human beings alone, and the freedom to use these words even to express one's own most forbidden desires, slows down the time of the impulse towards pathological and aggressive actions. Or, as in the case of the tricycle, words could put psychic inertia gradually into motion. Words take time to be uttered, a time that suspends the pathological act; words do not afford immediate gratification but time for reflection, and in the Maison Verte setting they become a means for unconscious elaborations. We do not give up our desire if we can express it rather than act it out. But, in the suspension of the act which speaking involves, the process of thought and inventiveness will find an opening in which to enter. Keeping this opening of the mind is the foundation of mental health for psychoanalysis

Difference and immigrant families

The difference and the inventiveness of each host, child, and adult, is put to work in an architecture of co-existence, the poor and the rich, the young and the old, the immigrant and the native. The analytical practice has no home or fatherland; it is a welcoming in the form of listening and of living attention towards psychic as well as social and cultural particularities.

La Maison Verte can be particularly useful to immigrant families, where not only the child, but the parents, and especially the mother, find themselves far away from their roots, their culture, and their habitual forms of social communication. Often with several children, the mother in such families is usually closed in her purely domestic role within an environment that is alien, if not hostile, to her. More often than not, the immigrant mother finds herself closed in a fusional isolation with her children as her only emotional shelter. A centre like a Maison Verte could offer her time to break away from this isolation and from her everyday difficulties. She will be welcomed and listened to without her maternal role being put into question or having to feel rivalry with the hosts themselves. A meeting between different cultures will become possible where the culturally "different" guests will not have a therapeutic duty or social integration imposed on them, something they resent as the price to pay to the hosting culture and as a rejection of their own. They are not being requested to adapt to new rules or to re-educate themselves, but to find pleasure in the sociable situation, not only with people from their own ethnic group, but also with people from the hosting ethnic group. Class and cultural differences, which in everyday life are barriers to common topics of conversation, will be more easily overcome here by the common experience of being parents and by the opportunity to express difficulties and doubts. La Maison Verte will be a place to abandon control for a while without feeling guilty about "wasting time". Each will be able to speak their own language with other parents from their country of origin and the hosting language with everyone else, so that children will be able to listen to both languages from their mothers' conversations. This cordial relationship between La Maison Verte hosts, the representative of the hosting culture, and the mother allows children to play and mix with other children who speak another language without feeling obliged to deny their own. At the same time, playing and conversation will provide the best conditions to achieve two results: learning the hosting language as the language of their games with friends and not the language of the hostile other; and the prevention of low school results among many immigrant children. These will be given the opportunity to freely play and explore, manipulating sand and water and a range of objects that they do not have or are not allowed to have because of restricted living spaces at home or for cultural reasons. In this way they will also learn "the limit", the basic rules of the social life they are about to live in: sharing toys with other children, washing their hands before touching food in the kitchen, and so on. This training for minimum rules to follow, based on play, is of great preventative interest, especially for boys, who, as the experience of countries with an immigration dating back through several generations show, tend to deviant behaviour, especially during adolescence. This phenomenon can be explained in several ways: a form of ethnic revenge, often inherited from the previous generation, absence or only occasional presence of the father figure (often a humiliated one who feels held to ransom), violence within the family.

All these experiences, taken together, lead children born into immigrant families to a kind of sociability not based on hostility, charity, or social humiliation, but to one where their psychic and ethnic identity will be recognized and respected. So, even if the condemnation or rejection of the other will not be allowed, the expression of one's own differences, even the emergence of occasionally rough exchanges, will not be censured, because expressing these cultural or psychic differences without rejection starts off an authentic process of dialogue, a taking the other to heart: we do not waste time arguing with people who are indifferent to us. Dolto used to say to a child who was hitting another, "You must be very interested in this child; maybe you want to be him and his friend at the same time." Socialization, as Dolto conceives it, is not just a group in harmony, one generally based on denial of conflicts but, on the contrary, is based on recognition and expression of conflicts which need to be negotiated. Humanization seems to be, for Dolto, like the child who hits the other child, encountering others whom we want both to have and be like, because s/he is the subject of our interest. The different view of another can irritate us at first, but it also makes new questions and new psychic processes emerge.

La Maison Verte is not, then, a cosy little home, nor is it a utopian space, but a complex attempt to host any vision of the world (any desire) so that it can find a place from which it can be heard and responded to (at times even by being hit on the head). Visitors who came to the Casa Verde were struck by the fact that in spite of so many people and children in one room, there was absolutely no sense of chaos; they all seemed at ease moving within their own trajectories, in spite of all sorts of clashes or alliances which were part of those trajectories.

For this to happen there must be transference at work, too, and if this is conjugated through various figures, not necessarily the worker, but also other mothers, and new-born friendships, transference arises from the place as such. Pleasure of playing or its adult equivalent, the disengaged chat (not engaged in a neurotic psychic fixity), rather than feeling oppressed by guilty feelings and a duty for sacrifice, opens up, similarly to dreams, the royal road to the unconscious, if there is someone who can hear it. But it is the permission for a convivial pleasure to evade the barriers of resistance, guardian of consciousness. Of course, the opening of the unconscious causes anxiety and, as a consequence, a new closing up, as happens in any analytical work. The unconscious pulsates, says Lacan; like a heart, it opens, and closes up again. Any sensible idea, any stereotype kind of discourse or reply, can only function as an obstruction to the opening of the unconscious which is here at work in the form of the everyday simplicity of a Maison Verte.

References

Brennan, T. (2004). *The Transmission Of Affect*. Ithaca: Cornell University Press.

Dolto, F. (1984). *L'Image inconsciente du corps*. Paris: Le Seuil, coll. "Points Essais", 1992.

Dolto, F. (1986). Esquisses psychanalytiques n. 5, section *Actualitès*, F. Bètournè & C. Boukobza (Eds.) 1985, from a paper given at the Centre de Formation et de Recherches Psychanalytiques.

Winnicott, D. W. (1971a). *Playing and Reality*. London: Tavistock/Routledge, 1989.

CHAPTER TEN

Desire, Dire, Dieu, and Dolto

Guy Hall

There is a Zen Buddhist story (Reps, 1971, p. 98) that tells of a teacher who, when he wanted to emphasize a point, would raise his finger into the air. One of his pupils started doing the same thing when repeating what he had learnt. It was not long before the teacher heard of this, and one day when the student made this gesture, the teacher leapt forward and, with a knife, cut off the student's finger. It is said that it is only from that moment that the student was truly able to teach and not simply repeat the lessons that he had previously learnt. Such a story would have appealed to Françoise Dolto, not only for the symbolic castration contained within it, but also because it mirrors so much of her own experience and understanding about the nature of education. Simply repeating the lessons and understanding of previous generations is not sufficient. Each generation has to add its own insights, so that there is the potential of exploring other options. Freud opened the door to a new way of conceptualizing what happens in the mind. His was not the final word, just the first step in what was at the time a revolutionary direction. Those who have made the most interesting contributions to psychoanalysis since Freud have often been *apart* from, as well as *a part* of, what went before.

When Freud describes religion as an illusion, he does not mean that it is necessarily false, just that it cannot be proved by scientific methods. He did consider religion to be a universal neurosis, and that it was often obsessional in nature, an expression of the search for an exalted father figure. He considered the mystic's oceanic feeling to be an expression of the omnipotent and narcissistic feelings that a child has in the womb, or in very early childhood, but he also recognized that religious traditions could have therapeutic qualities. However, the classical attitude within psychoanalysis is to suspect any manifestation of religion to be an expression of an individual's, or group's, psychopathology. Such an approach overlooks one of Freud's own obsessions, that psychoanalysis be only seen as a science and the consequent material, deterministic, reductionism that ensues. The contemporary high profile exponents of militant atheism, such as Richard Dawkins (2007), or Christopher Hitchens (2008), make use of a very similar argument, claiming that, in essence, religion is no more than an unfounded infantile superstition.

It is worthy of note that Darwin was born a Christian, and, although he later considered himself to be an agnostic, he was never an atheist. For a while, he had been a country parson and supported missionary activity in South America. He said in a letter to John Fordyce, on 7 May 1879, "It seems to me absurd to doubt that a man may be an ardent Theist and evolutionist" (Woodall, p. 61).

It is also quite possible to be an observant Jew and accept Darwin's theories on evolution. Rabbi Shlomo Yitzhaki, better known as Rashi, had already pointed out in the eleventh century, in his commentary on Genesis 1.1, that, "the text does not indicate the sequence of the acts of creation" (Rosenbaum & Silberman, 1946). In other words, this part of the Bible should not be read as a literal and historical document.

Freud could appear somewhat intolerant about other conceptions about psychoanalysis, particularly if he had not been the first to think of them. The result, in the institutions that he and his immediate followers set up, was that legitimate variations from accepted Freudian ideas have been considered as tantamount to heresy, often leading to the equivalent of excommunication. Freud thought that atheism did not need to be explained, where as religion did. Perhaps this is because atheism, for many people, is devoid of the emotional energy so often found in religion. It is doubtful whether even Dawkins and Hitchens would see in atheism a cause for which they would be prepared to die as martyrs, in a similar manner that many religious people have had to endure. If religion is excluded, it is often replaced by other emotive passions such as nationalism, sports, and certain causes. Both Sigmund Freud and Françoise Dolto make universal claims about religion with an air of certainty and confidence that are sometimes hard to substantiate. On the other hand, she seemed to be much more willing to acknowledge when she had made a mistake then many of her colleagues and contemporaries, and unlike Freud, whose authority appears often to have been no less absolute than that of the Pope.

One of the problems with any study of religion is that it manifests itself in such a wide variety of different expressions that it is difficult and possibly misleading to make universal observations about it. A psychoanalyst visiting a suburban European church, temple, mosque, or synagogue would have a difficult task diagnosing the majority of worshippers as displaying serious neurotic symptoms, compared to a group who did not attend such places of worship. The classical psychoanalytic approach to religion has its origins in Freud's complicated relationship to his father, the anti-Semitism to be found in Austria, and his feelings towards, as he saw it, Jung's defection, to a greater degree then is usually recognized. The problem remains that psychoanalysis does not adequately explain, or understand, either religion or religious experience. It may be that the psychoanalytic model needs to be refined to allow for other states of consciousness, or the possibility that consciousness is there from the beginning and is beyond physicality. The classical view of psychoanalysis, that expressions of religious behaviour are always manifestations of psychopathology, can be contrasted usefully with that of the Royal College of Psychiatrists, who have a page on their website dedicated to spirituality. They recognize that it can offer potential benefits for improving a person's mental heath.

There have been alternative viewpoints and psychoanalysts who do not view religion in only negative terms. Donald Winnicott (1989, p. 13) viewed religion as a cultural phenomenon, such as art. He associates it to a child's transitional object, or space. Harry Guntrip (1956) and, to a lesser degree, Ronald Fairbairn, show how religion can support the psyche, as well as trap it. Bion (1965) describes transcendent mystical states expressed as "O", while Kristeva (2008), although a non-believer, is constantly fascinated by religion. She shares with Françoise Dolto the influence of Christian Orthodox liturgy and the consequences of working in Paris in a male dominated society. There is surely a book to be written that compares and contrasts the lives and work of both these interesting women.

Clearly, there has been a return to trying to improve the understanding of religion since the start of psychoanalysis. It is as if something has remained repressed and not fully understood. The promise by Freud and other rationalists of the period that religion would soon cease in the face of science has not been borne out by subsequent history. Psychoanalysts who write positively about religion tend to be strongly attacked by colleagues. The strength of feeling is so powerful that one cannot help but wonder why. What is it about this issue that is so disturbing that any dissention from the establishment position leads to such a strong reaction? The impression is given that the whole edifice of psychoanalysis would be fatally undermined if such unorthodox views were to become accepted. It was certainly Françoise Dolto's experience to be continually pilloried by other analysts for her theological views. They appeared unwilling to engage in a serious, if critical, dialogue with her.

The psychoanalytic understanding of religion continues to produce many books on the subject, which suggests some dissatisfaction with the established theory. It certainly remains an issue for many Jews and Catholics, in particular, although not exclusively. There have been publications on psychoanalysis and Buddhism and Hinduism. There is slowly a development of a dialogue with Islam (Benslama, 2002; Chebel, 2002), although little of this is available in English.

Relatively few prominent psychoanalysts have been able to accept religion in largely its own terms. Oscar Pfister (1948), while being a Protestant Pastor and practitioner of psychoanalysis, managed to maintain a friendship with Freud that outlasted many others, despite their differences on this issue. In a short book, Leavy (1988) combines a Christian view about the goodness of humanity with psychoanalysis. Meissner (1984) has authored an interesting book, which is well worth reading, not least because he is both a Jesuit and a psychoanalyst. It does seem to be easier for Christians, and especially Roman Catholics, to simultaneously retain an insider's understanding in both fields. In one exceptional case, the opposite applies. The German former Catholic priest, theologian, and psychotherapist, Eugen Drewermann, uses psychoanalysis as the critical apparatus for examining the church's problems over sexuality (Beier, 2006). There has been no shortage of clergymen wishing to attack psychoanalysis, but also quite a number who appreciate what it has to offer. I suspect that the number of theologians who study psychoanalysis is greater then the number of psychoanalysts who have a serious interest in religion.

Lacan maintains his Freudian atheism in regard to religion, reflecting not only his personal feelings towards the subject, but also the cultural approach of the French. However, he is not indifferent to religion, and there are many references to religion throughout his written works, some of them quite surprising (Haddad, 2007). Lacan's philosophy is to follow Spinoza, and that joy, or *jouissance*, is the greatest virtue. When a patient can find pleasure in living, there is no call for the analysis to continue. For Françoise Dolto, there is an internalized "devil" that resists human destiny, and all desire is in part divine. She sees in Jesus a prefiguration of the work of the psychoanalyst. Her conception of what it means to be a psychoanalyst is to carry out, similar work to that of Jesus in clarifying unconscious desires. If the New Testament speaks of Jesus casting out evil spirits from the possessed, then this might equate, for Françoise Dolto, to a psychoanalyst working with a psychotic or neurotic. For Lacan, the analyst is in the imaginary and symbolic registers of the patient, the subject who is supposed to know (Lacan, 1977, p. 233). The analyst is in the place of god and able to understand the hidden meaning of the patient's words. It allows the transference to start. Françoise Dolto shows greater humility and does not seek to replace the numinous.

Françoise Dolto audaciously claimed that not only does psychoanalysis not obstruct access to spirituality, but, on the contrary, being in analysis is a path that people should be encouraged to take to find their religious identity. Françoise Dolto was a classically trained psychoanalyst, but with a radically different approach to religion. Her training analysis with René Laforgue was an experience that enabled her to discover her adult religious faith. Although one can respect Françoise Dolto's experience, there should be some caution in extrapolating from such a single experience to a general application, as it can lead to the kind of rigidity found earlier in the Buddhist story. Laforgue was very critical of Freud's *The Future of an Illusion*. Unlike Freud, he considered religion to be a normal part of the psyche, like dreaming. In the same way that one needed to sleep in order to remain physically healthy, so one needed religion to maintain a healthy mental balance (Laforgue, 1995). Françoise Dolto pointed out that, whenever one comes to the end of psychoanalytic thinking, something else appears, which is not psychoanalytic. Such a notion appears to have annoyed and confused many of her colleagues, possibly because it is a reminder that psychoanalysis has its limits, but possibly also because she went on to express herself in what appears to be a quasi-mystical manner.

Childhood

Religion clearly was an important influence on Françoise Dolto. The family could trace their roots to both Protestant and Roman Catholic branches of Christianity. Her great-grandfather, who was originally from Alsace, created the first Lutheran parish in Bourg-la-Reine, a suburb to the south of Paris. He brought together a number of Protestant families and together they built the church. (The original church no longer exists, but a more contemporary one can be found at the Eglise évangélique luthérienne de France, 26 rue Ravon, F-92340 Bourg-la-Reine.) Françoise was brought up in a Catholic home, as her parents considered that this was the normal thing to do in France.

Françoise must have been a very precocious chid, or else her reminiscences of her childhood have been influenced by ideas that she had later. However, there is no evidence that her recollections are anything other than accurate. By the age of seven, while her mother was pregnant with her brother Philippe and mourning the death of her uncle, Françoise was already asking herself:

> How is it that people can live without knowing where they are going and that they find that amusing and good? I must be as

stupid as adults. It's so odd to live when we do not know what there is after. [Dolto, 1989, pp. 70–71]

As a child, she found the local Catholic Abbot, Father R, a rather nervous man. He was later to become a Monsignor. He asked the young Françoise to read St Matthew's gospel as part of the preparation classes for her first communion. She did so, and subsequently asked, why did people speak so badly of Judas? He had an exclusive role that was necessary to bring about the Passion and Jesus encouraged him to do what was required. As Françoise saw it, Judas had only arranged to appear to betray Jesus so that he could go before the Sanhedrin and prove that he really was divine. When subsequent events did not go as anticipated, Judas was overcome with guilt. Anyone who dedicates everything to express such love can only be a saint, a category to which Judas clearly belongs. The priest replied that people do not have the right to hang themselves, in the same way that they cannot decide whether they wish to be born. In a private conversation with her, he later added: "I would ask one thing from you. Tomorrow when you receive Jesus, you will pray that he gives you the grace not to think, because when you think, it isn't good" (*ibid.*, pp. 21–22).

Francois found this extraordinary, but she tried to follow his request. This is remarkable, not only because Françoise demonstrated a sophisticated understanding in her exegesis of the text, but an innocent trust in the authority of the clergy. Interestingly, later, as a psychoanalyst, she took the view that babies do indeed choose whether to be born and live. She maintained throughout her life a sensitivity to what is said to children before their first communion and any possible consequent difficulties.

In her memoires, she recounts listening to sermons in which the meaning of gospel stories such as the story of the Good Samaritan was changed, even corrupted, the result being that the local mothers abandoned their children and followed the instructions of the priest, in order to please him, by making clothes for poor children. This was to be the answer to the question supposedly posed by Jesus: who is your neighbour? In Françoise Dolto's perception, these mothers not only misunderstood the meaning of the text, but also got involved in something that did not concern them at great cost to their own children. She had a similar experience listening to a sermon on the subject of the Prodigal Son (Winter & Dolto, 2002, pp. 145–146). Françoise, while she was a teenager, clearly had a vivid internal world. She believed she had a guardian angel to whom she spoke and for whom she would make room in her bed. The dialogue with this invisible friend helped her make sense of the world and deal with her sense of guilt for various injustices that she felt (Dolto, 1986, pp. 20–21). She describes the family being believers, but not very observant. Like many Catholic families of the period, they would go regularly to mass on Sundays and have fish to eat on Fridays.

At her first communion, Françoise's mother had commanded her to pray for the life of Jacqueline, her terminally ill sister. It was thought that the pure innocence of young girls at their first communion could bring about miracles, as they were considered to be in a special state of grace. In 1920, Jacqueline's parents had asked her where she would like to spend the summer. She had replied at the lake near Annecy. Her father rented part of a former Benedictine Abbey near the lake, but Jacqueline's condition deteriorated and it was decided to return to Pairs. She died en route and was buried in the family crypt at Bourg-la-Reine. Following the death of Françoise's sister, her mother asked Françoise to read to her books by Charles Richet (1850–1935). Richet's interests were wide-ranging and included aviation and pacifism. In 1913, he was awarded the Nobel Prize for Medicine. He also wrote about spiritualism and how ectoplasm appeared to allow the dead to speak. There was a great interest in spiritualism following the end of the First World War, as a means of dealing with the trauma of so many dead and mutilated people. Françoise considered herself at this young age to be a war widow, having been, at least in play, "engaged to be married" to her Uncle Pierre, who died in battle. Talking about such things gave Françoise sleepless nights, and she asked her mother to allow her to stop. However, her mother said that Françoise was the only one she could talk to about such things. She was already in a therapeutic role, aged twelve.

Roman Catholicism

Françoise Dolto's independence of thought can be seen against some of the traditional teachings of the Roman Catholic Church.

She is not against gay and lesbian marriages. She is aware of a French priest who blesses such couples. Françoise Dolto points out that the difference between a blessing and a marriage is very slight. In the eyes of the church, getting married is a sacrament. In her view, it is a promise and commitment given and received by the couple themselves, and this is as true for homosexuals as for heterosexuals. Françoise Dolto makes a comparison with heterosexual couples in the Resistance during the Second World War, who entered into long-term relationships, before witnesses, but without the benefit of clergy, but who were added to the church registers after 1946 with a nuptial blessing. For the church, the act of commitment need not always match its official recognition. For Françoise, homosexual couples can be as faithful and fertile, socially, culturally, and in terms of being a family, as any heterosexual couple (Dolto, 1994, pp. 345–346). Neither is she against artificial contraception, but considers it a wonderful discovery (Dolto, 1979, p. 9).

Françoise Dolto thought she lived in a perverse society, because laws and words are used in a misleading way. Values said to be Christian were, in fact, secular, with no reference to God as Creator, or as a God in which all humanity can find themselves. In regard to divorce, Françoise Dolto takes a liberal attitude, but thought that judges should make clear to those involved in a divorce, including the children, their responsibilities and duties, and not to be so concerned with their rights (Dolto, 1998, p. 270). She is particularly concerned to express and understand how a divorce affects children, both consciously and unconsciously. However, she disapproves of single mothers, believing that they encourage in children phantasies of an incestuous nature.

In regard to abortion, she took a view close, although not identical, to that of the Roman Catholic church. She thought that abortion should only be allowed for certain rare and very particular circumstances. She justifies her position through ostensibly psychoanalytic and medical reasons (Dolto, 1998, pp. 201–236). However, she does not counter any of the arguments put forward in support of more liberal views for abortion, nor does her morality entertain any conception about the value of individual conscience on this issue. That abortions are legalized is, in her view a misnomer. They should only be viewed as being decriminalized, rather then being morally acceptable (Dolto, 1994, p. 261).

Françoise Dolto's view of religious education is that it should be more than to patronize children, because they are small, by exposing them to gaudy images of sentimental saints, pious miracles, dubious morality, or the singing of dreary hymns. Rather, children should be shown and educated about the great works of art and music, and sacred texts with all their difficult words. Education in a religious context should not be limited to obedience, knowing what is forbidden, rituals, inducing guilt and crushing the independence of developing minds. Religions are often at their best when in a prophetic mode; they defy authority and are subversive and challenging to authority. A child's metaphysical questions, the sense of what is holy, spiritual, and sacred, should be taken seriously. Otherwise how else will a child learn about the symbolic value of even the simplest of religious acts (Chérer, 2008, pp. 180–181)?

Françoise Dolto used to say, regarding life after death, that all we can say is that when we are dead we are no longer alive. However, on her deathbed, she said that she was about to go into the presence of one who was unknown to her and that this would mark the start of a new relationship. She was sure that she would also meet her late husband again.

Eastern Orthodoxy

A new aspect of religion became a part of Françoise's life when she married Boris Dolto, who was Russian Orthodox. The Orthodox liturgy had a major impact on Françoise's understanding of theology. It was, she says, as great as her encounter with psychoanalysis. She was particularly impressed with the way the Orthodox Church dealt with failed marriages, which she considered to be more honest and symbolically more helpful for the community (Dolto, 1989, p. 176), and how it ensured that every child knew who were its parents. She admired the liturgy that even young children knew by heart, and how the funeral service started in mourning but ended in joy, as the soul of the deceased is greeted by an invisible presence to guide it to the next world. The deceased is forgiven through the grace of the living saying liturgical prayers. Françoise Dolto, considered the Orthodox Church to be the true successors to Judaism, having been neither subject to Roman law, nor "latinized" (*ibid.*, p.176). She is moved as people talk to God, even if at times she feels they are also self-deluded. She understands the phantasmagoria found in the Bible to be human beings speaking to another idealized human being, who is divine.

She thought that psychoanalysis could never have been discovered in Russia, since all the phantasies that people speak about on the couch are lived there by everyone, when they get drunk. The next day they may see the destruction, but have no memory of how it was caused. In Russia, it would not be possible to say, "Pray so as not to think." Russians do not know how to think—to think is to "vatinicate" (make pompous pronouncements)—and the only real thinkers in Russia are Jewish. She said that Russians eat, die, fornicate, argue, love, hate, run, pray, and are violent. It is very Christian, because God is always present, in the corner, reminding Russians that although they exaggerate they remember that Jesus died for them (*ibid.*, p. 181) How much of this was said tongue in cheek by Françoise Dolto, and how much is said with a straight face, is difficult to ascertain.

Judaism

Psychoanalysis, claims Françoise Dolto, is one of the long-term consequences of the words and sayings of Jesus of Nazareth. It was necessary that Freud should not have practised his religion, otherwise he would not have discovered psychoanalysis. He was only able to do so by sublimating his suffering and frustrations with Judaism. He only had to dare to give words to this frustration in order to become aware of unconscious processes (Winter & Dolto, 2002, pp. 13–15). In her autobiography, Françoise Dolto confirms that Christianity makes no sense without Judaism, but she also stresses the importance of Freud being Jewish, although he denied being religious. Freud was challenged about what was left in Judaism if he was a non-believer? He replied by saying that it was the most important part, but he did not specify what this might be. However, a combination of ethics, belonging to a fraternity, and Zionism might seem to be among some of the more possible options. Françoise Dolto made an error that others have pointed out in thinking that being Jewish depends on holding certain beliefs. It is quite possible to be Jewish, like Freud, but not a believer. Judaism is not a faith religion, in the sense that most Jews are recognized as being Jewish because they have a Jewish parent, usually their mother. People identify themselves as Jewish not because of their belief, but because of shared sense of values, their biology, followed by environment and a shared sense of history. Certainly, Françoise Dolto thought that psychoanalysis could only have begun with someone who was Jewish, even if she thought that Jews are Christians without knowing it (Dolto, 1989, p. 160). This is, to say the least, rather patronizing, but injury is added to insult when she goes on to explain that the reason for this is because Jews are afraid to let go of their neurosis. However, she shows a greater insensitivity in her understanding when she said, "In any case, it was the Jews who were Christ during the war. The Jews were Christ on the cross. The Jews were the incarnation of Christ even though they did not know it" (*ibid.*, p. 161).

Now such a viewpoint is problematic for both Catholic and Jewish theologians. It is also part of another problem with Françoise Dolto's personality and outlook. She seems to find great difficulty with any connection to suffering, pain, aggression, sadism, or masochism to be found in the gospels. Nor does she share the negative outlook of Melanie Klein about children, in particular, or Freud's pessimistic regard for humanity in general. She saw Protestantism as a message that followed Jewish morality, having been reformed by Jesus and having also been reformed by Luther (Winter & Dolto, 2002, p. 144).

Françoise Dolto identifies which of her teachers are Jewish. The religious identity of others in her life, outside of her family, is rarely identified. It is not clear if this represents a fascination and respect for her colleagues in which she feels their very Jewishness, as with her view on Freud, added some quality to their work not found elsewhere. It might also represent an internalizing of an attitude of the period in which Jews were identified, either for anti-Semitic reasons or because they were refugees, as the symbolic outsider and a signified other.

When, in 1942, the Doltos were looking to move into a larger home, Françoise was surprised to be shown many furnished flats and to be informed that the owners were away on holiday, or had decided to return to their own country. These were the homes of

Jews who had fled, or been deported. Françoise advised her husband to be cautious, and they took up residence in a flat whose provenance was unambiguous. Françoise also shows some naïveté by innocently agreeing to go with a Jewish psychoanalytic colleague, recently arrived from Austria, to register with the German occupying authorities. After the war, she said that she was at the time completely unaware of the Holocaust, but not of Nazi-inspired hatred against the Jews. Her understanding of this historical period again echoes a problem she had through out her life of coming to terms with the existence of death and violence.

For example she felt acutely embarrassed when another Jewish psychoanalyst, Sophie Morgenstern, spoke about pogroms in Poland, or of concentration camps. Sophie was trained by Eugénie Sokolnicka (1884–1934), who lived in Paris from 1929, specializing in working with children. She came from a Jewish middle-class family, and was said to be temperamental and to have a difficult personality. Born in Warsaw, she helped introduced psychoanalysis into France. In 1919, she saw a boy from Minsk for about six weeks, and wrote a paper based on her experience titled, "Analysis of a case of infantile obsessional neurosis". It is one of the first cases of a child being treated by a psychoanalytical method more usually used with adults. Her life was very unsettled, and she was said to have had a turbulent sexual life and found it difficult to earn a living from her work. It seems likely that she suffered from depression, and she committed suicide just after her fiftieth birthday. Eugénie Sokolnicka, who had been analysed by both Freud and Ferenczi, had been the training analyst of René Laforgue. It was with René Laforgue that Françoise Dolto was in analysis for three years. Françoise Dolto clarifies in her autobiography that she would never have become a psychoanalyst if she had not been a religious believer, and that she would not have been a believer if she had not been in analysis. Indeed, at first, while seeing Laforgue, she had not wanted to be a psychoanalyst (Winter & Dolto, 2002, p. 166).

Sophie Morgenstern was the main guide and inspiration for Françoise Dolto during the early days of her work. Morgenstern was one of the first psychoanalysts to work with children and use drawings in the treatment of children. She committed suicide in 1940, the day before the Germans entered Paris. By the end of the war, some say there were only two psychoanalysts in Paris,

Françoise Dolto and John Leuba. The rest had either died or fled. Françoise Dolto spoke up in defence of René Laforgue after the war, when accusations were made that he had been a Nazi collaborator, when in fact he had hidden Jews in his farmhouse in the south of France,

Boris Dolto was denounced to the Nazis as a Jew and a Communist, although he was neither, because of his Russian roots and identity, of which he was very proud. He had to present himself in front of the German occupying authorities to prove that he was not Jewish. He did this by showing he was not circumcised. However, he felt so humiliated by this experience that it took him several days to tell his wife, and if she had not persuaded him otherwise, Boris would certainly have killed the man who he thought had betrayed him.

Religion

Françoise Dolto published a series of three interviews she had with another psychoanalyst, Gérard Sévérin. (Dolto & Sévérin, 2000) The title in French of the first of these was *La foi au risque de la psychanalyse*, translated into English as *Psychoanalysis: a Freudian Interpretation of the Gospel*. A second and third volume were published in French, the final book being called "Faith at risk from psychoanalysis". These three volumes have also been published together. It should be noted that the implication is that it is the gospels and faith that are threatened by psychoanalysis, and not vice versa. The first book was the partial inspiration for Jean-Luc Godard's film, *Je vous salue! Marie*. The film makes use of exact quotations from the book, although ultimately Godard appears to come to different conclusions that are critical of psychoanalysis.

Gérard Sévérin is a psychoanalyst who had worked with Françoise Dolto at the Trousseau hospital. He interviewed her about her views on religion and faith. Françoise Dolto's approach is that of a psychoanalyst with the text, as it were, on the couch. Her approach is not to give a classical theological exegetical interpretation, but to share her point of view. Not all the gospel stories are commented upon. For her, Jesus is not the incarnation of absolute love, but the indicator of unconscious desires. Some in the Roman Catholic church find this distinctly disturbing. The unconscious use of the body takes on a unique paradigm when Françoise Dolto considers the birth, death, resurrection, and divine incarnation of Jesus. The life of Jesus becomes a psychodrama, and he becomes the master of desire. He is the one who reveals the perverse desires in others and offers them the possibility of finding their true desires. The humanity of Jesus is emphasized, while a spark of the divine is found in every human being. She points out that these two thousand-year-old texts are not in contradiction with the unconscious desires of contemporary people. She does not hesitate to highlight significant conflicts, sexuality, and neurosis in the decisive moments of the life of Jesus that she interprets as castrations (Sauverzac, 1993, p. 357).

When Françoise Dolto speaks about *desire*, she is essentially referring to an inter-human communication. It is not a reference to a *need*. A need can be satisfied by an object. A *desire* cannot. At the start of life, there are three unconscious desires, that of the father, the mother, and the newborn child. This is not about envy, or pleasure. It is a process of exchange leading to an encounter. The baby represents the incarnation of the desire for life through an encounter between the parents. However, desire is not about physiology, but language, and is not satisfied through any bodily climax. Needs can be met, but not desires. Yet, desire can become a source of energy, leading to inventive, creative, and imaginative expressions. However, too much pleasure and satisfaction leads to a mutilation of creativity and the atrophy of communication. As a child internalizes the code that marks human relationships, its love of itself (narcissism) is joined with the love of others (altruism).

According to Françoise Dolto, the subject is not the sense of self, it is not the individual, but it is something that is dynamic, unconscious, and beyond time. It pre-exists humanity, but its temporal expression can be found in the human body. It follows its course after the death of the body. Françoise Dolto considered Jesus to represent the master of understanding as to what human beings carry within themselves. With Jesus, the demands of desire are silenced and liberated through love. In her view, there can be no subject without God (Ledoux, 2006, pp. 88–93, 328–333).

For Françoise Dolto, the proof of God's existence was a circular argument on the lines that, since she existed, so must the Divine and vice versa. Gerard Sévérin's view was that such an observation was not very helpful.

All human beings, from their birth to their death, carry within them the existential question and answer that can be expressed as where and by what will I be. This mirrors the description that God gives of himself in Exodus 3.14, אהיה אשר אהיה. (In Hebrew, *Ehyeh Asher Ehyeh,* usually translated either as "I am that I am", or "I shall be what I shall be".) The reference here is not to God's self-existence, but to what God has in mind to be for others. If Françoise Dolto believes that Jesus works in a prefiguration of psychoanalysis, then it follows that Françoise Dolto can to some degree occupy a place symbolized by Jesus through her work, just as Freud identified himself with Moses.

There is a difference between morality and ethics. It is Françoise Dolto's view that morality is about the conduct of the self in society. It belongs to the imaginary. Ethics is about an unconscious process concerning the subject. It is dynamically linked to desire and is found in the symbolic. To Freud's theories, Françoise Dolto also adds the word. It is a source of life; it makes sense of the world and civilizes it. In a baby, the word (of the parents) is made flesh and is primordial. To be effective and join together the symbolic, there must be security, a wish to meet and be met, and a recognition of individuality. The word must take account of experiences gained and the regressions that are at work. To be able to speak in this way is to be able to appreciate the unconscious image of the body. For Françoise Dolto, Jesus does not exist to tell humanity what to do, or how to behave, but to tell us what is going on in our unconscious. He creates different scenes in the parables to appeal to different people, and then reveals the dynamics of their desire.

Françoise Dolto soon realized that if she had merely been interested in religious responses to suffering she would never have studied psychoanalysis. She saw that what the Roman Catholic church offered was often a painful masochistic solution that required a believer to identify with Jesus on the cross. This was an idea that she had great difficulty accepting. Psychoanalysis gave her an understanding about the origin of the conflicts that exist within people and that create anxiety and freeze communication.

It was because Freud left the religious fold and identified with Greek humanism (and was phobic about Roman Catholicism) that he was able to discover psychoanalysis. It is because Freud did not accept the ready-made answers of his religion and of medical science to answer questions about God, or explain human nature, in the way he wanted to ask them, that he developed his own ideas. Similarly, Françoise Dolto thought that institutionalized expressions of Christianity pervert the desire of human beings by codifying morality in a way that has nothing to do with the gospels. Francis Martens, a Belgian psychoanalyst and anthropologist interested in the anthropology of racism, anti-Semitism, xenophobia, and the concept of the scapegoat, asked a similar question of Françoise Dolto to the challenge made by Gérard Séverin. She replied that her religious beliefs only became publically known through the books that appeared after she retired from direct clinical work. Since then, she had received many apologetic letters from those who had previously called her "a dirty Jew", and who thought that the religious icon that she had in her consulting room was to mislead people. While she was working as a psychoanalyst, people did not know what were her views about religion. These projections reflected the lacks and desires in both patients and colleagues (Dolto, 1998, p. 298).

Clearly, Françoise Dolto distinguishes between established or organized religion and the essential substance of religious sentiment, which she says exists in every human being. Seeking to define what this essence is, she explains that where there is change, or the potential for change, there is love. If there is change in the body, heart, and intelligence, then there is freedom. If we change it is because we have faith in such changes with all those around us. They need us and we need them. The human being is a being who is religious by nature, a being who wants to establish relationships, and it is not possible to differentiate between when these are with the Divine, or with others.

For Françoise Dolto, everyone has a spiritual life, but they do not know it, as it is unconscious, like the influences on their emotional life. She maintains that desire aims always at a higher level then the object of its pleasure.

She said, "There is only one kind of sin in my sense . . . the sin against one's desire . . . a sin is when one cannot risk living out one's desire" (Barral, 2000, p. 523).

For her, God is a continual development of infinite desire. It is God who is manifest in reconciling the subject between desire and the law. For Françoise Dolto, each human being symbolically incarnates the desires of its self and its parents, because all three are creatures who use language. It is the ability to keep the question open that allows the subject to exist and to be. Françoise Dolto maintains that answering a question might be a premature foreclosure that can put any question at risk and prevent it from keeping alive the desire that the subject can bring into creation. The answer can block the creativity of the question.

Françoise Dolto gave consideration to how a child evolves a sense of religion. To begin with, a child believes itself to be ruler of its own universe. As it is able to differentiate between itself and others, it first considers that its mother is godlike, as she rules over the child. When the child appreciates that even mother must have been created, it also understands that mother cannot be divine. The child then considers father to have these godlike qualities. Except it discovers that father too has been created, and that there must be some other originator in operation. It is at this point that a religious sentiment is born. The child might consider other objects, but comes to appreciate that these things do not move, create, or react, unless the child is there to make it happen, or for other factors to do so. For the child, the problem remains: where or what is the original first cause that makes, or denies all things from happening.

In the Maison Verte, Françoise Dolto would often explain how a child could make an object live, both for itself and, especially, for others, just by wanting it. If the biggest child in the group wants the object, usually a toy, then it becomes valuable for some of the other children in the room (Dolto, 1994, pp. 76–78). It is the same for adults, as modern advertising techniques repeatedly demonstrate. It is when someone is on their own that they can more clearly think about how to understand the origins of their world.

Françoise Dolto considers the creation stories found in Genesis, and whether God created the world essentially because he was bored and lonely.

God's desires are met through humanity. This is a God who does not want to be on his own, but creates humanity in order to have company. God cannot be fully God until he is named, known, and recognized as such by humanity. This mirrors the story in Genesis 2:19–20, in which God asks Adam to give names to all of creation. According to Françoise Dolto, citing Genesis 2:19–20, Adam is not able to recognize himself until after the creation of Eve. This is dubious, as it is not exactly what the Bible says. It is not the only place where Françoise Dolto is elastic with the biblical text. The reverse seems to be the case in that Adam names Eve (Genesis 2:23). The essential point that we are not known until we are with another is a discovery that couples make, a feature of social life, and is reflected in Françoise Dolto's habit, when first meeting a child, of asking it for its name and introducing herself with her name. Adam gives names to all the creatures in existence and discovers, according Françoise Dolto, that he is not able to name what kind of creature he is until there was another, who was both similar to and different from him. That Eve was made from a part of Adam allowed him to recognize himself in this other (Genesis 2.19–24). Eve represents that part of man that finds pleasure and joy through existence. God created the world and humanity to relieve himself of his solitude, so that, through the divine in humanity, God, too, was able to see and meet an aspect of the self that had previously been inaccessible. In this creation story, God was bored, and Adam on his own is anonymous, and creation takes place through the word (Dolto, 1994, p. 57).

Such ideas find their echo in the writings of rabbinic sages. However, a strict reading of the Bible does not support Françoise Dolto's contention that Eve was created so that Adam would be able to give himself a generic name, but because of his solitude. God had already named the creature made out of the ground as man. Françoise Dolto suggests that something similar happens for the very young child. For the dependent child, everything appears magical until the child attains some independence. It is then able to understand the world in a non-magical way, including the realization that its mother was also created from another and therefore cannot be a god. It is only when our false gods fail that we can become more human.

There are Christian counter arguments that flow along the following lines. God pre-existed the creation of the universe. God is outside of time and space and transcends existence. It is God who created time and space. In other words, God existed in non-existence, prior to his creation of existence. Existing in non-existence as the sole existent might lead some to think that God would appear to be very lonely. However, this cannot be the case, because of the lack of existence of time and space and because God, being perfect and complete, lacks for nothing. Loneliness implies a lack, a need and an imperfection. Since God cannot want for anything, he cannot create space and time, the universe and humanity for company. There are rabbinical commentaries that suggest that God is not perfect, and has lacks and needs, and is not complete, rather like his creation, and that one of the tasks of humanity is to finish the work of creation.

Françoise Dolto said that there is only one kind of sin and that is to go against one's desires. If religion is an illusion, it is not one like any other. She castigates Freud's *The Future of an Illusion* as one of the worst of his books, a view that Freud might well have shared. It is not enough to reduce religion to an obsessional neurosis. She says that the book is written by someone who feels they have not been respected and who projects this on to religion. With hindsight, one might also say this lack of respect was an issue for Françoise Dolto. Freud could not accept his father as his equal and Françoise Dolto's mother had difficulty in accepting the abilities of her daughter.

Françoise Dolto is not uncritical of organized religion and the way that some use and manipulate guilt feelings. She considered guilt to have nothing to do with religion, since desire should never lead to guilt. It is our impotence that we cannot forgive. For Freud, the origin of guilt exists even before the establishment of a super-ego. It is as the result of a feeling of anxiety before authority, in which satisfactions are given up in order not to lose the feeling of being loved. She saw Christianity as an advance on Judaism (Dolto, 2000, p. 277). It is the moment when the Divine, the subject of the law, becomes incarnated in humanity, even if the significance of the life of Jesus only becomes apparent after his death. Reality can be known to humanity, but what is real can be known only to God. We do not fully know if what God desires is the same as what we desire. It is only through our actions, our work, that we can mediate a desire in which God has a part. God is revealed through his creation, of which humanity is a partial element (*ibid.*, p. 317) When Christianity became institutionalized, it made of the Jews a people who are a living chain of believers and who represent a symbolic phallus, but also an impossible other. In Christianity, the truth is acted out through desire. Françoise Dolto found difficulty in accepting violence and hatred in the Bible. She sees Cain, before he killed his brother Abel, as the creator of the social space, of cities. If, afterwards, he feels guilty for killing his brother, it is not before the Eternal, but his own transcendent desire. It is this definition of God that condemns him (Sauverzac, 1995, p. 362). Interestingly, for Lacan, love originates from the Father. For Françoise Dolto, God is always female and maternal, it is just that most people take the Divine to be masculine. For the child, all adults are phallic. Great suffering arises from being abandoned by the Father and no longer being able to hear the word. It is desire that Françoise Dolto exalts, not suffering. She sees the work of psychoanalysis as a process of humanization of the subject. Spirituality is distinguished from religion and can find expression through desire.

For Françoise Dolto, true guilt is, or should be, the opportunity to develop the strength for new action, woven out of trust and love, while false guilt is a harmful source of depression and a lack of confidence that people have in both themselves and in life. This is not to say that all forms of depression are based on false guilt. It echoes the rabbinic notion that one deals with guilt not through forgiveness, but that when temptation is found in a similar situation, the previous action is not repeated. A healthy spirituality requires the possibility of an individual giving up remaining traces of a false conviction. Such a task is not easy, and the contribution of psychoanalysis here can be of great interest. Drewermann would say that the Roman Catholic church reinforces a false sense of guilt.

In her writings, Françoise Dolto gives clinical examples of children whom she has seen who experience disturbances as a result of what they had been told by institutionalized religious organizations. She cites the case of Leon, an obsessional boy from a poor, controlling, if self-sacrificing, family. His mother wanted nothing other the he should become *a gentleman*. As a child, Leon was very obedient, good, and polite. He was looking forward to his first communion. The church was, for him, a place of freedom in which he could escape from his controlling family. It gave him a space for his imagination to express all sorts of savage and murderous fantasies. However, he heard a sermon about the "wrong kind of thinking". It was not enough, suggested the priest, to be good and polite, but all thoughts should be about what God would allow. God knew his secret thoughts. God is a mind reader and knows the secrets of the heart. Leon had a new understanding which he took literally, but this revelation led to a terrifying sense of false guilt and paranoia. Now, at his first communion, Leon lost faith, hope, and the possibility of ever being loved. He was both unacceptable and damned. Françoise Dolto says that, for many children, the period leading up to the first communion brings together feelings of love towards God, but also magical feelings of guilt linked to archaic and filial feelings, which are all awoken by this mysterious meal. For Leon, belief in God meant belief in an almighty jealous voyeur. Leon used to confess himself and feel redeemed for his aggressive wicked thoughts, but now, with this new understanding of the power of God, such life-saving redemptive acts no longer worked. God had become like "Big Brother", a tricky and knowing peeping Tom, from whom there was no escape. Christianity, being a faith religion, makes the internal world an essential area of theological examination. In Judaism, with the possible exception of the kabbalah, its mystical tradition, there is no such thought police. It is much more concerned with external reality and, while it is often too behaviourist, there is at least much more scope about what can or cannot be believed without it feeling life, or after-life, threatening.

Another example was of a ten-year-old girl who, as her first communion approached, was anxious that in biting into the host she would hurt Jesus. She was unable to sleep or eat, and started to bite herself. She explained this by saying that Jesus would not be troubled when she bit the host, because he would know how she had suffered. Françoise Dolto pointed out to her that when Jesus had said, "Eat my flesh", he had not said, "But do not bite". It is the priests who say this, just as they said that worshippers should line up and genuflect before them as a sign of deference. It is not a sin not to do so. Eating Jesus was a way of maintaining a spiritual life, just as eating elsewhere was a means of maintaining a physical body (Dolto, 1995, pp. 209–213).

According to Françoise Dolto, one has to distinguish between objective morality and subjective morality, not only for adults, but also for children. A child expresses its desires and needs through words and gestures, but is not able to always recognize within them the deep subjective significance that they find. Jesus famously chased away the merchants in the temple. Françoise Dolto said, "Too often we turn him [Jesus] into a merchant who in the temple of our children's hearts, and evaluate their actions into good and bad" (*ibid.*, pp. 218–219).

These values belong uniquely to parents and teachers, and it would be a mistake to equate the thoughts of Jesus with the thoughts of the child's parents. Some of the metaphors used in Françoise Dolto's exegesis of the gospels seem stretched. When Jesus says, "I will make you fishers of men" (Mark 1:16), Françoise Dolto sees this as an instruction that they should fish people from their amniotic waters to appreciate that there is another kind of respiration that is available to them. One can admire the idea and admit that it is imaginative, but, as an expression of unconscious desire, it is not very convincing.

Conclusion

Despite her background, when Françoise Dolto speaks about religion, it is not the understanding of theologians, or of the Roman Catholic church. It may be what some consider natural religion, for it is faith in something that is greater than the mind, the self, the ego, and the power of the physical religious establishment. Her understanding of desire and the subject is unique, even if it makes use of a vocabulary used by other psychoanalysts. Desire is an energy that has a transcendent quality to it. The subject is both mystical and seemingly infinite. The castrations of life momentarily liberate desire that may otherwise be fixed on an object, so that the subject becomes able to consider what it lacks, rather then what it needs. This enables it to achieve the potential that is in its being. Françoise Dolto is trying to explain religious redemption in psychoanalytic terms. She believes in Jesus as a source of salvation, because he teaches about desire as a pathway to God. The gospels are a proof of the living dynamism of the human psyche, with all its strengths and failings, but through Christian perspectives. Françoise Dolto moves from the sign that is the body of Jesus to the word that is God, and which is not limited by death. What happens after desire has reached its full potential is not explained.

Françoise Dolto was a courageous, independent woman who made her mark and had original ideas while working in a chauvinistic environment and in a culturally atheist country. Unlike the

Buddhist student, she did not religiously copy what she had learnt, nor did she want those she taught to slavishly copy her. She acknowledged that more then psychoanalysis was required to understand spirituality, which is a rare admission for any analyst to make. Those who are against her will see in her books proof that Freud was right to take a reductionist view, that individual religiosity is an expression of an obsessional neurosis. Those who largely agree with her can acknowledge, even if they do not completely agree with everything that she says, that she is still worth reading and should be taken seriously.

References

Barral, W. (2000). La psychanalyse est-elle une bonne nouvelle? In: *C. Dolto, Françoise Dolto, aujourd'hui présente: Actes du colloque de l'Unesco, 14–17 janvier 1999*. Paris: Gallimard.

Beier, M. (2006). *A Violent God-Image: An Introduction to the Works of Eugen Drewermann*. Harrisburg, PA: Continuum International.

Benslama, F. (2002). *La psychanalyse à l'épreuve de l'islam*. Paris: Aubier.

Bion, W. (1965). *Transformations*. London: Heinemann.

Chebel, M. (2002). *Le Subjet en Islam*. Paris: Seuil.

Chérer, S. (2008). *Ma Dolto*. Paris: Stock.

Dawkins, R. (2007). *The God Delusion*. London: Black Swan.

Dolto, F. (1979). *Lorsque l'enfant paraît*, Tome 3. Paris: Seuil.

Dolto, F. (1986). *Enfances*. Paris: Seuil.

Dolto, F. (1989). *Autoportrait d'une Psychanalyste*, 1934–1988. Paris: Le Seuil.

Dolto, F. (1994). *Solitude*. Paris: Gallimard.

Dolto, F. (1995). *La difficulté de vivre*. Paris: Gallimard.

Dolto, F. (1998). *Le Féminin*. Paris: Gallimard.

Dolto, F., & Sévérin, G. (2000). *Les évangiles et la foi au risqué de la psychanalyse*. Paris: Gallimard.

Guntrip, H. (1956). *Mental Pain and the Cure of Souls*. London: Independent Press.

Haddad, G. (2007). *Le péché original de la psychanalyse: Lacan et la question juive*. Paris: Broché.

Hitchens, C. (2008). *God is Not Great: How Religion Poisons Everything*. London: Atlantic Books.

Kristeva, J. (2008). *Thérèse Mon Amour*. Paris: Fayard.

Lacan, J. (1977). *The Four Fundamental Concepts of Psycho-Analysis*, A. Sheridan (Trans.). London: Hogarth.
Laforgue, R. (1995). *Au-delà du scientisme*. Paris: Maisnie Tredaniel.
Leavy, S. (1988). *In the Image of God*. New Haven, CT: Yale University Press.
Ledoux, M. (2006). *Dictionnaire raisonné de l'oeuvre de F. Dolto*. Paris: Payot.
Meissner, W. W. (1984). *Psychoanalysis and Religious Experience*. New Haven, CT: Yale University Press.
Pfister, O. (1948). *Christianity and Fear*. London: Allen & Unwin.
Reps, P. (1971). Zen flesh, Zen bones. Harmondsworth: Penguin.
Rosenbaum, M., & Silberman, A. (1946). *Pentateuch with Targum Onkelos, Haphtaroth and Prayers for Sabbath and Rashi's Commentary*, Vol. 1. London: Shaprio, Vallentine and Co.
Sauverzac, J.-F. (1993). *Françoise Dolto: Itinéraire d'une psychanalyste*. Paris: Flammarion.
Winnicott, D. W. (1989). *Playing and Reality*. London: Routledge.
Winter, J.-P., & Dolto, F. (2002). Les images, les mots, le corps. Paris: Gallimard.
Woodall, E. (1884). *Charles Darwin. A Paper Contributed to the Transactions of the Shropshire Archaeological Society*. London: Trubner & Co.

APPENDIX I

Chronology of the life of Françoise Dolto

1874 Birth of father, Henri Marette.
1879 Birth of mother, Suzanne Demmler.
1901 Wedding of Henri Marette and Suzanne Demmler.
1902 Birth of Jacqueline Marette.
1903 Birth of Pierre Marette.
1906 Birth of Jean Marette.
1908 Birth of Françoise Marette.
1909 Irish nanny forced to leave the Marette family.
1913 Birth of Philippe Marette.
1915 Birth of André Marette.
1916 Death of Pierre Demmler, uncle (and "fiancé") to Françoise Marette.
1920 Jacqueline Marette dies from cancer.
1922 Birth of Jacques Marette.
1925 Françoise Marette passes the second part of the Baccalauréat. For the oral in her philosophy exam, she chooses a text by Freud.
1929 Begins studying to become a nurse at Hôpital-école de la Croix-Rouge.
1930 Graduated as a nurse.
1932 First year as a medical student.

1933 Philippe Marette starts his analysis with René Laforgue.
1934 Françoise Marette starts her analysis with René Laforgue.
1936 Meeting with Sophie Morgenstern at Heuyer's and of Mélanie Klein at Marie Bonaparte's.
1936 Françoise Marette leaves her family home.
1936 End of her training analysis with Laforgue.
1937 Trainee at the Enfants Malades hospital in Professor Darre's department, *consultation de la porte.*
1938 Françoise Marette becomes a member of the Société Psychanalytique de Paris (SPP).
1939 Works in Professor Pichon's hospital department.
1939 Graduates as a medical doctor with PhD thesis titled, *Psychanalyse et Pédiatrie.*
1940 Begins consultations at Hôpital Trousseau and stays until 1978.
1941 Meets Boris Dolto.
1942 Françoise Marette marries Boris Dolto.
1953 First split: Dolto, Lagache, Reverchon-Jouve, Favez-Boutonnier, and Lacan leave the SPP.
1960 Dolto gives her paper, "Sexualité feminine", at the Amsterdam Conference.
1962 Starts working at Centre Etienne Marcel, with Bernard This.
1964 Second split: Dolto and Lacan leave the SFP.
1964 Lacan founds l'Ecole Française de Psychanalyse, later to be l'Ecole Freudienne de Paris.
1967 One day conference on "Psychosis" under the patronage of Maud Mannoni.
1967 First introduction to *Le Cas Dominique.*
1969 Dolto broadcasts her first radio programmes using the name of Docteur X.
1971 Republication of *Psychanalyse et Pédiatrie.*
1976 Beginning of France Inter radio programmes: *Lorsque l'enfant paraît.*
1978 Dolto stops seeing patients.
1979 Creation of la Maison Verte.
1980 Lacan closes l'Ecole Freudienne de Paris.
1981 Death of Boris Dolto.
1981 Death of Jacques Lacan.
1988 Death of Françoise Dolto.

INDEX

For Product Safety Concerns and Information please contact our EU representative GPSR@taylorandfrancis.com Taylor & Francis Verlag GmbH, Kaufingerstraße 24, 80331 München, Germany

Batch number: 10726011

Printed by Printforce, the Netherlands